Strategies for Risk Communication

Strategies for Risk Communication

Anurag Sharma

ADHYAYAN

ADHYAYAN PUBLISHERS & DISTRIBUTORS

NEW DELHI (INDIA)

Published by
ADHYAYAN PUBLISHERS & DISTRIBUTORS
4378/4B, 105, J.M.D. House, Murari Lal Street
Ansari Road Darya Ganj, New Delhi - 110002
Ph.: 011-23263018, 011-23277156, Fax: 011-23280028
Email: adhyayanpublishers@yahoo.com

Strategies for Risk Communication

Edition 2011
ISBN 978-81-8435-232-0

Printed in India

Published by Harish Chandra Yadav for Adhyayan Publishers & Distributors, Laser Typeseting at A.V. Rao and Printed at Tarun Offset Printers, Delhi

Preface

Risk communication is an interactive process of exchange of information and opinion on risk among risk assessors, risk managers, and other interested parties. It is an integral and ongoing part of the risk analysis exercise, and ideally all stakeholder groups should be involved from the start. Risk communication makes stakeholders aware of the process at each stage of the risk assessment. This helps to ensure that the logic, outcomes, significance, and limitations of the risk assessment are clearly understood by all the stakeholders.

Risk communication is most effective if undertaken in a systematic way, and generally starts with the gathering of information on the risk issue of concern. Therefore the risk manager and risk assessor must be able to briefly and clearly summarise what this issue encompasses, at an early stage, in order to elicit interest and stakeholder input. Problems for risk communicators involve how to reach the intended audience, to make the risk comprehensible and relatable to other risks, how to pay appropriate respect to the audience's values related to the risk, how to predict the audience's response to the communication, etc.

Combining in-depth scientific underpinnings and the greatest breadth of information available, this book makes the topic of risk communication accessible to those who need it most. It is intended as an introduction to the field as well as a refresher and reference book for those communicating environmental, safety, and health risks. It will be a trusted compendium of strategies and guidance for effectively conveying risk information. Managers, engineers, students, communication specialists and healthcare professionals will be benefited from its contemporary, practical advice on what to do and what to avoid for successful risk communication.

Anurag Sharma

Contents

1

Introduction to Risk Communication

Risk communication is an interactive process of exchange of information and opinion on risk among risk assessors, risk managers, and other interested parties.It is an integral and ongoing part of the risk analysis exercise, and ideally all stakeholder groups should be involved from the start. Risk communication makes stakeholders aware of the process at each stage of the Risk Assessment. This helps to ensure that the logic, outcomes, significance, and limitations of the Risk Assessment are clearly understood by all the stakeholders. Information may be available from the stakeholder. Industry stakeholders may, for example have unpublished data crucial to the risk assessors, which may be an essential part of the data needed for the risk assessment. There is also information that is typically presented to the stakeholders (both industry and consumers), as an integral part of the risk analysis process.

The identification of particular interest groups and their representatives should comprise a part of an overall risk communication strategy. This risk communication strategy should be discussed and agreed upon between risk assessors and managers early in the process to ensure two-way communication. This strategy should also cover who should present information to the public, and the manner in which it will be done.

Decisions on risk communication, including what, whom and how, should be part of an overall risk communication strategy. Risk communication is most effective if undertaken in a systematic way, and generally starts with the gathering of information on the risk issue of concern. Therefore the risk manager and risk assessor must be able to briefly and clearly summarize what this issue encompasses, at an early stage, in order to elicit interest and stakeholder input Communication must then continue throughout the entire process. Once available information has been used to fully identify the hazards, and decide on and assess the appropriate risks, then the preparation and dissemination of this information is required. This will be followed by further discussion with stakeholders, leading to corrections, amendments, and additions as appropriate, resulting in the final Risk Assessment and risk analysis reports.

1.1. Emergence of Risk Communication

Why has the concept of risk communication suddenly become a widely discussed framework for public policy in the environmental and health areas? Prior to 1986 there were only a few essays in the scholarly and policy literature with "risk communication" in their titles. Since that year, however, scores of titles with the term have appeared along with conferences, special sessions in scientific meetings, agency-sponsored workshops, and grants. From one perspective this is not so unusual. New problems often capture the attention of researchers and become the centerpiece of academic and policy research for a period of time. Scientific subfields both from within and across disciplines are constantly emerging.

Risk communication might be just another fashionable rubric for the activity of a specialised group of researchers. If that were the case, then its birth as an area of study would be of interest primarily to historians and sociologists of science. The emergence of risk communication as a research theme cannot be fully appreciated or accounted for without understanding its link to a set of issues that symbolise the discord between scientific experts and the public around the issue of risk. These tensions are played out in disputes between different research traditions on fundamental questions regarding the perception of risk and the essential nature of human rationality. Federal regulatory agencies in the health and environmental areas draw on this diverse and at times conflicting body of research very selectively, choosing analytical frameworks that are most compatible with their policy agendas. Citizen groups, less concerned with formal theories, are increasingly aware that getting a message across to government in disputes over health and environmental hazards is essentially a political activity. On the other hand, experts in risk analysis have come to appreciate the gap between their analytically derived conclusions and the conceptions of popular culture. In the final analysis, those who control the discourse on risk will most likely control the political battles as well.

In this chapter we will analyse the emergence of risk communication as a significant new organising theme for a set of diverse but conceptually related problems concerning the political management of public risk perceptions and individual behavioral responses to risks. Our discussion begins with a brief look at the historic conditions that gave rise to the current thematic focus on risk communication in the social and behavioral sciences; we then examine the role of heuristics in defining the legitimate areas of study; and finally we argue that the research activities centered on risk communication have precipitated new debates over technical and cultural meanings of rationality.

Risk communication is more than a research framework. It has become a concept that is strongly marketed by specific interest groups and used instrumentally to achieve particular ends. At the federal policy level, the Environmental Protection Agency (EPA) has been the strongest marketer of the concept of risk communication. Its chief administrator has stated: "On the national level we will build risk communication into regulatory policy whenever possible." The EPA has elevated the concept of risk communication to a strategic level of importance in both its regulatory activities and its research agenda.

In the public health area the terminology of risk communication is slightly different (federal health officials speak about educating the public about risks) but the concept is equally important. The current policy discourse on preventing health problems such as AIDS, teen pregnancy, and substance abuse focuses on communicating risk to a target population. This emphasis has gone beyond the health education strategies of an earlier era in public health. It incorporates slick national media campaigns developed by public relations or advertising firms in conjunction with science-based strategies in the attempt to change "unhealthy" personal behaviors.

Risk communication has always been an important component in medical practice, particularly in doctor-patient relationships. More recently, with the rise of chronic disease as a major source of health problems and the uncertainty associated with the risk factors for these diseases and the course of treated illnesses, risk communication in medicine has attained a more central and visible role.

Although the study of risk communication is considered new, the practice of it may be as old as human culture itself. There is also nothing new about the social problems that shape the public discourse on risk. Throughout human history individuals and groups have had to contend with a variety of risks for survival and personal wellbeing. Risk is inherent to the human condition. The vagaries of an ever-changing environment, incurable diseases, and manmade threats like war have presented risks to both individual and collective survival.

The origins of structured risk analysis have been traced to the Babylonians in 3200 B.C. All of human history is very much a story of assessing and adapting to risks. Methods used by the ancients to predict risks and to communicate knowledge about avoiding hazardous situations were based on myths, metaphors, and ritual. Risk communication was embedded in folk discourse.

1.2. Professionalisation of Risk

The transition from folk discourse about risk to an expert-centered communication was preconditioned by a series of key historical events beginning in the late 18th century and continuing through the present time. One necessary condition was the rise of the modern state with an implied responsibility for general social welfare functions. The modern state's legitimacy, in part, derives from its claim to protect the population from physical harm.

By the early 20th century the development of public health institutions provided a second condition that furthered the professionalisation of risk. Medicine emerged as an influential profession which defined health risks and controlled intervention strategies. Public health departments began the first large-scale environmental risk monitoring in the sanitation and food safety areas under new governmental mandates. Formal risk messages communicated the danger of hazards such as unsafe water and unpasteurised milk and indicated that experts should be trusted to apply new technologies to reduce the risks of infectious diseases.

A third tributary to the expert-driven field of risk assessment is decision analysis. During World War II the government's need for scientifically based decision methodologies gave rise to a new era of federal research support that spawned fields like operations research and systems analysis. In the late 1940s a variety of quantitative methodologies were introduced to promote understanding of chance processes and to create a rational framework for economic and strategic military decisions. Eventually, these models were applied to the practical problems of predicting and altering the course of risk factors in public health, medicine, and the environment. The methods first used in mathematics, economics, and statistics slowly diffused into the social and health sciences and gave rise to a number of hybrid approaches for calculating risks and quantifying decisionmaking. By the late 1960s the decision methodologies brought promise of a systems science that could provide a rational basis for complex policy decisions concerning technological risks. This was a compelling idea to federal regulators. The schools of rational risk analysis assumed a great burden, namely, to create a bridging logic between the assessment of risk and political decisions concerning the types, levels and distribution of risks acceptable to society. The results have not fulfilled the original expectations. It has been difficult to find common ground between the social world of risk perceptions guided by human experience and the scientists' rational ideal of decisionmaking based on probabilistic thinking.

The modern field of risk analysis is concerned primarily with predicting or quantifying the risks of "scientifically identified hazards" (i.e., toxicity of chemicals, probabilities of accidents, spread of a disease). The communication of information about risks usually occurs within a context of fear and uncertainty. Nuclear radiation, toxic wastes, AIDS, asbestos, and other hazards invoke a range of responses in the scientific, regulatory, and lay communities. Questions of the acceptability of any identified risk are deeply connected to perceptions of fairness and justice. There is wide agreement within the professions that value and equity problems in making decisions about risk are serious. There is less consensus about the extent to which political and ethical choices are an unavoidable part of risk assessment.

With the passage of the Environmental Policy Act of 1969 and the Occupational Safety and Health Act of 1970, the creation of the

Office of Technology Assessment in 1972 and the development of a host of other programs in the early 1970s, the institutionalisation of risk evaluation has been realised, making equal weighting of technical and value considerations difficult to achieve in practice. Legislation requires a formal and legally defensible assessment of risk as exemplified by the requirement of environmental impact statements for most federal agencies. Consulting firms marketing their quantitative expertise blossomed in response to the national emphasis on risk and risk management. Concurrently, graduate schools of public policy and public health, responding to the new role of quantitative decisionmaking within the federal government, began to require courses in decision analysis. In schools of public policy the effective management of environmental and health risks is synonymous with quantitative assessment of problems. Within this orientation, the social and cultural context of risk is of marginal concern.

Quantitative models of risk including comparative risk assessment disregard the many value issues embedded in risk analysis. These problems reemerge in the domain of risk management when regulatory agencies must decide what actions to take once risk assessments have been accomplished. William Ruckelshaus defines risk management as "the distribution of current resources to shape some desirable future state; risk management in its broadest sense means adjusting our environmental policies to obtain the array of social goods—environmental, health-related, social, economic, psychological—that forms our vision of how wc want the world to be." While these certainly are the factors that must be considered if equitable decisions on risk are to be made, there is no public consensus that government can conduct this broad social management of risk in a fair and equitable manner. Thus, the rise of environmental advocacy in the 1970s challenged the expert model of risk management.

Environmentalism became a powerful social movement. Regulatory policies evolved that gave greater attention to the need for public participation. Inevitably, conflicts arose between the rational quantitative approach to risk assessment and public perceptions of risk. The dilemmas of reconciling democratic ideals and citizenc-entered values with the rationality of elite institutions and formal decision processes became more pronounced. While some experts and regulators lamented the rise of "irrational" discourse in environmental debates (the dreaded "not-in-my-backyard" response to siting issues), this same discourse was an expression of their own democratic ideals, which included the opportunity to oppose official decisions that ignored the experiential context of risk.

In the field of public health, the risk debate during the 1970s began to focus on the individual's responsibility for poor health outcomes. Health care costs increased from 7 to 10% of the gross national product, and the complex patchwork of federal health policy seemed unmanageable. To some policymakers, the greatest risk area in the late 1970s was containing costs of medical care. Prevention became more focused on poor health outcomes related to lifestyle variables such as smoking, diet, exercise, and sexual behavior.

Risk factor research and intervention programs increasingly focused on the risky individual and less on the social and cultural context of risk. Personal health risk assessment shares with environmental risk assessment the notion of the "irrational individual." In the former, the individual does not make rational choices about risky behaviors such as smoking and not wearing a seat belt and therefore the individual takes irresponsible risks. In the latter case the faulty logic is reversed: The individual maintains an "exaggerated" fear of hazards which experts consider to be relatively safe. The field of comparative risk assessment actually connects both of these constructions of the irrational individual.

A partial answer to the question of why risk communication has emerged as a framing issue for environmental issues can be found in the differences between professional risk analysts and popular culture. To explore this further we shall look at how risk communication has been conceptualised within the policy sciences.

1.3. From Definitions to Heuristics

The term "risk communication" describes a wide range of activities. It has both a conventional definition and a symbolic definition. The former reflects the use of the term in risk management while the latter derives from the role of risk in political discourse. To frame the concept exclusively in conventional terms restricts the meaning of risk communication to surface behavior or what natural scientists like to call "the phenomenon of the event." The conventional account neglects cultural themes, motivations, and symbolic meanings which may be of equal or greater importance to the technical understanding of how and why a risk message gets transmitted. When risk communication becomes embedded in the political arena, it is less about risks per se than about responsibility or accountability for certain events.

"Risk communication" can refer to any public or private communication that informs individuals about the existence, nature, form, severity, or acceptability of risks. In this broad use of the term, risk communication may be directive and purposeful or nondirectiye and fortuitous. It may describe the controlled release of information toward certain well-defined ends or it may represent the unintended consequences of informal messages about risks. This broad interpretation has been adopted by Kasperson and Palmlund; they state that risk communication "enters our lives in a multitude of forms, sometimes part of the imagery of advertising, sometimes a local corporation's formal statement, or its failure to say anything, sometimes a multivolumed and impenetrable technical risk assessment." Almost any communication from any source that speaks to the issue of risk satisfies the authors' definition.

In risk management a narrower use of the concept usually focuses on an intentional transfer of information designed to respond to public concerns or public needs related to real or perceived hazards. Thus, risk communication incorporates tacit or explicit goals for targeted groups Sbout specific events or processes. The information is channeled from experts to a general audience.

The conventional definition of risk communication centers on the intentionality of the source of information and the quality of the information. Covello and his colleagues have defined risk communication as "any purposeful exchange of scientific information between interested parties regarding health or environmental risks" This definition constraining risk communication to scientific information between interested parties raises several questions. For example, are the claims of lay people in news reports about environmental hazards excluded under this definition? Further, it is not clear what relevance the term "interested parties" has in this definition; the Surgeon General may receive a bored or disinterested response to his reports of the risks of cigarette smoking, but few would disqualify these messages as risk communication.

We can envision risk communication as having five components in its definition: intentionality; content; audience directed; source; and flow. Different definitions of risk communication are narrow or broad depending on the latitude of interpretation of these elements. RThe most restricted interpretation would define a risk communication as a plan executed by a regulatory body targeted to a special audience and embodying specific outcome goals for behavior or attitudinal change.

The conventional definition of risk communication restricts the purview of its study to how "experts" inform others about the truth. Under this notion, some researchers view the exchange of risk information as flowing from technical elites to the polity as a form of scientific noblesse oblige. The process involves the transfer of "scientific" facts and a set of conclusions drawn from those facts. In the broader and more comprehensive definition, technical elites are not the exclusive trustees of risk information. For those who study social process, this broader definition highlights the importance of nonelites as risk communicators.

To understand the symbolic meaning of risk communication, we have to study risk in its social context. A scientist speaking to a community about the health risks of a chemical dump may be carrying out a ritual that displays confidence and control. The technical information (the message) is secondary to the real goal of the communicator: "Have faith; we arc in charge." Local residents citing a litany of symptomatology that they attribute to contaminated water are using risk communication as a channel for their anxieties over environmental overload. "Popular" or "barefoot" epidemiologists are lay people who spot disease clusters and use risk communication to organise for additional public health studies and eventual toxic cleanup.

For a company, risk communication is frequently not about risks but about safety and confidence. When a contract research firm in Cambridge, Massachusetts, wrote a "Dear Neighbor" letter to thousands of residents on the issue of its research with chemical warfare agents, risk communication meant "we wouldn't dream of doing anything hazardous to the community, trust us." In the area of public health, risk communication is the final result of a complex political process through which a problem gets a relatively simple policy construction and is brought to the public consciousness in a restricted form. For community organisers, risk communication is a strategy for solidifying a movement and rebuilding the social complexity of an adverse health or environmental outcome. The symbolic definition of risk communication differs substantially from the conventional view. While the former includes cultural and experiential inputs, the latter generally is reductionist, focusing on quantifiable variables.

1.4. Risk, Rationality, and Culture

Risk communication evolved out of a need of risk managers to gain public acceptance for policies grounded in risk assessment methodologies. The prevailing view of many experts and risk managers is that local communities and the general public react to limited, false, or inadequate information. These lay groups exercise a personal or democratic prerogative in response to "bad" information that is inconsistent with the more fully informed conclusions of risk assessment experts on whom policymakers depend for developing rational responses to complex problems. Frequently, the exercise of local democracy and personal choice is at odds with the rationality of technical experts. Quantitative risk analysis, rather than narrowing differences, may actually exacerbate antagonisms between the technosphere (the culture of experts) and the demosphere (popular culture). Casting the issues in a technical language reduces the possibility of a dialogue between the public and elites.

Recent studies in the risk perception literature reinforce the conception that rationality and democracy are antagonistic to one another. There are many areas where public perceptions about hazards are inconsistent with so-called objective information. For example, people are said to exhibit too little concern about some hazards (smoking, auto accidents, geological radon, and exposure to sunlight) and too much concern about others (nuclear power, toxic wastes, pesticides, and genetic engineering).

Recently, the EPA convened experts from its principal divisions to determine which events, technologies, and situations represented the greatest environmental risks. The results were not surprising^The experts' inventory of environmental priorities did not correlate positively with the agency's regulatory priorities. The EPA was allocating a large share of its resources for reducing adverse environmental effects in areas its own experts did not consider to warrant the most attention.

The discrepancy between what experts deem most important and what the public demands of its government raises difficult policy questions. Two things deserving respect, namely, scientific rationality and democracy (the rights of local communities to express their will on issues of health and safety), are in conflict. How does one proceed? The options that policymakers usually consider include:

1. Circumventing the public by avoiding disclosure, by distraction, by preemption, or by citing social contract doctrine according to which agencies represent the public through their elected officials and can decide for the people.
2. Appealing to some exemplary and independent authoritative body that will apply the rational decision framework and secure public confidence.
3. Communicating the risks and educating the public into thinking about the problem the way the experts do. Public perception must be brought into conformity with scientific rationality.

Of the three options, only the last is directed specifically at reducing the opposition between the demosphcre and the technosphere from the experts' perspective. The emphasis is on a restricted notion of informed democratic practice. Within this context, risk communication is the responsibility of elites and falls into the general rubric of "public understanding of science." The success of risk communication is measured by the degree to which popular attitudes reflect the technical rationality of risk and the extent that popular behavior conforms to technocratic values. A lack of convergence is attributed to a failure of risk communication.

The rapid growth in research on risk perception began to cast doubt about the public education model. Popular conceptions of risk resisted the conclusions of elites despite clear presentation of the "facts." Studies appeared that purported to explain the discrepancies between expert and lay perceptions of risk. Variables that are intended as proxies for cultural determinants were introduced to account for the differences. Two events with the same risk (probability of mortality) evoke different risk perceptions in experimental studies. One event is perceived as voluntary while the other is perceived as involuntary. Lay people do not compare events strictly in terms of actuarial risks.

Psychologists began codifying these and other factors that appeared to explain the discrepancies between technical risk assessment and public perceptions. This has resulted in a labeling of risk events according to the restricted logic of cognitive science. The conventional risk communication approach was modified to accommodate adjustment parameters (voluntary vs. involuntary; familiarity vs. unfamilianty; natural vs. manmade). However, instead of building a culture-based theory of risk perception, psychometricians isolated the cultural factors and treated them as another variable in an experimentally derived technical framework. Every risk event possesses objective hazard estimates and certain qualities that begin to take on ontological status. Thus, a risk event that is voluntary would not be compared on pure rational grounds to one that is involuntary. This system preserves the dichotomy between expert judgment and lay perception of risk. It merely categorises "irrationalities" and does not explore the cultural underpinnings of risk perception. Moreover, cultural noise affecting the popular response to risk is rationalised. This form of the analysis treats the cultural inputs into risk perception as deviant but comprehensible. Risk communication is still viewed as information transfer from experts to lay people.

A cultural approach that seriously considers popular behavior and symbolic dimensions distinguishes two foims of rationality applied to risk: technical and experiential. Both make contributions to the problem of constructing and analysing a risk event, but neither is sufficient. Deviance is not the appropriate metaphor to understand differences between the demosphcre and the technosphere. Once these distinct modes of rationality are understood, the problem of risk communication is transformed; the problem becomes one of mutual understanding and mutual learning. This cultural model is based on the notion that expert and popular approaches to a risk event can each be logical and coherent on their own terms but may exhibit differences in how the problem is articulated, in the factors relevant to the analysis, and in who the experts are.

1.4.1. Technical Rationality

This form of thinking rests on explicitly defined sets of principles and scientific norms. These include hypothetico-deductive methods, a common language for measurement, and quantification and comparison across risk events. In its more advanced forms technical rationality encompasses a mature theory with predictive power. The emphasis is on objeptive (nonpcrsonal) inputs rather than subjective (experiential) information. Perceived responses to risk are important only in understanding the extent to which ordinary people's ideas deviate from the truth. Logical consistency is an imperative. Two events that have an identical risk profile are treated the same—they are interchangeable.

1.4.2. Cultural Rationality

One of the common mistakes in attempting to codify the public attitudes about risk is to measure people's responses to hypothetical questions. Cultural rationality can only be understood when people's cognitive behavior is observed as they are threatened by a real risk event. It is only then that the full panoply of factors come into play that create a complete picture of a public response. To understand cultural rationality, one must address anthropological and phenomenological issues as well as behavioral ones. Technical rationality, on the other hand, believes that risk can be studied independently of context. Mary Douglas provides some insight on this point: "The question of acceptable standards of risk is part of the question of acceptable standards of morality and decency, and there is no way of talking seriously about the first while evading the task of analysing the cultural system in which the second take their form."

Lay people bring many more factors into a risk event than do scientists. For technical experts, the event is denuded of elements that arc irrelevant to the analytical model. Table 1.1 illustrates some of the differences. Many events that are deemed to have very low or insignificant risk by experts are viewed as serious problems by the laity. Burial of low level radioactive wastes and releasing a natural organism minus a few genes into the environment are among such cases. Where there has been discussion of rationality, it has focused on the scientific grounds of a decision. And yet there are clear instances of reasonable decisionmaking at the community level that are inconsistent with expert opinion. Once it is accepted that two inconsistent decisions can be rational and consistent on their own grounds, it is possible to reach beyond the deviant model of risk communication.

Cultural reason does not deny the'role of technical reason; it simply extends it. The former branches out, while

Table 1.1. Factors relevant to the rationality of risk.

Technical Rationality	Cultural Rationality
Trust in scientific methods, explanations; evidence	Trust in political culture and democratic process
Appeal to authority and expertise	Appeal to folk wisdom, peer groups, and traditions
Boundaries of analysis are narrow and reductionist	Boundaries of analysis are broad; include the use of analogy and historical precedent
Risks are depersonalised	Risks are personalised
Emphasison statistical variation and probability	Emphasis on the impacts of risk on the family and community
Appeal to consistency and universality	Focus on particularity; less concerned about consistency of approach
Where there is controversy in science, resolution follows status	Popular responses to scientific differences do not follow the prestige principle
Those impacts that cannot be uttered are irrelevant technical and cultural	Unanticipated or unarticulated risks are relevant

Two issues seem important: First, experts and institutions have developed models of risk and communicated them in various forms throughout history. Conflicts between groups over risk assessments (should we go to war will there be a famine] are fundamental to all cultures. The current discourse on risk and its reliance on sophisticated quantitative models of assessment and cognitive typologies of perception represent a change in the form of risk communication but not in the underlying value controversies over the social context of risk. What we have are new methods addressing persistent structural problems.

The second issue centers on the fit between these new methods and the structural problems of risk communication. Research on the risks described in this essay has an overwhelming tendency to avoid the experiential context of risks—that is, actual people considering real threats to their well-being or other persons' well-being. Laboratory experiments of cognitive psychologists represent risk perception within the bounded models of experts. These models reveal more about the cognitive context of the research tradition than about how persons construct and experience a risk event in a social context. Researchers who view the differences between popular culture and technical rationality as a form of deviance are not likely to generate better strategies for risk communication.

We argue that risk communication has emerged from a context of political conflict. The analytic models attempted to respond to real problems. However, the dominant model of risk communication creates a template that trivialises the complexity of cultural factors. We regard this as an imbalance in the research agenda which should be corrected.

References

Susskind, Lawrence, & Field, Patrick. (1996). *Dealing With an Angry Public.* NewYork: The Free Press.

Swets, Paul, W. (1992). *The Art of Talking So That People Will Listen.* New York: Simon & Schuster.

Timm, Paul, R. (1981). *Functional Business Presentations.* Englewood, NJ: Prentice Hall, Inc.

Turkington, Carol. (1999). *The Complete Idiot's Guide to Cultural Etiquette.* Indianapolis: Macmillan USA, Inc.

Ury, William. (1993). *Getting Past No: Negotiating your way from confrontation to cooperation.* New York: Bantam Books.

Yale, David, R. (1991). *The Publicity Handbook.* Chicago: NTC Business Books.

2

Cycle of Risk Communication

Communication theorists today are apt to slice and dice their definitions quite finely. For the purposes of this course, we will define crisis communication, issues management communication, risk communication, and crisis and emergency risk communication in ways that should be acceptable to most communication theorists and still give the practitioner a firm foundation for discussing with others the differences and similarities among the fields of communication. Call it what you will, but the fact is that communication expertise that fulfils the needs of public health professionals responding to a public health emergency or crisis will borrow from many areas of communication study. This course calls this special combination "crisis and emergency risk communication."

2.1. Crisis Communication

Crisis communication can be defined in two ways and, therefore, can cause some confusion for a practitioner looking for expert training and counsel. Today, the term is most often used to describe an organisation facing a crisis and the need to communicate about that crisis to stakeholders and the public. Typically, a crisis is an event that occurs unexpectedly, may not be in the organisation's control, and may cause harm to the organisation's good reputation or viability. An example of an organisation facing a crisis is the occurrence of a mass shooting of employees by a disgruntled employee. In most instances, the organisation is facing some legal or moral culpability for the crisis (unlike a disaster in which a tornado wipes out thc production plant), and stakeholders and the public are judging the organisation's response to the crisis.

A simple definition of crisis communication separates the judgment or reputation factors in the communication and deals primarily with factual communication by an involved organisation to its stakeholders and the public. Crisis communication could simply be the effort by community leaders to inform the public that, by law, they must evacuate in advance of a hurricane. In this definition, the organisation is not being overtly judged as a possible participant in the creation of the disaster, and the information is empirically sound, so the individual can judge its veracity without the help of an expert.

The underlying thread in crisis communication is that the communicating organisation is experiencing an unexpected crisis and must respond. Crisis also implies lack of control by the involved organisation in the timing of the crisis event.

— *Communicator*: Participant
— *Time Pressure*: Urgent and unexpected
— *Message Purpose*: Explain and persuade

2.2. Issues Management Communication

Issues management communication is similar to crisis communication; however, the organisation has the luxury of foreknowledge of the impending crisis and the opportunity, to some extent, to choose the timing of its revelation to stakeholders and the public and reveal the organisation's plan to resolve the issue. Again, the organisation is central to the event.

— *Communicator*: Participant
— *Time Pressure*: Anticipated; timing somewhat in control of the communicator
— *Message Purpose*: Persuade and explain

2.3. Risk Communication

Risk communication is a field that has flourished in the area of environmental health. Through risk communication, the communicator hopes to provide the receiver with information about the expected type (good or bad) and magnitude (weak or strong) of an outcome from a behavior or exposure. Typically, it is a discussion about an adverse outcome and the probability of that outcome occurring. In some instances, risk communication has been employed to help an individual make a choice about whether or not to undergo a medical treatment, continue to live next to a nuclear power plant, pass on genetic risks, or elect to vaccinate a healthy baby against whooping cough. In some cases, risk communication is used to help individuals adjust to the knowledge that something that has already occurred, such as an exposure to harmful carcinogens, may put them at greater risk for a negative health outcome, such as cancer, in the future. Risk communication would prepare people for that possibility and, if warranted, give them appropriate steps to monitor for the health risk, such as regular cancer screening.

- *Communicator*: Expert that did not participate in the event and is neutral regarding the outcome
- *Time Pressure*: Anticipated communication with little or no time pressure
- *Message Purpose*: Empower decision-making

2.4. Crisis and Emergency Risk Communication

Crisis and emergency risk communication encompasses the urgency of disaster communication with the need to communicate risks and benefits to stakeholders and the public. Crisis and emergency risk communication differs from crisis communication in that the communicator is not perceived as a participant in the crisis or disaster, except as an agent to resolve the crisis or emergency. Crisis and emergency risk communication is the effort by experts to provide information to allow an individual, stake-holder, or an entire community to make the best possible decisions about their well-being within nearly impossible time constraints and help people ultimately to accept the imperfect nature of choices during the crisis. This is the communication that goes on in emergency rooms, not doctors' offices. Crisis and emergency risk communication also differs from risk communication in that a decision must be made within a narrow time constraint, the decision may be irreversible, the outcome of the decision may be uncertain, and the decision may need to be made with imperfect or incomplete information. Crisis and emergency risk communication represents an expert opinion provided in the hope that it benefits its receivers and advances a behavior or an action that allows for rapid and efficient recovery from the event.

— *Communicator*: Expert who is a post-event participant invested in the outcome
— *Time Pressure*: Urgent and unexpected
— *Message Purpose*: Explain, persuade, and empower decision-making

2.5. Emergencies, Disasters, and Crises

What do emergencies, disasters, and crises have in common? Simply, that something bad has happened or is happening. When something bad and/or unexpected happens, it may be called an emergency, a disaster, or a crisis depending on the magnitude of the event and the current phase of the event.

Disasters are the ultimate test of emergency response capability. The ability to deal effectively with disasters is becoming more relevant as the factors that tend to increase risk are also increasing. Some of these factors include the following:

— *Increasing Population Density*. As areas become more densely populated, there are more potential victims when a disaster strikes.
— *Increased Settlement in High-Risk Areas*. Another reason for rising disaster losses is that part of this increase in population density is occurring in disaster-prone areas. There is greater settlement in such high-risk areas as floodplains; earthquake faults; coastal hurricane areas; unstable hillsides; areas subject to wild land fires; and areas adjacent to hazardous waste landfills, airports, and nuclear power plants.
— *Increased Technological Risks*. New technology is adding to the list of disaster agents at an ever-increasing rate. One of these is the 4 billion tons of hazardous chemicals that are shipped annually in this country. Our society is also becoming more dependent on technology and specialisation, making us more vulnerable to such disasters as a mass power outage.

— *Aging U.S. population.* The United States is on the brink of a longevity revolution. By 2030, the number of older Americans will have more than doubled to 70 million, or 1 in every 5 Americans. The growing number and proportion of older adults is placing increasing demands on the public health system and on medical and social services. More than 65 percent of Americans ages 65 years or older have some form of cardiovascular disease, and half of all men and two-thirds of women older than age 70 have arthritis. Of older adults not living in institutions in 1994, nearly 40 percent—12 million seniors were limited by chronic conditions. Of these, 3 million were unable to perform the activities of daily living—such as bathing, shopping, dressing, or eating—placing caregiving demands on family and friends. A large body of evidence indicates that the health conditions and needs of older adults are different from other segments of the population. An aging population offers new challenges for disaster response.

— *Emerging infectious diseases and antimicrobial resistance.* Infectious diseases are a continuing danger to all people, no matter their age, gender, lifestyle, ethnic background, or economic status. They are still among the most common causes of suffering and death, and they impose an enormous financial burden on society. Because we do not know which new diseases will arise, we must always be prepared for the unexpected.

Throughout history, humanity has fallen victim to pandemics of cholera, plague, influenza, typhoid, tuberculosis, and other infectious maladies so widespread that most people rarely survived into middle age.

In the years following World War II, it was widely believed that humans were winning the centuries-long war against infectious microbes. Such life-threatening bacterial diseases as tuberculosis and typhoid fever could be treated by antibiotics. Dread diseases of childhood such as polio, whooping cough, and diphtheria, could be conquered through vaccination. Coupled with earlier improvements in urban sanitation and water quality, vaccines and antibiotics dramatically lowered the incidence of infectious diseases. Thus, it became possible to imagine a world in which infectious pathogens would no longer prey upon humanity.

However, this optimism was premature. As early as the 1950s, penicillin began to lose its power to cure infections caused by *Staphylococcus aureus*, a common bacterium that can cause serious illness. In 1957 and 1968, new strains of influenza emerged in China and spread rapidly around the globe, and in the 1970s, there was a resurgence of sexually transmitted diseases. Also during the 1970s, several new diseases were identified in the United States and elsewhere, including Legionnaires' disease, Lyme disease, toxic shock syndrome, and Ebola hemorrhagic fever. Antibiotic-resistant bacteria are becoming more common in hospitals, among patients, and in communities.

Looming over the yearly routine of preparing for each flu season is the threat that a pandemic strain might emerge—a virulent new type of flu that can span the globe in months and decimate the world's population—the kind that killed more than 20 million people in 1918–1919. Such a lethal virus can sweep the world without warning. The recent avian influenza scare in Hong Kong in 1997 raised the specter of a possible global pandemic and jolted the world from any renewed complacency about infectious diseases.

Increased International Travel. International travel and trade play a role in the development of microbial resistance. A microbe originating in Africa or Southeast Asia can arrive on North American shores within 24 hours. In the United States, published reports show that the majority of multidrug-resistant typhoid cases originated in six developing countries. The future will bring, by all indications, megacities. In the next 25 years, the world may have as many as 20 cities with populations above 20 million. Most of these cities will be in developing countries where poverty, population density, and lack of sanitation will allow microorganisms to incubate and spread rapidly. Add to that the speed of travel, and the global threat is obvious.

The rapid geographic movement of products and populations, changes in lifestyles and behaviors, the emergence of new infectious diseases, and the deliberate use of microorganisms and toxins as terrorist weapons add to the current public health risks. In addition, unforeseen interactions, such as those that may allow disease agents to cross species' barriers, also add to the unpredictability of public health risk.

Increased Terrorism. The threat from terrorism is real. it is immediate, and it is evolving. State-sponsored terrorism appears to have declined over the past 5 years, but transnational groups—with decentralised leadership that makes them harder to identify and disrupt—are emerging. The world is seeing fewer centrally controlled operations and more acts initiated and executed at lower levels.

Terrorists are also becoming more operationally adept and more technically sophisticated in order to defeat counterterrorism measures. For example, as security around government and military facilities has been strenghtened, terrorists are seeking out "softer" targets that provide opportunities for mass casualties. Employing increasingly advanced devices and using such strategies as simultaneous attacks, the number of people killed or injured in international terrorist attacks rose dramatically in the 1990s, despite a general decline in the number of incidents. Approximately one-third of these incidents involved U.S. interests.

An act of biological or chemical terrorism may range from the dissemination of aerosolised anthrax spores to food product contamination; predicting when and how such an attack may occur is impossible. The probability of biological or chemical terrorism cannot be ignored, especially in light of the events of the past 10 years.

2.6. Crisis Communication Lifecycle

Understanding the pattern of a crisis can help communicators anticipate problems and respond effectively. For communicators, it's vital to know that every emergency, disaster, or crisis evolves in phases and that the communication must evolve in tandem. By dividing the crisis into the following phases, the communicator can anticipate the information needs of the media, stakeholders, and the general public. (Digure 1) Each phase has its unique informational requirements. The movement through each of the phases will vary according to the triggering event. Not all crises are created equally. The degree or intensity and longevity of a crisis will impact required resources and staff.

2.6.1. Pre-crisis Phase

Communication objectives during the precrisis phase are the following:

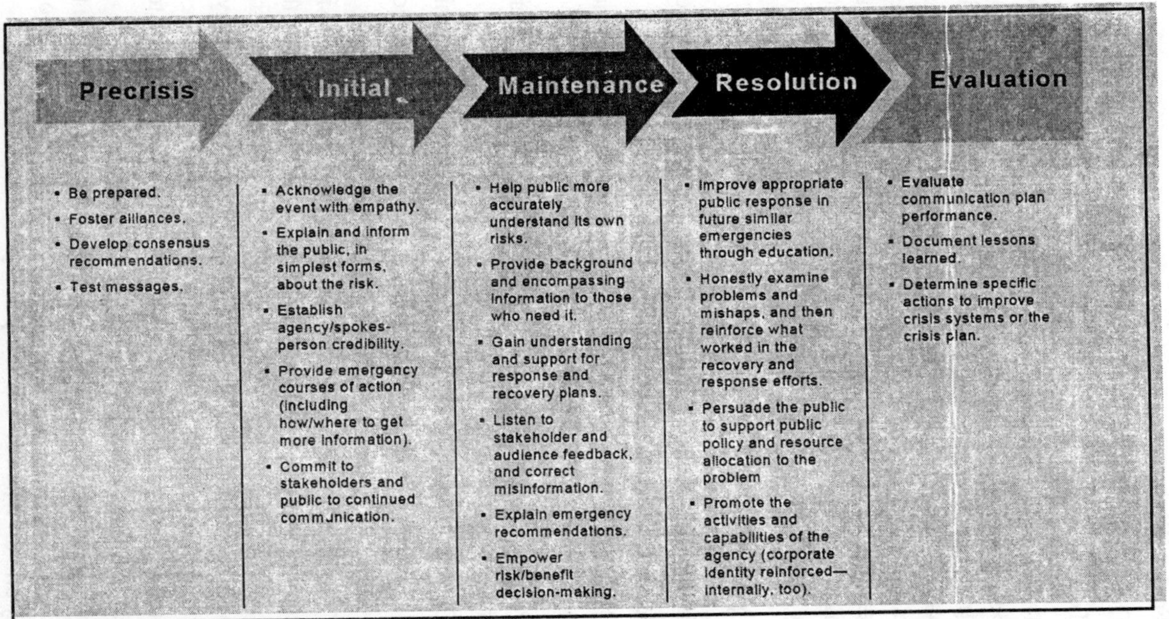

Figure 1. Crisis Communication Lifecycle

— Be prepared.
— Foster alliances.
— Develop consensus recommendations.
— Test messages.

This is where all the planning and most of the work should be done. Types of disasters that your organisation may need to address can be anticipated. Reasonable questions can be anticipated, and preliminary answers can be sought. Initial communication can be drafted with blanks to be filled in later. Spokespersons, resources, and resource mechanisms can be identified. Training and refinements to plans and messages can be made. Alliances and partnerships can be fostered to ensure that experts are speaking with one voice.

2.6.2. Initial Phase

Communication objectives during the initial phase are the following:

— Acknowledge the event with empathy.
— Explain and inform the public, in simplest terms, about the risk.
— Establish organisational/spokesperson credibility.
— Provide emergency courses of action (including how/where to get more information).
— Commit to stakeholders and public to continued communication.

Simplicity, credibility, verifiability, consistency, and speed count when communicating in the initial phases of an emergency.

The initial phase of a crisis is characterised by confusion and intense media interest. Information is usually incomplete, and the facts are disperse. It's important to recognise that information from the media, other organisations, and within your organisation may not be accurate. Your role is to learn the facts about what happened, to determine your organisation's response is to the problem, and to verify the true magnitude of the event as quickly as possible.

In the initial phase of a crisis, there is no second chance to get it right. Your organisation's reputation depends on what you do and do not say and on when or whether you say it.

One of the best ways to limit public anxiety in a crisis is to provide useful information about the nature of the problem and what the public can do about it. During the initial phase of an event, establish your organisation as a credible source of information. Even when there is little information to offer, you can still communicate how the organisation is investigating the event and when more information will be available. At the very least, messages should demonstrate that your organisation is addressing the issues head-on that its approach is reasonable, caring, and timely.

Of course, the pressure to release information prematurely can be intense. Remember that all information must be approved by the appropriate managers before its release to the media.

In the initial phase of a crisis or emergency, people want information—*now*. They want timely and accurate facts about what happened, and where, and what is being done. They will question the magnitude of the crisis, the immediacy of the threat to them, the duration of the threat, and who is going to fix the problem. Communicators should be prepared to answer these questions as quickly, accurately, and fully as possible.

2.6.3. Crisis Maintenance

Communication objectives during the crisis maintenance phase are as follows:

— Help people more accurately understand their own risks.

— Provide background and encompassing information to those who need it.

— Gain understanding and support for response and recovery plans.

— Listen to stakeholder and audience feedback and correct misinformation.

— Explain emergency recommendations.

— Empower risk/benefit decisionmaking.

As the crisis evolves, anticipate sustained media interest and scrutiny. Unexpected developments, rumors, or misinformation may place further media demands on organisation communicators. Experts, professionals, and others not associated with your organisation will comment publicly on the issue and sometimes contradict or misinterpret your messages. Expect to be criticised about your handling of the situation.

Staying on top of the information flow and maintaining tight coordination are essential. Processes for tracking communication activities become increasingly important as the workload increases.

The crisis maintenance phase includes an ongoing assessment of the event and allocation of resources.

2.6.4. Resolution

Communication objectives for the resolution phase are as follows:

— Improve appropriate public response in future similar emergencies through education.

— Honestly examine problems and mishaps, and then reinforce what worked in the recovery and response efforts.

— Persuade the public to support public policy and resource allocation.

— Promote the activities and capabilities of the organisation (corporate identity reinforced—internally, too).

As the crisis resolves, there is a return to stasis, with increased understanding about the crisis as complete recovery systems are put in place. This phase is characterised by a reduction in public/media interest. Once the crisis is resolved, you may need to respond to intense media scrutiny of how the event was handled. You may have an opportunity to reinforce public health messages while the issue is still current. A public education campaign or changes to a Web site may be necessary. Research has shown that a community is usually most responsive to risk avoidance and mitigation education directly after a disaster has occurred.

2.6.5. Evaluation

When the crisis is over, evaluate communication plan performance, document lessons learned, and determine specific actions to improve crisis systems or the crisis plan.

2.7. Role of Risk Communication

Crises, emergencies, and disasters happen. One of the reasons disaster response is difficult to coordinate is that disasters are different from routine daily emergencies. The difference is more than just one of magnitude. Disasters generally cannot be adequately managed merely by mobilising more personnel and material. During crisis situations, decision-makers are often unable to collect and process information in a timely manner and, thus, rely on established routines for situations that are, by definition, novel. Communication during a crisis cannot be managed solely by mobilising more people and material the communication itself must change because crises are inherently low-probability but high-impact events in which established frames of reference for understanding may breakdown. In major disasters, the incident is so shattering that both the sense of what is occurring and the means to rebuild that sense collapse simultaneously. Crisis and emergency risk communication is a vital component to help people cope and begin to rebuild a sense of order and understanding in their lives.

Crisis and emergency risk communication can work to counter some of the harmful human behaviors that are known to arise during a crisis. These potentially harmful individual, group, or community behaviors include:

— Demands for unneeded treatment
— Disorganised group behavior (stealing/looting)
— Bribery and fraud
— Reliance on special relationships
— Increased alcohol and tobacco use
— Increased multiple unexplained physical symptoms (MUPS)
— Unreasonable trade and travel restrictions.

Add bad communication practices to a crisis situation and the odds of a negative public response increase. Some of the bad communication practices that contribute to a poor public response that can be overcome with planning, coordination, research, and training include:

— Mixed messages from multiple experts
— Information released so late that events make the issue moot
— Messages that are over-reassuring
— Recommendations to the public without a reality check
— Leaving myths, rumors, and doom-sayers unchallenged or corrected

— Spokespersons who engage in improper behavior, exhibit a lack of affect, or use inappropriate humor

— Public power struggles and confusion.

The purpose of a public health response to a crisis is to efficiently and effectively reduce and prevent illness, injury, and death and return individuals and communities to normal. The possibilities of harmful human behaviors, combined with bad communication practices, can lead to overwhelming harmful public health outcomes during the crisis response. The following are some of the negative situations public health professionals could face:

— Public demand for misallocation of limited emergency response resources

— Public mistrust or circumventing public health recommendations

— Opportunists who play on peoples' fear or uncertainties to provide fraudulent alternative treatments

— Increased disease and death

— Overreaction and wasted fiscal and medical resources during the emergency response.

Communication can reduce the tendencies of detrimental human behavior and prevent negative public health response outcomes by:

— Executing a solid crisis communication plan

— Being the first source for information

— Expressing empathy and caring

— Exhibiting competence and expertise

— Remaining honest and open

— Committing and remain dedicated to the response and recovery

— Applying emergency risk communication principles to the message.

Way to good crisis and emergency risk communication and help organisation reserve limited resources, fulfil its mission, and maintain public trust.

References

Rodman, George. (1981). *Mass Media Issues: Analysis and Debate*. Chicago: Science Research Associates, Inc.

Sandman, Peter M., Ph.D. (1993). *Responding to Community Outrage: Strategies for Effective Risk Communication* (Fairfax, VA: American Industrial Hygiene Association).

Shewe, Charles D.; Smith, Reuben M. (1983). *Marketing Concepts and Applications*. New York: McGraw- Hill Book Company.

Smith, Larry. (2001). *The ICM Crisis Management Certification Course*. Louisville, Kentucky: Institute for Crisis Management.

3

Psychological Approach to Risk Communication

Effective communication is a "resource multiplier" during a crisis, disaster, or emergency. Many of the expected harmful individual and community behaviors can be mitigated with effective crisis and emergency risk communication. Each crisis will carry its own psychological baggage. The practitioner must anticipate what mental stresses the population will be experiencing and apply appropriate risk communication strategies to attempt to manage these stresses in the population. Risk communication is a fully legitimate tool of response and recovery just like any other resource applied to the disaster. It is not an attempt at mass mental therapy. It is a reasoned and mature communication approach to the selection of message, messenger, and method of delivery.

3.1. Psychological Manifestations in Crisis

Contrary to what one may see in the movies, people seldom act completely irrationally or panic during a crisis. We do know that people have run into burning buildings, have refused to get out of a car stuck on the tracks with a train speeding close, and have gone into shock and become paralysed to the point of helplessness. The overwhelming majority of people can and do act reasonably during an emergency. However, the following are some of the stresses and expected psychological manifestations that do occur during a crisis. These can be addressed through effective risk communication:

— *Vicarious rehearsal.* Interestingly, experience has shown that people farther away (by distance or relationship) from the threat may actually exercise less reasonable reactions than those who are facing the real crisis. The communication age allows some people to vicariously participate in a crisis in which they are not in immediate danger of harm. These people will mentally rehearse the crisis as if they are experiencing it and "try on" the courses of action presented to them. Because these "arm chair" victims have the luxury of time to decide their chosen course of action, they may be much more critical about its value to them. In some cases, these people may reject the proposed course of action and choose another or insist that they too are at risk and need the recommended remedy themselves, such as a visit to an emergency room or a vaccination. In its most troublesome form, these "worried well" will heavily tax the recovery and response.

— *Denial.* Members of the community will experience denial.

  – Some people choose not to get warnings or action recommendations.
  – Some people may become confused by the warning.
  – Some people may not believe the threat is real.
  – Some people may not believe the threat is real to them.

An individual experiencing denial may not take recommended steps to safeguard safety and life until the absolute last moments, and then, perhaps, when it's too late.

— *Stigmatisation.* In some instances, victims may be stigmatised by their communities and refused services or public access. Fear and isolation of a group perceived to be contaminated or risky to associate with will hamper community recovery and affect evacuation and relocation efforts. In a disease outbreak, a community is more likely to separate from those perceived to be infected.

— *Fear and avoidance.* Fear is an important psychological consideration in the response to a crisis. The fear of the unknown or the fear of uncertainty may be the most debilitating of the psychological responses to disaster. With fear at the core, an individual may act in extreme and sometimes irrational ways to avoid the perceived or real threat.

— *Withdrawal, hopelessness, and helplessness.* Some people can accept that the threat is real, but the threat looms so large that they feel the situation is hopeless. They feel helpless to protect themselves and thus withdraw.

3.2. Crisis-related Psychological Issues

The negative emotions commonly experienced in a crisis or disaster left without mitigating communication from a trusted source may lead to harmful individual or group behaviors that can adversely affect the public's safety by hampering the speed, quality, and appropriateness of the crisis response and recovery. What's at stake are loss of life, health, safety, and property. This may be manifested when harmful actions lead to:

— Misallocation of treatments based on demand, not need

— Needless destruction of an industry or product through avoidance or boycotting

— Accusations of preferential treatment and bias in aid

— Unreasonable trade and travel restrictions

— Attempts at fraud

— Creation and propagation of damaging rumors and hoaxes directed at people or products

— Doomsayers that encourage distrust of government

— Attempts at bribery for scarce or rationed treatments and resources

— Dependence on special relationships to ensure special considerations based on desire, not need.

Self-destructive behaviors among adults as reactions to stress may include increased alcohol and tobacco use, inattention to family responsibilities, depression, anxiety, and compromised immune systems contributing to health complications.

— Research shows increased incidences of "multiple unexplained physical symptoms (MUPS)" among populations experiencing a crisis. In emergencies involving a biological disease, these symptoms could confound the effort to identify those people who need immediate care versus those who need limited treatments or pharmaceuticals.

3.3. Levels of Risk Communication

The public must feel empowered to take action in the event of a crisis to reduce the likelihood of victimisation and fear. Physical and mental preparation will relieve anxiety despite the expectation of potential injury or death. An "action message" can provide people with the feeling that they can take steps to improve a situation and not become passive victims of the threat.

How people absorb or act on information they receive during an emergency may be different from non-emergency situations. Research provides some clues about the receiver of information during an emergency. While it can be expected that normal communication psychology principles apply during a crisis, research has shown that in a dire emergency, people or groups may exaggerate their communication responses as they revert to more rudimentary or instinctual "flight or fight" reasoning, caused in part by the increase of adrenaline and cortisol in the blood system.

Studies show that the amount of media coverage of a traumatic event directly affects audience response. In some instances, information can hurt. The media affects segments of the population differently. The effects of television coverage of disasters on children can be especially troubling because the context of the disaster may not be understood. The 24-hour-a-day coverage following the Oklahoma City bombing gave local children the illusion that the entire town had been demolished. Most studies show that more information leads to decreased anxiety.

3.3.1. Decision-making

Decision-making is also affected during a crisis. The following behaviors are commonly exhibited:

3.3.1.1. Simplify

Under intense stress and possible information overload, people will miss the nuances of messages or avoid the effort to juggle multiple facts by simplifying what they've heard. To cope, people may not attempt an analytical and reasoned approach to decisionmaking. Instead, they may rely on habit, long-held traditions, following the lead of others, and such stereotyping as classifying participants as "good" and "bad" guys.

3.3.1.2. Maintain Current Beliefs

If your communication requires asking people to do something that seems counter-intuitive (e.g., getting out of a safe car and lying in a ditch instead of outrunning a tornado), it may be difficult to change beliefs during a crisis or emergency. People are adept at maintaining faith in their current beliefs. People tend not to seek out contrary evidence. They also exploit the conflicting or contradictory information about a subject by interpreting it as consistent with existing beliefs.

3.3.1.3. Believe assumed, Incorrect, or Conflicting Information

People remember what they see. They tend to believe what they've experienced in their own lives; however, faced with new risks in an emergency, people must rely on experts. The concern today is that supposedly reputable experts may disagree regarding the level of threat, risks, and appropriate recommendations. The natural give and take among experts and their tendency to enjoy the peer process could leave the general public with increased uncertainty and fear. Research indicates that, often, the first message to reach the listener may be the accepted message even though more accurate information may follow.

Simplicity, credibility, verifiability, consistency, and speed count when communicating in an emergency. An effective message must be repeated, come from a legitimate source, be specific to the emergency being experienced, and offer a positive course of action.

3.3.2. Perception of Risk

The perception of risk is also vitally important in emergency communication. Not all risks are created equally. A wide body of research exists on issues surrounding risk communication, but the following emphasises that some risks are more accepted than others.

— *Voluntary versus involuntary*: Voluntary risks are more readily accepted than imposed risks.

— *Personally controlled versus controlled by others*: Risks controlled by the individual or community are more readily accepted than risks outside the individual's or community's control.

— *Familiar versus exotic*: Familiar risks are more readily accepted than unfamiliar risks. Risks perceived as relatively unknown are perceived to be greater than risks that are well understood.

— *Natural origin versus manmade*: Risks generated by nature are better tolerated than risks generated by man or institution. Risks caused by human action are less well tolerated than risks generated by nature.

— *Reversible versus permanent*: Reversible risk is better tolerated than risk perceived to be irreversible.

— *Statistical versus anecdotal*: Statistical risks for populations are better tolerated than risks represented by individuals. An anecdote presented to a person or community, i.e., "one in a million," can be more damaging than a statistical risk of one in 10,000 presented as a number.

— *Endemic versus epidemic (catastrophic)*: Illnesses, injuries, and deaths spread over time at a predictable rate are better tolerated than illnesses, injuries, and deaths grouped by time and location (e.g., U.S. car crash deaths versus airplane crashes).

— *Fairly distributed versus unfairly distributed*: Risks that do not single out a group, population, or individual are better tolerated than risks that are perceived to be targeted.

— *Generated by trusted institution versus mistrusted institution*: Risks generated by a trusted institution are better tolerated than risks that are generated by a mistrusted institution. Risks generated by a mistrusted institution will be perceived as greater than risks generated by a trusted institution.

— *Adults versus children*: Risks that affect adults are better tolerated than risks that affect children.

— *Understood benefit versus questionable benefit*: Risks with well-understood potential benefit and the reduction of well-understood harm are better tolerated than risks with little or no perceived benefit or reduction of harm.

The principles of risk communication are vital when developing messages during an emergency. If it's the first emergency of its type—

manmade, imposed, or catastrophic—the communication challenges will increase.

Populations subjected to risks caused by human action and meant to destroy, hurt, and create terror will react with greater outrage. Unfairly distributed, unfamiliar, catastrophic, and immoral events create long-lasting mental health effects that lead to anger, frustration, helplessness, fear, and a desire for revenge.

In any discussion of risk, the scientist may perceive one risk in 10,000 as an acceptable risk when the listener may anecdotally be familiar with that one adverse outcome and believe that the risk is much greater to them. Perception of risk is not about numbers alone. These and other risk perceptions must be considered during a crisis.

3.4. EPA's Cardinal Rules of Risk Communication

3.4.1. Rule 1. Accept and involve the Public as a Legitimate Partner

Two basic tenets of risk communication in a democracy are generally understood and accepted. First, people and communities have a right to participate in decisions that affect their lives, their property, and the things they value. Second, the goal of risk communication should not be to diffuse public concerns or avoid action. The goal should be to produce an informed public that is involved, interested, reasonable, thoughtful, solution-oriented, and collaborative.

Guidelines: Demonstrate respect for the public by involving the community early, before important decisions are made. Clarify that decisions about risks will be based not only on the magnitude of the risk but on factors of concern to the public. Involve all parties that have an interest or a stake in the particular risk in question. Adhere to highest moral and ethical standards: recognise that people hold you accountable.

3.4.2. Rule 2. Listen to the Audience

People are often more concerned about issues such as trust, credibility, control, benefits, competence, voluntariness, fairness, empathy, caring, courtesy, and compassion than about mortality statistics and the details of quantitative risk assessment. If people feel or perceive that they are not being heard, they cannot be expected to listen. Effective risk communication is a two-way activity.

Guidelines: Do not make assumptions about what people know, think or want done about risks. Take the time to find out what people are thinking: use techniques such as interviews, facilitated discussion groups, advisory groups, toll-free numbers, and surveys. Let all parties that have an interest or a stake in the issue be heard. Identify with your audience and try to put yourself in their place. Recognise people's emotions. Let people know that what they said has been understood, addressing their concerns as well as yours. Recognise the "hidden agendas," symbolic meanings, and broader social, cultural, economic or political considerations that often underlie and complicate the task of risk communication.

3.4.3. Rule 3. Be Honest, Frank, and Open

Before a risk communication can be accepted, the messenger must be perceived as trustworthy and credible. Therefore, the first goal of risk communication is to establish trust and credibility. Trust and credibility judgments are resistant to change once made. Short-term judgments of trust and credibility are based largely on verbal and nonverbal communications. Long term judgments of trust and credibility are based largely on actions and performance.

In communicating risk information, trust and credibility are a spokesperson's most precious assets. Trust and credibility are difficult to obtain. Once lost they are almost impossible to regain.

Guidelines: State credentials; but do not ask or expect to be trusted by the public. If an answer is unknown or uncertain, express willingness to get back to the questioner with answers.

Make corrections if errors are made. Disclose risk information as soon as possible (emphasising appropriate reservations about reliability). Do not minimise or exaggerate the level of risk. Speculate only with great caution. If in doubt, lean toward sharing more information, not less or people may think something significant is being hidden. Discuss data uncertainties, strengths and weaknesses including the ones identified by other credible sources. Identify worst-case estimates as such, and cite ranges of risk estimates when appropriate.

3.4.4. Rule 4. Coordinate and Collaborate with Other credible Sources

Allies can be effective in helping communicate risk information. Few things make risk communication more difficult than conflicts or public disagreements with other credible sources.

Guidelines: Take time to coordinate all inter-organisational and intra-organisational communications. Devote effort and resources to the slow, hard work of building bridges, partnerships, and alliances with other organisations. Use credible and authoritative intermediaries. Consult with others to determine who is best able to answer questions about risk. Try to issue communications jointly with other trustworthy sources such as credible university scientists, physicians, citizen advisory groups, trusted local officials, and national or local opinion leaders.

3.4.5. Rule 5. Meet the needs of the Media

The media are a prime transmitter of information on risks. They play a critical role in setting agendas and in determining outcomes. The media are generally more interested in politics than in risk; more interested in simplicity than in complexity; and more interested in wrongdoing, blame and danger than in safety.

Guidelines: Be open with and accessible to reporters. Respect their deadlines. Provide information tailored to the needs of each type of media, such as sound bites, graphics and other visual aids for television. Agree with the reporter in advance about the specific topic of the interview; stick to the topic in the interview. Prepare a limited number of positive key messages in advance and repeat the messages several times during the interview. Provide background material on complex risk issues. Do not speculate. Say only those things that you are willing to have repeated: everything you say in an interview is on the record. Keep interviews short. Follow up on stories with praise or criticism, as warranted. Try to establish long-term relationships of trust with specific editors and reporters.

3.4.6. Rule 6. Speak Clearly and with Compassion

Technical language and jargon are useful as professional shorthand. But they are barriers to successful communication with the public. In low trust, high concern situations, empathy and caring often carry more weight than numbers and technical facts.

Guidelines: Use clear, nontechnical language. Be sensitive to local norms, such as speech and dress. Strive for brevity, but respect people's information needs and offer to provide more information. Use graphics and other pictorial material to clarify messages. Personalise risk data: use stories, examples, and anecdotes that make technical data come alive. Avoid distant, abstract, unfeeling language about deaths, injuries and illnesses. Acknowledge and respond (both in words and with actions) to emotions that people express, such as anxiety, fear, anger, outrage, and helplessness. Acknowledge and respond to the distinctions that the public views as important in evaluating risks. Use risk comparisons to help put risks in perspective; but avoid comparisons that ignore distinctions that people consider important. Always try to include a discussion of actions that are under way or can be taken. Promise only that which can be delivered, and follow through. Acknowledge, and say, that any illness, injury or death is a tragedy and to be avoided.

3.4.7. Rule 7. Plan Carefully and Evaluate Performance

Different goals, audiences, and media require different risk communication strategies. Risk communication will be successful only if carefully planned and evaluated.

Guidelines: Begin with clear, explicit objectives such as providing information to the public, providing reassurance, encouraging protective action and behavior change, stimulating emergency response, or involving stakeholders in dialogue and joint problem solving. Evaluate technical information about risks and know its strengths and weaknesses. Identify important stakeholders and subgroups within the audience. Aim communications at specific stakeholders and subgroups in the audience. Recruit spokespersons with effective presentation and human interaction skills. Train staff—including technical staff—in communication skills: recognise and reward outstanding performance.

3.5. Be Careful about Risk Comparisons

The true risk and the perceived risk can be quite different. The source of the risk can be as troubling as the degree of risk. People do not like injustice. If they perceive that the risk has been imposed on them, that they have been unfairly singled out to experience the risk, or that a fellow human being deliberately put them in the position to be exposed to the risk, they are likely to perceive the risk with more concern or outrage. Explore both the true risk and the perception of that risk. "Hazard" is the seriousness of a risk from a technical perspective. "Outrage" is the seriousness of the risk in nontechnical terms. Experts view risk in terms of hazard; the rest of us view it in terms of outrage. The risks we overestimate are high-outrage and low-hazard. The risks we underestimate are high-hazard and low-outrage.

When technical people try to explain that a high-outrage, low-hazard risk isn't very serious, they normally compare it to a high-hazard, low-outrage risk. "This is less serious than that," the experts tell us, "so if you are comfortable with that, you ought to be comfortable with this." In hazard terms, the comparison is valid. But the audience is thinking in outrage terms and viewed in outrage terms, the comparison is simply false. "This" is lower hazard than "that," but it is higher outrage.

Bioterrorism is high-outrage and (for most of us, so far) low-hazard. You can't effectively compare it to a low-outrage, high-hazard risk such as driving a car which is voluntary, familiar, less dreaded, and mostly under our own control. Even naturally acquired anthrax fails to persuade as a basis for comparison. People are justifiably more angry and frightened about terrorist anthrax attacks than about natural outbreaks, even if the number of people attacked is low.

A volatile risk comparison can work if it is clear that you are trying to inform the public's judgment, not coerce it. If you're trying to inform the public about a risk, the natural thing to do would be to bracket the risk: bigger than X, smaller than Y. If you report only that it's smaller than Y, your audience can tell they're being coerced.

Risks for comparison should be similar in their characteristics that would generate outrage. Here is a risk comparison that can work:

Research indicates that, in Hawaii, a person is 10 times more likely to be killed by brain damage from a falling coconut than to be killed by a shark. In this case, the risks are both natural in origin, fairly distributed, exotic, and outside the control of the individual. Although being killed by a shark may cause greater terror or emotion, its comparison to being killed by a coconut helps the individual to see that he or she may be perceiving the risk as greater than it is. Most people have never considered their risk of dying by coconut.

Acknowledge to people the reasons that they are more worried about anthrax (which has been imposed on them) rather than, for example, auto accidents or flu deaths.

3.5.1. Don't Over-reassure

If an emergency event is catastrophic, unexpected, dreaded, unfamiliar, in someone else's control, morally repugnant, and memorable, expect high outrage.

Reassurance can backfire. Tell people how scary the situation is, even though the actual numbers are small, and watch them get calmer.

Even if over-reassurance worked, which it doesn't, it is important to remember that an over-reassured public isn't your goal. You want people to be concerned, vigilant even hypervigilant at first. You want people to take all available precautions; feel the fear, misery, and other emotions that the situation justifies; follow the crisis without obsessing over it; and still manage to live fairly normally. Over-reassurance is not the way to inspire that calm concern. If you have to amend the estimate of damage or victims, it's better to amend it down, not up. The public tolerates "It's less serious than we thought" better than "It's more serious than we thought."

3.5.2. Sensitive Syntax

You should, of course, give people reassuring information. But don't emphasise it. Especially don't emphasise that it is reassuring, or you will trigger your audience's ambivalence.

One very good approach is to put the good news in subordinate clauses, with the more alarmist side of the situation in the main clause. "It's too soon to say we're out of the woods, even though we haven't seen a new anthrax case in X days."

The main clause indicates that you are taking the situation seriously, how aggressively you are responding to every false alarm. Make sure that people have the data they need to put the risk in context and to judge how unlikely they are to get anthrax, but never put yourself in the position of minimising the risk or urging them not to worry.

3.5.3. Acknowledge Uncertainty

Professionals are taught to sound confident even when they are not. We imagine that this inspires trust. And when people are feeling extremely dependent, it does. But when something goes wrong and things always go wrong the overconfidence backfires badly. On an individual level, doctors who share their uncertainty (in tone as well as content), who make the patient a collaborator, and who work against inflated expectations are less likely to be on the receiving end of malpractice suits. The same is true of public experts in all fields.

Acknowledging uncertainty is most effective when the communicator both shows his or her distress and acknowledges the audience's distress: "How I wish I could give you a definite answer on that..."; "It must be awful for people to hear how tentative and qualified we have to be because there is still so much we don't know..."

3.5.4. Give People Things to Do

In an emergency, some suggested actions are directed to victims, persons exposed, or persons who may be exposed. However, those who do not need to take immediate action will be engaging in "vicarious rehearsal" of those recommendations and may need substitute actions of their own to ensure that they do not prematurely act on recommendations not meant for them. In an emergency, simple tasks will give people back a sense of control and will help to keep them motivated to stay tuned to what is happening (versus denial, where they refuse to acknowledge the possible danger to themselves and others) and prepare them to take action when directed to do so. When giving people something to do, give them a choice of actions matched to their level of concern.

3.5.5. Stop trying to Allay Panic

Panic is much less common than we imagine. The literature on disaster communication is replete with unfulfilled expectations of panicking "publics." It turns out that people nearly always behave extremely well in crisis. Recall the behavior of people in lower Manhattan on the morning of September 11! In the face of awful events, people become simultaneously resourceful and responsive. If told what to do by those in authority, we tend to do it; if no one is in charge, we figure it out for ourselves. When the crisis is over, we may feel anxiety, fear, even delayed panic attacks now that the time to panic is past. During the crisis, people may well take calm, self-protective actions that seem rational and appropriate to them, even if authorities recommend otherwise. Whether wise or unwise, securıng a personal stockpile of antibiotics is not a sign of panic.

The condition most conducive to panic isn't bad news; it is conflicting messages from those in authority. People are the likeliest to panic (though still not all that likely) when they feel that they can't trust what those in authority are telling them or when they feel misled or abandoned in dangerous territory. When authorities start hedging or hiding bad news in order to prevent panic, they are likely to exacerbate the risk of panic in the process.

Anyone involved in responding to the public during an emergency may feel that they've witnessed plenty of panic. Experience shows that in a true emergency, when life and death are at play, people respond exceptionally well. However, it also seems that the inverse is true the more removed people are from the real danger (in place and time), the more likely they are to allow their emotions full range. This vicarious rehearsal can be overwhelming in an emergency. Therefore, the communicator must recognise the differences among his or her audiences. The person anticipating the high risk is much more likely to respond inappropriately than the person in the heat of the battle who is primed to act on the information and doesn't have the time to mull it over.

3.5.6. Acknowledge People's Fears

What should you do with people who are vicariously rehearsing their responses? When people are afraid, the worst thing to do is pretend that they're not; second worst is to tell them they shouldn't be. Both responses leave people alone with their fears. (Mishandling people's fears Goes hand in hand with over-reassurance, but it's conceptually different: "Everything is under control" versus "Don't worry.")

Even when the fear is totally unjustified, it doesn't respond well to being ignored—nor does it respond well to criticism, mockery, or statistics. These approaches are less effective even when the fear is warranted. Instead, you can acknowledge fears even while giving people the information they need to put those fears into context.

Giving people permission to be excessively alarmed about a bioterrorist threat (but while still telling them why they needn't worry) makes it far likelier they will actually be reassured.

3.6. Communication during different Stages of Crisis

The principles of emergency risk communication should be considered during each phase of a crisis. These tenets are grouped below according to their importance during the precrisis, initial, maintenance, and resolution phases of the crisis:

3.6.1. Pre-crisis Phase

— *Stop trying to allay panic*. Panic stems from confusion, uncertainty, and lack of consistency. During the precrisis phase, information should be developed that anticipates and consistently answers the questions. In the precrisis phase, messages can be audience tested to ensure they are culturally and demographically valid. This effort allows the responders to speak with one voice. Don't patronise people before a crisis by telling them they have nothing to worry about *or* scare them by telling them they do—especially when there's little action that can be taken by an individual in anticipation of a crisis.

— *Emphasise that there is a process in place*. Define the process, describe the roles and responsibilities for response, and outline the solution.

3.6.2. Initial Phase

During the stage of acute danger, the priority for all is basic safety and survival. Most people respond appropriately to protect their lives and the lives of others. However, some may behave in a disorganised way and may not be able to respond appropriately.

The more the following stressors are experienced in a crisis, the more impact the crisis will have on the individual:

— Threat to life and encounter with death
— Feelings of powerlessness
— Loss (e.g., loved one, home, livelihood, possessions)
— Dislocation (e.g., separated from loved one or home)
— Feeling responsible (e.g., should be doing more)
— Inescapable horror (e.g., trapped, unable to escape, threat unseen)
— Human malevolence (e.g., deliberate evil to cause harm).

During the initial phase, violating the following emergency risk communication principles can spell immediate trouble. An inappropriate tone now will damage credibility.

— *Don't over-reassure*. The objective is not to placate, but to elicit accurate, calm concern.
— *Acknowledge uncertainty*. Offer only what you know. Show your distress and acknowledge your audience's distress about the uncertainty of the situation—"It must be awful to hear we can't answer that question right now..."
— *Emphasise that a process is in place* to learn more. "We have a system (plan, process) to help us respond (find answers, etc)."
— *Stop trying to allay panic*. Provide a consistent message that is qualified by the aspects of a changing situation. Alert the public that the message, recommendation, etc. may change as more information becomes available. Be sure that all responsible participants and any third-party validators are immediately aware when the message does change.

3.6.3. Maintenance Phase

During this phase the sense of the crisis magnitude, the concept of personal risk, and the initial steps toward recovery and resolution have begun. Emotional reactions will vary and will depend a great deal on perceptions about the risk and the stressors people face or may anticipate. During the early part of this phase, people may be perceived as elated—despite surrounding destruction or death—because of relief over their own survival. However, as the maintenance phase evolves, people may experience:

— Numbness

— Denial
— Flashbacks
— Grief
— Anger
— Despair
— Sadness
— Hopelessness.

The longer that individuals or communities are not allowed to return to "normal," the greater these reactions will be, as a sense of disillusionment may set in. Once the needs for basic survival are met, other needs for emotional balance and self-control emerge and people typically become frustrated and unfulfilled. The early altruistic response to the emergency may fall away to negative emotions and greater difficulty in recovering.

Therefore, the following emergency risk communication principles should be incorporated in messages:

— *Acknowledge fears*. Don't tell people they shouldn't be afraid. They are afraid, and they have a right to their fears. Don't disparage them for their misplaced fear. Acknowledge that it's normal and human to be frightened.

— *Express wishes*. "I wish we knew more." "I wish our answers were more definitive."

— *Give people things to do*. In an emergency, some suggested actions are directed to victims, persons exposed, or persons who may be potential to be exposed. However, those who do not need to take immediate action will be engaging in "vicarious rehearsal" of those recommendations and may need substitute actions of their own to ensure they do not prematurely act on recommendations not meant for them. In an emergency, simple tasks will give people back a sense of control and will help to keep them motivated to stay tuned to what is happening (versus denial, where they refuse to acknowledge the possible danger to themselves and others) and prepare them to take action when directed to do so. When giving people something to do, give them a choice of actions matched to their level of concern. Offer a range of responses—a minimum response, a maximum response, and a recommended middle response.

— *Acknowledge the shared misery.* Some people will be less frightened than they are miserable, feeling hopeless and defeated. Acknowledge the misery of a catastrophic event then help move people toward hope for the future through the actions of your organisation and through actions that they, too, can take.

— *Give anticipatory guidance.* If you are aware of future negative outcomes, let people know what to expect (e.g., side effects of antibiotics). If it's going to be bad, tell them.

— *At some point, be willing to address the "what if" questions.* These are the questions everyone is thinking about and wants answered by experts. Although it's often impractical to fuel "what ifs" when the crisis is contained and not likely to affect large numbers of people, it is reasonable to answer "what ifs" if they could happen and people need to be emotionally prepared for them. After all, if you do not answer the "what if" questions, someone with much less at risk regarding the response's outcome will answer them for you. If you are not prepared to address "what ifs," you lose credibility and the opportunity to frame the "what if" questions with reason and valid recommendations.

— *Be a role model and ask more of people.* Many trauma experts agree that the psychological outcome of a community as a whole will be resilience. Perhaps the most important role of the spokesperson is to ask people to bear the risk with you. People can tolerate considerable risk, especially voluntary risk. If you acknowledge the risk, its severity, and complexity and acknowledge fears, you can then ask them, to bear the risk during the emergency and work toward solutions. As a spokesperson, especially one who may be on site and at some personal risk, you can model the appropriate behavior—not false happiness, but true willingness to go on with life as much as possible and to make reasonable choices for yourself and your family. Don't be glib, but be stalwart. Your determination to see it through will help others who are looking for role models to face risk. Americans have great heart, a sense of selflessness, and a natural competitiveness. Sparking those inherent attributes will help people cope with uncertainty, fear, and misery.

3.6.4. Resolution Phase

At the time when the emergency is no longer on the front page, those who have been most severely affected will have significant emotional needs. Emotional symptoms may present as physical health symptoms such as sleep disturbance, indigestion, or fatigue as well as difficulties with interpersonal relationships at home and work. Organised support starts to erode and the realities of loss, bureaucratic constraints, and permanent life changes come crashing in.

To truly maintain trust and credibility at this point, the expressed commitments from the initial phases must be followed through.

— *Be regretful, not defensive*. Say "We are sorry..." or "We feel terrible that..." when acknowledging misdeeds or failures. Don't use "regret," which sounds like you're preparing for a lawsuit.

— *Express wishes*. Say, "I wish we all could have been spared this tragedy, incident, etc." or "I wish our answers were more definitive, but we will continue to investigate and monitor this problem and we will keep you posted on our developments."

3.7. Psychological Tensions during a Crisis

3.7.1. Effects of Traumatic Stress Disorder

— *Emotional effects*: Shock, terror, irritability, blame, anger, guilt, grief or sadness, emotional numbing, helplessness, loss of pleasure derived from familiar activities, difficulty experiencing loving feelings.

— *Cognitive effects*: Impaired concentration, impaired decisionmaking, memory impairment, disbelief, confusion, nightmares, decreased self-esteem, decreased self-efficacy, self-blame, intrusive thoughts/memories, worry, dissociation (e.g., tunnel vision, dreamlike "spacey" feeling).

— *Physical effects*: Fatigue, insomnia, cardiovascular strain, startled response, hyperarousal, increased physical pain, reduced immune response, headaches, gastrointestinal upset, decreased appetite, decreased libido, vulnerability to illness.

— *Interpersonal effects*: Increased relational conflict, social withdrawal, reduced relational intimacy, alienation, impaired work performance, impaired school performance, decreased satisfaction, distrust, externalisation of blame, externalisation of vulnerability, feeling abandoned and rejected, overprotectiveness.

3.7.2. Positive Responses following a Disaster

These include resilience and coping, altruism, relief and elation at surviving the disaster, sense of excitement and greater self-worth, changes in the way the future is viewed, and feelings of strength and growth from the experience.

3.7.3. Post-traumatic Stress Disorder (PTSD)

PTSD is a mental disorder resulting from exposure to an extreme traumatic stressor. Unique identifying features include the following:

— Exposure to a traumatic stressor

— Re-experiencing symptoms

— Avoidance and numbing symptoms

— Symptoms of increased arousal

— Duration of at least one month

— Significant distress or impairment of functioning.

PTSD sufferers tend to have abnormal levels of key hormones involved in response to stress. Some studies have shown that cortisol levels are lower than normal and epinephrine and norepinephrine are higher than normal. When people are in danger, they produce high levels of opiates, which can temporarily mask pain. Scientists have found that PTSD sufferers continue to produce those higher levels even after the danger has passed.

Most trauma survivors will be upset for several weeks following an event but recover to a variable degree without treatment. The majority of traumatised individuals do not develop PTSD. The frequency varies from about 4 to 30 percent.

The percentage of those who continue to have problems or develop PTSD depends on many factors, including the severity of trauma exposure:

— Natural disaster: 4–5 percent

— Bombing: 34 percent
— Plane crash into hotel: 29 percent
— Mass shooting: 28 percent.

Certain types of exposure place survivors at high risk for a range of postdisaster problems:

— Exposure to mass destruction or death
— Toxic contamination
— Sudden or violent death of a loved one
— Loss of home of community.

The rate of acute stress disorder (ASD) varies with higher rates reported for human-caused trauma:

— Typhoon: 7 percent
— Industrial accident: 6 percent
— Violent assault: 19 percent
— Motor-vehicle accident: 14 percent
— Assault: 13 percent.

Associated disorders from PTSD and ASD include:

— Depression
— Substance abuse
— Panic disorder
— Obsessive-compulsive disorder
— Sexual dysfunction
— Eating disorders.

3.7.3.1. Media Coverage and PTSD

In a study of 85 adults seeking mental-health services 6 months after the Oklahoma City bombing, the number of hours of bombing-related television watched did not correlate with increased PTSD symptoms.

Children in the group who watched bombing-related television reported more PTSD symptoms 7 weeks after the bombing than children who did not watch as much.

In a second study, television exposure was directly related to PTSD only in children who did not see, hear, or feel the explosion and who did not know anyone who was killed or injured. These findings suggest that watching bombing-related television may have contributed to an increase in PTSD symptoms. However, only the most distressed children may have chosen to watch bombing-related television.

3.7.3.2. Other Studies

In an Israeli study, 237 adults were divided into 2 groups. One group was exposed to television clips of terrorism and political violence; the other group was exposed to news clips unrelated to national threat. Individuals who watched the terrorism clips reported more anxiety than those who watched clips unrelated to terrorism.

A sample of adults who had an intimate friend or relative killed in the Mount Saint Helens explosion reported that the media were a hindrance to recovery. Adults who suffered property loss reported that the media were neither a help nor a hindrance.

Common experiences of those exposed to poisonous gas in a Japanese subway included anxiety, fear, nightmares, insomnia, depression, and fear of subways.

3.7.4. Understanding concepts of Death, Dying, and Grief

In a catastrophic event in the United States, communities or the nation may face what experts call "death out of time." The death of someone who is not advanced in age and sickly (e.g., the death of a child) can be much more difficult to cope with. People communicating to an individual or community experiencing the extreme pain and grief that accompanies loss through death must be especially aware of how this grief is suffered. Grief is experienced in a broad social context. The view of a particular society, culture, or subculture with its expectations of "appropriate grieving" influences the experience of loss and the "performance" of grief for those in that society.

Grief is a universal emotion, but no two people experience grief in exactly the same manner. Experts have given name to this process, which includes the following:

— *Bereavement* is the state that results from a significant loss and encompasses a wide range of reactions—emotional, cognitive, spiritual, behavioral, and physical. Bereavement is a normal, natural experience, although it is traumatic and emotionally disruptive.

— *Grief* refers to the intrapsychic process of regaining equilibrium after a loss. Manifestation includes emotional catharsis and obsessive thoughts of the deceased. Re-evaluating spiritual issues and experiencing physical symptoms may also be occurring.

— *Mourning* is the public expression or sharing of the feelings of grief. Such rituals as funeral services or the wearing of black are expressions of mourning.

— *Anticipatory* grief is an experience that occurs before the expected death of a loved one and is a projection of emotional pain and the life change that the loss will bring.

Growth should be the outcome of the grief process. The individual and the context of the death will affect the grief process.

The tasks of grief work include:

— Acceptance of the reality of the loss

— Experiencing the pain of grief

— Adjusting to an environment without the deceased

— Withdrawing emotional energy for the relationship with the deceased and investing it in new or existing relationships.

Several contexts have an influence on the grief process:

— The circumstances of the death

— The nature of the relationship with the deceased

— Has the individual experienced a prior loss?

— Are there secondary losses?

References

Cohn, Victor. (1990). *Reporting on Risk.* Washington D.C.: The Media Institute

Cooper, Lane. (1932). *The Rhetoric of Aristotle.* Englewood Cliffs, NJ: Prentice Hall, Inc.

DiGiovanni, C. (1999). "Domestic terrorism with chemical or biological agents: psychiatric aspects."*American Journal of Psychiatry*, 156, 1500–1505.

Everly, George S. Jr., Ph.D. (2001). "America Under Attack: The '10 Commandments' of Responding to

Lum, Max R., Ed.D.; Tinker, Tim L. Dr.P.H., M.P.H. (1994). *A Primer on Health Risk Communication Principles and Practices*. Atlanta: Division of Health Education, Agency for Toxic Substances and Disease Registry.

Mass Terrorist Attacks" *International Journal of Emergency Mental Health*, 3(3), pp 133–135.

Novac, Andrei, M.D. (April 2001). "Traumatic Stress and Human Behavior," *Psychiatric Times*, website:http://www.mhsource.com.

4

Risk Communication and Audiences

Risk communication began in the late 1970s with efforts by the nuclear and chemical industries in the United States to counteract widespread public concern about those technologies. It was believed that clear, understandable information was all that was needed to make people see that the risks were lower than many feared. To this day, many still believe risk communication is just a matter of making information understandable. This is particularly true in fields like nuclear technology, strongly influenced by people with scientific and engineering backgrounds.

For decades this approach has failed, and most risk communication experts say it is inadequate. The perception of risk, and the behaviors that result, are a matter of both the facts and our feelings and instincts and personal life circumstances. Communication that offers the facts but fails to account for the affective side of our risk perceptions is simply incomplete.

Risk communication is also commonly thought of as what to say under crisis circumstances. This too is inadequate. While it is certainly true that communication in times of crises is important in managing public response, countless examples have taught that a great deal of the effectiveness of risk communication during a crisis is based on what was done beforehand.

Finally, risk communication is widely thought of as what is said, a matter of which words and messages are delivered. Again, this approach is incomplete. Risk communication is implicit in the actions an agency, industry or company takes. Nowhere could it be more true that "actions speak louder than words" than when people are alert to anything that might threaten their health or survival.Here, then, is a more complete definition of risk communication:

> Actions, words, and other interactions that incorporate and respect the perceptions of the information recipients, intended to help people make more informed decisions about threats to their health and safety.

This definition emphasizes that:

— Risk communication is a matter of what an organization does, not just what it says.

— Risk communication must account for the affective component in people's perceptions of risk.

— Risk communication will be more effective if it is thought of as dialogue, not instruction. It will be more successful if the goal is to encourage certain behaviors, not simply to expect that the information recipients will think and do what the communicators want them to.

This approach recognizes findings in the fields of neuroscience and psychology which have established that the perception of risk is a dual process of fact and feeling. We use the information we have and a set of instincts which help us gauge how frightening something feels. Instinctive factors that bear on public concern about radiation include:

— *Pain and Suffering.* The greater the pain and suffering from a risk, the greater our fear. Radiation is associated with cancer, widely perceived as a particularly painful way to die.

— *Unknowability.* People are generally more afraid of things they can not detect with their own senses, like ionizing radiation

— *Is the threat natural or human-made?* A natural risk, like radon, evokes less fear than the same type of ionizing radiation that comes from a human-made source.

— *Risk versus Benefit.* The greater the benefit, the less we fear the risk. Many people who willingly subject themselves to medical radiation still fear nuclear waste.

— *Choice.* A risk taken voluntarily, such as when communities offer to host a waste disposal facility or nuclear power plant, is less frightening than the same risk if it is imposed, as the people in Nevada in the U.S.A. feel about Yucca Mountain.

— *Control.* The more we feel we can affect events as they occur, the less afraid we will be. (This is not a matter of whether to engage in the risk voluntarily in the first place, but how much actual control we feel over what's happening to us.) Airborne radiation from a radiological dispersal device or nuclear plant accident feels like something we can't do anything about.

— *Is the risk Catastrophic or Chronic*? Risks that threaten large numbers at one time evoke more fear than statistically greater causes of injury or death where the victims are spread out geographically and temporally. Images of Hiroshima and Nagasaki and Chernobyl associate safety-related events at nuclear power plants as potentially catastrophic.

— *Trust.* We are more afraid when we don't trust the agencies or officials supposed to protect us, or the industries creating the risk. Do we trust their competence? Their honesty? Their motives? Incompetent performance, keeping secrets, and inconsistent information are trust-destroying hallmarks of the way officials have behaved in many nuclear and radiological events.

Consider this example, irradiating food to make it safer. In many places where this process has been approved by the government, it is not widely used because of industry concerns about public apprehension. Yet studies have found that effective risk communication can increase consumer acceptance of food irradiation, which directly improves public health.

The risk communication offered to prospective consumers in these studies went beyond clear, understandable language. It included a discussion of both risks and benefits. The communications acknowledged people's apprehensions about radiation, rather than dismissing them by only offering information about how irradiating food poses no risk, or just talking about the benefits. It asked people to say what they would choose, including offering a policy to require labeling to identify irradiated products.

In short, clear and understandable messages were important, but they were not enough. Clear and understandable information is part of any communication. Risk communication also must account for people's affective perceptions, and demonstrate respect for those perceptions in actions as well as words (the policy of labeling).

4.1. The Message

The receiver of your communication will be judging the content of the message, the messenger, and the method of delivery. Each of these aspects must be considered in planning for crisis and emergency risk communication. The public's awareness of government is heightened during a crisis. A lack of continuity, control, adequate resources, or full knowledge of the event can invoke fear and threaten social unity. Your audience's needs can be judged three ways:

(1) their relationship to the incident,

(2) their psychological differences, and

(3) their demographic differences.

Possible audiences for your crisis and emergency risk communication:

1. *Public within the circle of disaster or emergency for whom action messages are intended* Concerns: Personal safety, family safety, pet safety, stigmatisation, property protection
2. *Public immediately outside circle of disaster or emergency for whom action messages are not intended* Concerns: Personal safety, family safety, pet safety, interruption of normal life activities
3. *Emergency response and recovery workers, law enforcement involved in their response* Concerns: Resources to accomplish response and recovery, personal safety, family safety, pet safety
4. *Public health and medical professionals involved in the disaster response* Concerns: Resources adequate to respond, personal safety, family safety, pet safety
5. *Family members of victims and response workers* Concerns: Personal safety, safety of victims and response workers
6. *Health care professionals outside the response effort* Concerns: Vicarious rehearsal of treatment recommendations, ability to respond to patients with appropriate information, access to treatment supplies if needed/wanted
7. *Civic leaders, local, state, and national* Concerns: Response and recovery resources, liability, leadership, and quality of response and recovery planning and implementation; opportunities for expressions of concern; trade and international diplomatic relations

8. *Congress* Concerns: Informing constituents, review of statutes and laws for adequacy and adjustment needs, opportunities for expressions of concern
9. *Trade and industry* Concerns: Business issues (loss of revenue, liability, business interruption) and protection of employees
10. *National community* Concerns: Vicarious rehearsal, readiness efforts started
11. *International neighbors* Concerns: Vicarious rehearsal, readiness efforts started
12. *International community* Concerns: Vicarious rehearsal, exploration of readiness
13. *Stakeholders and partners specific to the emergency* Concerns: Included in decision-making and access to information
14. *Media* Concerns: Personal safety, access to information and spokespersons, deadlines

Figure 4.1. Audience Relationship to the Event

Each of these audiences will be looking for a specific message. Priorities the development of messages for each audience based on their involvement.

Remember the basics when creating your messages. Audience segmentation and demographics are still relevant during a crisis. Always consider the following:

— Education
— Current subject knowledge and experience
— Age
— Language spoken/read
— Cultural norms
— Geographic location

4.2. Audiences' Judgement

Expect your audiences to immediately judge the content of your message in the following ways:

— *Speed of communication.* Was the message timely? Research indicates that the first message received on a subject sets the stage for comparison of all future messages on that subject. If the public hears that the world is flat, and then someone comes along and says "the world is round," that message may face some resistance because of preconceived ideas on the subject. Also, the speed with which you respond to the public can be an indicator of how prepared you are to respond to the emergency, that there is a system in place, and that needed action is being taken. If the public is not aware that you're responding to the problem, then you're not! The public may then lose confidence in the organization's ability to respond, and you will be attempting to catch up in convincing the public that the system for response is working.

First impressions are lasting impressions. If you shoot out of the gate and fall flat, it won't matter much if you get back up and flawlessly jump all of the hurdles in record time. This doesn't necessarily mean having all the answers; it means having an early presence so the public knows that you are aware of the emergency and that there is a system in place to respond. A great message delivered after the audience has moved on to other issues is a message not delivered at all.

— *Factual content of the message*. The public will be listening for factual information, and some will be expecting to hear a recommendation for action. Get the facts right, repeat them consistently, avoid sketchy details early on, and ensure that all credible sources share the same facts. Speak with one voice. Again, preparation counts. Consistent messages are vital. Inconsistent messages will increase anxiety and will quickly torpedo credibility of experts.

During the mid-1990s, the U.S. Midwest was badly crippled by a number of floods. Response officials cautioned citizens to boil their water to make it safe for drinking. Most citizens sought out more specific information. Unfortunately, various response agencies offered different guidance about how long and to what temperature water should be boiled to make it safe for drinking. The public and media were quickly indignant about the response operation and the government's ability to get the job done. Consistent messages are vital, especially when asking the public to perform an action or take a step that is unfamiliar.

— *Trust and credibility of the message*. Research by Dr. Vincent T. Covello shows that there are four basic elements to establishing trust and credibility through communication. You can't fake these. They must be truly present in the message. All messages, written or spoken, can incorporate these elements and should, especially when attempting to communicate during an emergency.

- *Empathy and caring*. Empathy and caring should be expressed within the first 30 seconds.

  According to research, being perceived as empathetic and caring provides greater opportunity for your message to be received and acted upon. Acknowledge fear, pain, suffering, and uncertainty.

- *Competence and expertise*. Obviously, education, position title, or organisational roles and missions are quick ways to indicate expertise. Previous experience and demonstrated abilities in the current situation enhance the perception of competence. Another useful means is to have established a relationship with your audiences in advance of the emergency. If that is not possible, have a third party, who has the confidence of the audience, express his or her confidence in you or your organisation.

- *Honesty and openness*. This does not mean releasing information prematurely, but it does mean facing the realities of the situation and responding accordingly. It means not being paternalistic in your communication but, instead, participatory giving people choices and enough information to make appropriate decisions. Be realistic about your communication systems and procedures and, if they do not permit you to comment on something or reveal information, don't pretend you don't have the information; tell the public why the information isn't available for release at the time (e.g., verifying information, notifying your organisation, not your information to release, etc.). It means allowing the public to observe the process while reminding them that this process is what drives the quality of the emergency response. Cut the professional jargon and euphemisms; they imply insecurity and lack of honesty.
- *Commitment and dedication*. State up front what your organisation's objective is in this emergency response, and commit to reaching that objective. Show dedication by sharing in the sacrifices and discomforts of the emergency. Don't fake hardship for the cameras. Effective Governors know that they'd better walk the territory in which they're declaring a state disaster area. Dedication means not leaving the emergency until the community is recovered. This often means staying in touch with the community long after the media lose interest in the story. Resolution and follow-up should be committed to from the start and carried through to the end.

4.3. How to Give Effective Messages

Consider the following when creating your initial communication to your audiences:

— For the general public, present a short, concise, and focused message (6th-grade level). It's difficult in a heightened state of anxiety or fear to take in copious amounts of information. Get the bottom line out first. In time, the public will want more information.

— *Cut to the chase* relevant information only at this time. Don't start with a lot of background information. Don't spend a lot of time establishing yourself or your organisation. One sentence should be enough.

— *Give action steps in positives*, not negatives (e.g., "In case of fire, use stairs," "Stay calm," are positive messages. Negative messages are "Do not use elevator" and "Don't panic.") Use positives, not negatives.

— *Repeat the message* repetition reflects credibility and durability. Correct information is correct each time you repeat it. Reach and frequency, common advertising concepts, tell us that your message is more apt to be received and acted upon as the number of people exposed to the message (reach) and the number of times each person hears the message (frequency) go up.

— *Create action steps in threes or rhyme, or create an acronym.* These are ways to make basic information easier to remember, such as "stop/drop and roll" or "KISS—keep it simple, stupid." Three is not a magic number, but in an emergency, you should expect someone to absorb three simple directions. Research indicates that somewhere between three and seven bits of information is the limit for people to memorise and recall. It makes sense in the stress of an emergency to ask your audience to remember fewer bits of information.

— *Use personal pronouns for the organisation.* "We are committed to..." or "We understand the need for..."

4.3.1. Avoid

— *Technical jargon*

- Instead of saying "people may suffer morbidity and mortality," say, "people exposed may become sick or die."
- Instead of "epidemic" or "pandemic," say "outbreak" or "widespread outbreak."

- Instead of "deployed," say "sent" or "put in place."
- Instead of "correlation" say "relationship" (avoid using "cause").

— *Unnecessary filler*—background information (save for other outlets/times)

— *Condescending or judgmental phrases*—(e.g., "You would have to be an idiot to try to outrun a tornado." "Only hypochondriacs would need to walk around with a prescription for Cipro.") Many of us are neither idiots nor hypochondriacs, and both ideas have crossed our minds. Don't insult your audience by word or tone. That doesn't mean condoning the behavior; instead, validate the impulse but offer a better alternative and the reasons why it's better.

— *Attacks*—Attack the problem, not the person or organisation.

— *Promises/guarantees*—only what you can deliver. Otherwise, promise to remain committed throughout the emergency response.

— *Speculation*—don't play "worst-case scenario." Stick to the known facts. If you don't know it's an outbreak of Ebola, then why talks about Ebola? If the facts are not known, don't fall into the "what ifs." Instead, concentrate on describing the steps in place to get the facts and help the audience deal with the uncertainty while that process goes on. Speculation weakens your credibility. Do you want to be the Ebola expert or the emergency response expert who knows how to get the answers and empower the public to make the best possible response? "What ifs" are usually topics for times when there are no emergencies?

— *Discussion of money*—In the initial phase, discussion of the magnitude of the problem should be in the context of the health and safety of the public or environment. Loss of property is secondary. Also, a discussion of the amount of money spent is not a surrogate for the level of concern and response from your organisation (what does that money provide?).

— *Humor*—Seldom is humor a good idea. People seldom "get the joke" when they are feeling desperate. Humor is a great stress-reliever behind closed doors. Anyone who has responded to emergencies knows that sometimes-inappropriate humor creeps in as a coping mechanism. Be careful not to offend others responding to an emergency, even behind closed doors. Be especially sensitive when speaking to the public. One person's attempt at humor may be another's insult.

4.4. Building Consensus for Actions

In the precrisis phase, when consensus on recommendations is being built and implementation planning is being developed, consider the following to make recommendations more appealing to the target audience:

— Increase the expected gains

— Decrease the expected costs

— Increase the present social pressure

— Improve the individual's ability to act

— Decrease the desirability of competitive alternative actions

For example, you want to encourage a community to prepare "family survival kits," so consider doing the following:

— *Increase expected gains*—give anecdotes about successful families who had kits and how they benefited in earlier disasters; offer lots of possible expected uses for the kit.

— *Decrease the expected costs*—decrease the expectation of the monetary cost for a kit and explain its longevity as a safety product for the home.

— *Increase social pressure*—involve the community neighborhood watch program in promoting the concept. Ask neighbors to help each other develop kits specific to the community's anticipated needs. Saturate communication channels with information about the civic groups involved in the kit project.

— *Improve the individual's ability to act*—Make the list of kit items easy to use and widely available; encourage partner retailers to discount safety kit items during key times of the year.

— *Decrease competitive alternatives*—Explain how putting together your own kit need not cost much nor take much time, and that expensive prepackaged kits are less desirable because they are not customised to the individual family's needs.

— *Increase the expected gains*—Self-imposed isolation will protect people from unnecessary exposure. They can cut through the red tape and emergency room waiting time by first calling a community nurse hotline. A trained nurse will assess their risk immediately by phone and empower them to make the best decision about additional care during the crisis.

— *Decrease the expected costs*—If the nurse agrees that a doctor or hospital visit is needed, an e-mail of the hotline contact with the patient's name will be placed on a reservation list at the medical facility, giving the patient priority in the waiting room before those who have not gone through the screening process.

Increase the present social pressure—Engage community and civic leaders and trusted health care professionals to present the individual benefits of using the hotline, and applaud the expected reduction of chaos at the medical facilities, so that dedicated health care workers can effectively treat those in dire need of care—who might someday be a family member.

Improve the individual's ability to act—Publicise widely the toll-free number, ensure that contact is made with little or no waiting, and ensure that a "satisfaction" check is made before the call is ended.

4.5. Culture and the Message

Culture is a complex amalgam of values, ideas, attitudes, and symbols that shape our behavior as they transmit from one generation to the next. People can belong to several cultural groups. The largest is our national heritage; we identify with the people of our nation. But people are also members of smaller groups within the larger society, such as where we live in the nation, our religion, or our ethnicity. Culture is adaptive. As the needs of a society change, its values change to meet those needs. Because cultural norms influence how people live and behave, culture has important implications to communication, including emergency communication. Reference groups influence individual behaviors. Of the reference groups, the family is the most influential.

4.6. Emergency Response Presentations

Public health emergencies can come in various sizes and durations.

After the initial response occurs, health officials and emergency responders may need to present updates or background information to community leaders, Congress, or citizen forums. They may also have to explain certain recommendations made at each step of the recovery effort. Depending on the purpose of the presentation and any expected resistance to the message, the pattern in which you choose to present the information can help open your audience to receiving it. A careful arrangement of your key ideas goes a long way toward helping your audience understand your message.

If a message arouses exceptionally intense feelings of anxiety, people tend to ignore the further content of the message. People must be prepared for messages, especially those likely to evoke emotional responses. Give listeners a "preparatory set" to increase their recognition and attention level. Your introduction should prepare the audience for the subject, recognise its emotional impact and tell them that you will review the material as many times as necessary. Listeners will tune the speaker out if they suspect that his or her message will not confirm their beliefs or opinions. Look for those elements that you know you and your audience share and build on those elements.

Research indicates that you can "inoculate" your audience by providing a small dose of the counterargument, just as a person can be inoculated by a mild dose of a disease organism.

4.6.1. Sharing New Information

Consider first using the direct pattern which presents your main idea or conclusion. The idea is then developed with supporting information. Most busy decision-makers prefer not to be teased; they want the bottom line up front. If you save the big idea until last, you may increase expectations. At the end of your talk, when you say that you can decrease the spread of infection by 25 percent but the audience thought your proposal would stop all spread of the disease, they will be disappointed. Lower expectations by declaring the expected outcome first.

Persuasive presentations, however, benefit from an indirect pattern of presentation; building the argument with ancillary concepts until you offer your most potent ammunition. You could list each of the benefits of a public health policy and finish by saying, "it will save billions in the next 10 years while saving lives."

4.6.2. Progress Reports

Often, progress reports are best organised chronologically. The same is true for step-by-step instructions. This helps the listener follow where you've been and where you're going. This technique can be overused, especially if these are frequent updates. It is a useful pattern if your listeners need to understand the ongoing development of your ideas. You may also wish to consider a priority order pattern for progress reports. In this pattern, you present the most significant point first with other developments following in descending order of importance.

4.6.3. Problem-solving

If your presentation is meant to offer a solution to a problem, the criteria-application pattern is a strong approach. Early in the presentation, criteria or standards for evaluation are suggested. Then, solutions or choices are compared against those standards. This approach highlights your underlying reasoning and can be very convincing as long as the audience agrees with your decision criteria. The criteria should describe the best possible case, and then explore the available alternatives.

4.6.4. Explain Why Something Happened

A cause-effect pattern for your presentation can explain how something occurred or predict the consequences of an action. It's easy to confuse cause and effect, so apply this pattern carefully. Causality is not always clear. Be careful not to simplify your conclusions or make them too optimistic (e.g., "If only we had a training program for administrators, we wouldn't have such difficulty getting decisions finalised in an emergency.").

4.6.5. Teach A New Concept or Process

To teach, a speaker begins with something familiar or already known by the listeners and moves to the unknown or more complex. By using an increasing magnitude of difficulty pattern, you can help your audience take in complex information in a way they can "own" it.

Table 1. Arranging Main Points in a Presentation

Kind of presentation	Purpose of presentation	Recommended method of organization
Persuasive	Have the audience accept ideas Get the audience to act	Inductive pattern: show several specific examples, lines of reasoning, that lead to a general conclusion Problem-solving pattern: Describe a problem vividly to create a "need," then offer a solution. Criteria-application pattern: Describe criteria which pose a "best possible case." Then compare alternatives against these. Your solution fits the best.
Informational	Inform or teach the audience	Deductive pattern: Present the conclusion first, then explain details. Chronological pattern: Show how several events developed over a period of time. Increasing difficulty pattern: Start with something known by the audience, then add more complex concepts.
Progress report	Inform or update knowledge of a familiar subject	Chronological pattern Deductive pattern Order of importance pattern: Start with most significant finding and arrange others in ascending or descending order.

Presentation flops that destroy credibility:

— The apologetic beginning such as "Unaccustomed as I am to public speaking," or "I'm here to bore you with a few more statistics."

— The offensive beginning. An off-color joke, sarcastic or ridiculing statement.

— The same opening regardless of audience or situation.

— The gimmicky beginning, such as writing the word "sex" on your overhead.

4.6.6. Receivers of Behaviour Change Messages

Communication is two-way. When the purpose of your communication is to make a call to action or change behavior, you must be especially aware of your target audience. "Who are they?", "What do they believe now?", "Are you a credible source of information for them?" etc. In addition to knowing the audience specifically, there are a number of general aspects of audiences you should keep in mind when building your reasoned case for a recommendation of action.

— Audiences selectively receive and interpret messages based on their existing knowledge, attitudes, beliefs, and current needs.

— Listeners are more receptive to a message that is consistent with their attitudes and beliefs.

— Messages phrased in terms of the listener's interests and needs are more successful than if given from the speaker's perspective. A "you viewpoint" helps. Show benefits, with "What this means to you."

— Persons with high self-esteem are less readily influenced that those with low self-esteem.

— Those overtly hostile or excessively apathetic are not likely to be influenced by your message.

— Mental or verbal participation by listeners improves the chance that your message will influence them.

4.6.7. Group influences on the Effects of Your Message

Social pressure involves the consideration that a person's intention to take a particular action will depend not only on his or her perceived perception of personal consequences, but also on the perception of others' wishes. Health care workers and physicians can be very important sources of social pressure. However, for someone to move to action, he or she must not only see personal benefit or accept the social pressure to take the action, but must also believe that the action can actually be accomplished. Perceived consequences of a behavior involve a trade-off between positive and negative consequences.

— Listeners are influenced by beliefs shared by those around them. There is a tendency to conform.

— If the speaker's message is counter to the norms of the group, a listener's tendency to accept that message is inversely proportional to the value he or she places on group membership.

— Audience members will be searching for nonverbal cues from other audience members to confirm or refute the speaker's message.

Internally, your target population will be asking these questions:

— What will I gain if I undertake this proposed behavior?

— What will it cost me to do it?

— What do those who are important to me want me to do?

— Can I actually carry it out?

If you satisfactorily answer those questions with candor, the action may be more readily accepted. The more socially desirable and easily undertaken a recommended action is, the more likely that it will be accepted.

4.6.8. Communicating about Death One-on-one

In a catastrophic event, many people are ill, dying, or in need of treatment and it may be your job to talk with individuals about what is happening. There is a great body of work about expressing empathy and empowering decision-making between the medical professional and the patient in a medical care setting. However, most of this work assumes the luxury of time that is non-existent in an emergency situation. Some people, who may not have much experience in this patient-professional dialogue, may be recruited for the first time to educate patients or groups during a crisis.

In addition, if an evolving disease outbreak in a community begins to involve members of your response teams or their families, supervisors and team leaders may find themselves attempting to engage in supportive conversations. The following are some basic thoughts about communication styles in an intimate but highly emotional health emergency situation:

4.6.8.1. Empathise with the Patient and Family

— People indulge in serious, meaningful communication only for short spans.
— Chitchat is a treasure trove of meaningful "hints" about what a person is worried about.
— Privacy is an important requirement. Assure that information shared will be kept private.
— Allow communication free from interruptions (e.g., crying shouldn't be interrupted).
— Try not to answer questions outside your area of expertise. Get permission from the individual to refer him or her to an expert.

4.6.8.2. Listen Carefully

— Place the speaker's needs above your own.
— Use open and accepting body language (e.g., no crossed arms).
— Always be honest in responding.
— Try not to interrupt to give advice.
— Accept moments of silence.
— As much as 90 percent of communication is nonverbal.

4.6.8.3. Be Careful

— Don't miss the meaning of the words and the gestures.
— Value judgments hinder communication.
— Teasing belittles the individual.
— Blame cuts off communication.

4.6.8.4. Better Communication

— Use the person's name in the conversation.

— Ask a clarifying question: "Can you help me understand?"
— Allow the conversation to evolve—don't push it where you hope it will go.
— Allow time for silence.
— Be sensitive to a person's nationality, ethnicity, religion, age, and feelings.
— When possible, use the words the person uses.
— Self-disclosure may help the person expand on the topic.
— When responding to someone, say "you're crying" instead of "you're sad;" allow the person the opportunity to express the feeling behind the action.
— How something is said is often more important than what is said.

4.6.8.5. When speaking to grieving Family Members

Your presence is more important than conversation. Family members may voice feelings with such strong emotion as "I don't know how I'm going to live without my husband," or "Why would God allow this to happen?" Short statements of condolence, such as "I'm so sorry," "This is a sad time," or "You're in my prayers," are enough of a response. If a persons tenses at your touch, withdraw.

Use "death" or "dying" not softer euphemisms. Many people feel patronised by words like "expired" or "received his heavenly reward." Use the same words as the grieving person to respect cultural differences.

Refrain from platitudes—"She lived a good life," or "She is no longer suffering." These statements can trivialise the family's loss.

Avoid sharing your personal experiences of death and grief so you can keep the focus on the family member.

Careful to avoid sending signals that you are distracted or need to do something else. Don't glance at papers, your watch, the elevator, the clock, or others in a conversation. Focus on the person and speak gently and without haste.

4.7. Audience Feedback

In pre-event planning, identify the mechanisms you will use to obtain and analyse feedback from target populations. In addition, state how this information will be used in reassessing your communication and response operations. The methods of obtaining feedback are straightforward. You will hear from your target populations directly or through the media, community leaders and advocates, Congressional representatives, and lawyers. Be sure that there are open channels between the public and your organisation and solicit public feedback.

Toll-free public information lines, an e-mail address and a "snail mail" address for comments should be provided to the public before and during the emergency. The more public outrage the event generates the more opportunities people will need to vent. That venting can be valuable to you as a communicator. It will tell you what questions they want answers to, what upsets them, what needs more explanation and which recommendations are not working.

A citizen may begin with a question during a phone call, but will end with a concern. Be sure that your public response services can answer questions and detect trends in the public's comments. It's not just about pushing information out of your organisation, it's also about taking it in.

Use common content or trend analyses to compile a report that will be useful to your public health emergency leadership. Tell them quickly when your analysis shows that something is or is not working. You may not be the most popular member of the team in this role, but it's vital that public input is taken into account.

In addition to monitoring direct feedback, you can also get a feel for the public's responses to the emergency through media and Internet monitoring. If a rumor takes flight on the Internet, you must know about it in order to respond. The media can reflect public reaction. Immediately after the Sept. 11, 2001 tragedy, Centers for Disease Control and Prevention (CDC) public response lines were indicating topic trends from the public before that information reached the media. It's possible that the questions you're getting directly from the public may clue you in to what the media will soon be asking. The predictive value of early feedback can help your communication team *manage* issues instead of simply *reacting* to issues.

REFERENCES

Andreasen, Alan R. (1995). *Marketing Social Change: Changing Behavior to Promote Health, Social Development, and the Environment*. San Francisco: Jossey-Bass Publishers.

Cohn, Victor. (1990). *Reporting on Risk*. Washington D.C.: The Media Institute

Graeff, Judith A., et. al. (1993). *Communication for Health and Behavior Change*: San Francisco: Jossey- Bass Publishers.

Lum, Max R., Ed.D.; Tinker, Tim L. Dr.P.H., M.P.H. (1994). *A Primer on Health Risk Communication Principles and Practices*. Atlanta: Division of Health Education, Agency for Toxic Substances and Disease Registry.

Timm, Paul, R. (1981). *Functional Business Presentations*. Englewood, NJ: Prentice Hall, Inc.

5

Risk Communication Planning

Understanding the pattern of a crisis can help communicators anticipate problems and respond effectively. For communicators, it's vital to know that every emergency, disaster, or crisis evolves in phases and that the communication must evolve along with it. By dividing the crisis into the following phases, the communicator can anticipate the information needs of the media, stakeholders, and the general public. Each phase has its own unique informational requirements.

For communication purposes, the phases of an emergency, disaster, or crisis include:

— Precrisis

— Initial

— Maintenance

— Resolution

— Evaluation

The movement through each of the phases will vary according to the triggering event. Not all crises are created equally. The degree or intensity and longevity of a crisis will impact required resources and manpower.

5.1. Pre-crisis Phase

Communication objectives during the precrisis phase:

— Be prepared

— Foster alliances

— Develop consensus recommendations

— Test messages

This is where all of the planning and most of the work should be done. You can usually predict the types of disasters that your organisation is likely to encounter. Reasonable questions can be anticipated and preliminary answers sought. Initial communication can be drafted with blanks to be filled in. Spokespersons and resources, and resource mechanisms, can be identified. Training and refinements of plans and messages can be made. Alliances and partnerships can be fostered to ensure that experts are speaking with one voice.

Conduct an emergency public health communication needs assessment.

5.2. Initial Phase

The initial phase of a crisis is characterised by confusion and intense media interest. Information is usually incomplete and the facts scattered. It's important to recognise that information from the media, other organisations and within your organisation might not be accurate. Your role is to learn the facts about what happened, to determine what your organisation's response is to the problem, and to verify the true magnitude of the event as quickly as possible.

There is no second chance to get it right in the initial phase of a crisis. Your organisation's entire reputation is on the line, based on what you say and what you don't say; based on when you say it or that you never say it.

Communication objectives during the initial phase:

— Acknowledge event with empathy

— Explain and inform the public, in simplest forms, about the risk

— Establish organisation/spokesperson credibility

— Provide emergency courses of action (including how/where to get more information)

— Commit to stakeholders and public to continued communication

Simplicity, credibility, verifiability, consistency, and speed count when communicating in the initial phases of an emergency.

One of the best ways to limit public anxiety in a crisis is to provide useful information about the nature of the problem, and what the public can do about it. Hence, during the initial phase of an event, seek to establish your organisation as a credible source of information. Even when there is little information to offer, you can still communicate how the organisation is investigating the event and when more information will be available. At the very least, messages should demonstrate that your organisation is addressing the issues head-on—that its approach is reasonable, caring, and timely.

Of course, the pressure to release information prematurely can be intense. Remember, the appropriate managers must approve all information before release to the media.

In the initial phase of a crisis or emergency, the public wants to know what they want to know *now*. They want timely and accurate facts about what happened and where and what is being done. They will question the magnitude of the crisis, the immediacy of the threat to them, the duration of the threat to them, and who is going to fix the problem. Communicators should be prepared to answer these questions as quickly, accurately, and fully as possible.

5.3. Crisis Maintenance

Communication objectives during the crisis maintenance phase:

- Help the public more accurately understand its own risks.
- Provide background and encompassing information to those who need it (How could this happen? Has this happened before? How can we keep this from happening again? Will I be all right in the long term—will I recover?)
- Gain understanding and support for response and recovery plans
- Listen to stakeholder and audience feedback and correct misinformation
- Explain emergency recommendations
- Empower risk/benefit decision-making

As the crisis evolves, anticipate sustained media interest and scrutiny. Unexpected developments, rumors, or misinformation may place further media demands on organisation communicators. Experts, professionals, and others not associated with your organisation will comment publicly on the issue, and sometimes contradict or misinterpret your messages. Expect to be criticised about your handling of the situation.

Staying on top of the information flow and maintaining tight coordination is essential. Processes for tracking communication activities become increasingly important as the workload increases.

The crisis maintenance phase includes an ongoing assessment of the event and allocation of resources.

5.4. Resolution

Communication objectives for the resolution phase:

— Improve appropriate public response in future similar emergencies through education.

— Honestly examine problems and mishaps and then reinforce what worked in the recovery and response efforts

— Persuade the public to support public policy and resource allocation to the problem

— Promote the activities and capabilities of the organisation (corporate identity reinforced—internally too)

As the crisis resolves, there is a return to stasis with increased understanding about the crisis. Complete recovery systems are in place. This phase is characterised by a reduction in public/media interest. Once the crisis is resolved, you may need to respond to intense media scrutiny about how the event was handled. You may have an opportunity to reinforce public health messages while the issue is still current. A public education campaign or changes to a Web site may be necessary. Research has shown that a community is most responsive to risk avoidance and mitigation education usually directly after a disaster has occurred because they have been sensitised.

5.5. Evaluation

When the crisis is over, evaluate communication plan performance, document lessons learned, and determine specific actions to improve crisis systems or the crisis plan.

5.6. Finding Risk Communication

A critical element in your crisis communication plan is its integration into the overall emergency response plans for your organisation. After all, a "perfect" media and public information plan that can't be executed because of resistance or lack of understanding by the response leadership is a failed plan.

The following are some thoughts about "getting a permanent seat at the table."

1. In FY 2002, DHHS leadership insisted that a new and distinct "focus area," of the bioterrorism and emergency public health response cooperative agreements between the Department and the 62 project areas, include separate plans and funding for public information and risk communication. This new "Focus Area F" garnered about $46 million in initial funding for states, cities and territories to plan crisis communication responses.
2. Be ambassadors of communication. Every element of your organisation involved in emergency planning and response should know you by first name AND face. Meet the planners informally and ask them how they think better communication to the public, partners, and stakeholders would help them accomplish their mission.
3. Engage the leadership with straightforward objectives for communication in a crisis. (Note: most emergency operations planners think "two-way radio" when they hear the word "communication." It might be a good idea to stick with public information, to distinguish what you do.)
4. Tell leadership how the overall response and recovery operation benefits through an investment in public information activities.

5.6.1. Key Concepts to Stimulate Proactive Thinking

Following are a few key concepts to stimulate proactive thinking:

— Customer focus

- Acquire necessary facts.
- Empower decision-making.
- Be an involved participant, not a spectator.

- Provide feedback to responders.
- Watch guard resource allocation.
- Recover or preserve well-being and normalcy.

— Organisational focus

- Execute response and recovery efforts.
- Gain support for crisis management plans.
- Avoid misallocation of limited resources.
- Ensure that decisions-makers are well informed.
- Reduce rumors.
- Decrease illness, injury, and deaths.
- Avoid wasting of abundant resources. You will go a long way toward getting a seat at the table if your leadership understands the following:

— Contributors to a poor public response to recovery plans

- Mixed messages from multiple experts
- Tardy release of information
- Paternalistic attitudes
- No reality check on recommendations
- Not immediately countering rumors and myths
- Public power struggles and confusion

— Formula to meet customer and organisation goals

- Execute a solid communication plan.
- Be the first source of information.
- Express empathy early.
- Show competence and expertise.
- Remain honest and open.
- Remain dedicated to customer.
- Apply emergency risk communication principles.

Any worries about "not being heard" at the table during a crisis event must be addressed in the precrisis planning. Don't be a wallflower get in and get talking *now* with EOC planners and leaders. Recent national events give you plenty of examples (both good and bad) to help decision-makers in your organisation "get it." Your participation, education, and credible execution during the planning phases will help to ensure your seat at the table when a crisis hits.

5.7. Developing a Crisis Communication Plan

The crisis communication plan must be planned with the worst case scenario in mind. An organisation's crisis communication plan should be fully integrated into the overall emergency response plan for the organisation and the local, state, or national response plan. A true public health emergency will involve a number of agencies and departments, and a good plan will reflect that coordination. An important benefit is the opportunity to mobilise shared resources; for example, a city-wide telephone number to respond to public concerns.

An emergency risk and crisis communication plan should include the following elements:

— Signed endorsement from your director
— Designated line and staff responsibilities for the public information teams
— Internal information verification and clearance/approval procedures
— Agreements on information release authorities (who releases what/when/how)
— Regional and local media contact list (including after-hours news desks)
— Procedures to coordinate with the public health organisation response teams
— Designated spokespersons for public health issues and third-party validators in an emergency
— Your organisations emergency response team after-hours contact numbers
— Contact numbers for emergency response information partners (e.g., Governor's public affairs officer, local FBI public information special agent in charge, local or regional department of agriculture or veterinarian public information officers, Red Cross, and other nongovernmental organisations)

- — Agreements/procedures to join the joint information centre of the emergency operations centre (if activated)
- — Procedures to secure needed resources (space, equipment, people) to operate the public information and media operation during a public health emergency 24 hours a day/ 7 days a week, if needed
- — Identified vehicles of information dissemination to public, stakeholders, partners (e.g., e-mail list serves, broadcast fax, door-to-door leaflets, and press releases) during a crisis.
- — The plan is not a step-by-step "how to." It is the bones of your work. It should systematically address all of the roles, lines of responsibility, and resources you are sure to encounter as you provide information to the public, media and partners during a public health emergency. More than anything, your crisis communication plan is a resource of information—the "go to" place for must-have information. Many communication professionals keep media contact numbers jotted in phone books, or their directors' home telephone number on the scrap of paper it was originally written on during a quick Friday afternoon planning session from a previous "crisis." These must be collected, organised, and updated.

The single most important responsibility that can be assigned to someone in your organisation is the duty to keep the plan alive. Update the plan regularly all of the elements. Schedule the review; don't just wait for so many changes to occur that the plan is useless when you take it off the shelf.

Longer is not better. Again, the plan will be the bones of your work. It does not have to spell out every required task. It must be the reference that will keep everyone on track and enable the tasks to get done with a minimum of scrambling. Emergencies are chaotic enough without the disorganisation of a plan less office. You don't build lines of authority and relationships with your response partners during the crisis. Too often, the initial confusion and mixed messages that cripple an organisation's credibility come from a lack of clear role and responsibility definition, and undefined lines of authority.

5.7.1. Signed Endorsement from Your Director

This is a must. Your director should know that you've thought through the process, that you've coordinated your response planning, and that he or she has an important role in the ownership of this plan. Keep it to a couple of simple paragraphs that endorse the plan. Have it signed and dated. Get it re-signed and re-dated to keep the plan fresh. It also helps keep you accountable for getting it updated. Here's an example of an introduction for a crisis communication plan from a director at CDC:

> "CDC comes together during a crisis to help protect the health and safety of Americans. We also need to calm public fears during a crisis by communicating credible information and by promoting appropriate health actions.

Experts agree that most crises take an organisation by surprise. Appropriate and timely communication allows CDC to work effectively with partners, engender public trust in its scientifically based health recommendations, and perform its public health mission.

Crisis communication planning helps CDC deal effectively with those unexpected disasters or emergencies. This framework of action incorporates the ethical, professional, and guiding principles needed by CDC during a crisis to communicate to the media and public with confidence and credibility. We cannot predict or always avoid future crises, but we can do our part to be prepared."

5.7.2. Responsibilities of Media and Public

Someone must be in charge of the release of information to the media, public and partners. This is information not moving through official command channels as part of the emergency response. This is information to keep partners and the public up to date on the process, response outcomes, and any public health recommendations. It is also the information needed to respond to the public and partners based on their feedback to the organisation. Whether you have teams of people to attend to these tasks or single individuals, the work must be done. If your organisation is incapable of meeting the likely media, partner, and public information needs during a public health emergency internally, ensure that your plan identifies from where this response support will come, including your role as part of the city's or state's emergency operations centre. Regardless of who does it, the work must be done, and it's your responsibility to ensure that appropriate public health information is reaching the public and partners, either through the media or through a direct communication channel, such as a town hall meeting.

Here are some of the responsibilities that must be planned for as part of the emergency response:

5.7.2.1. Command and Control

— Directs the work related to the release of information to the media, public, and partners

— Activates the plan based on careful assessment of the situation and the expected demands for information by media, partners, and the public

— Coordinates with harizontal communication partners as outlined in the plan to ensure that messages are consistent and within the scope of the organisation's responsibility

— Provides updates to organisation's director, EOC command and higher headquarters, as determined in the plan

— Advises the director and chain of command regarding information to be released, based on the organisation's role in the response

— Ensures that risk communication principles are employed in all contact with media, public, and partner information release efforts

— Knows incident-specific policy, science, and situation

— Reviews and approves materials for release to media, public, and partners

— Obtains required clearance of materials for release to media on policy or sensitive topic-related information not previously cleared

— Determines the operational hours/days, and reassesses these throughout the emergency response

— Ensures that resources are available (human, technical, and mechanical supplies)

5.7.2.2. Direct Media

— Assesses media needs and organises mechanisms to fulfil those needs during the crisis (e.g., daily briefings in person, versus a Web site update)
— Triages the response to media requests and inquiries
— Ensures that media inquiries are addressed as appropriate
— Supports spokespersons
— Develops and maintains media contact lists and call logs
— Produces and distributes media advisories and press releases
— Produces and distributes materials (e.g., fact sheets, B-roll)
— Oversees media monitoring systems and reports (e.g., analysing environment and trends to determine needed messages, determining what misinformation needs to be corrected, identifying concerns, interests, and needs arising from the crisis and the response)
— Ensures that risk communication principles to build trust and credibility are incorporated into all public messages delivered through the media
— Acts as a member of the joint information centre or field site team for media relations
— Serves as a liaison from your organisation to the Joint Information Centre (JIC)

5.7.2.3. Direct Public Information

— Manages the mechanisms to respond to the public who request information directly from the organisation by telephone, in writing, or by e-mail.
— Oversees public information monitoring systems and reports (e.g., analysing environment and trends to determine needed messages, determining what misinformation needs to be corrected, identifying concerns, interests, and needs arising from the crisis and the response)
— Activates or participates in the telephone information line
— Activates or participates in the public e-mail response system

— Activates or participates in the public correspondence response system
— Organises and manages emergency response Web site and Web pages
— Establishes and maintains links to other emergency response Web sites

5.7.2.4. Direct Partner/Stakeholder Information

— Establishes communication protocols based on prearranged agreements with identified partners and stakeholders
— Arranges regular partner briefings and updates
— Solicits feedback and responds to partner information requests and inquiries
— Oversees partner/stakeholder monitoring systems and reports (e.g., analysing environment and trends to determine needed messages, determining what misinformation needs to be corrected, identifying concerns, interests, and needs arising from the crisis and the response)
— Helps organise and facilitate official meetings to provide information and receive input from partners or stakeholders
— Develops and maintains lists and call logs of legislators and special interest groups
— Responds to legislators, special interest group requests, and inquiries

5.7.2.5. Content and Material for Public Health Emergencies

— Develops and establishes mechanisms to rapidly receive information from the EOC regarding the public health emergency
— Translates EOC situation reports and meeting notes into information appropriate for public and partner needs
— Works with subject matter experts to create situation-specific fact sheets, Q/As, and updates
— Compiles information on possible public health emergency topics for release when needed

— Tests messages and materials for cultural and language requirements of special populations
— Receives input from other communication team members regarding content and message needs
— Uses analysis from media, public, and partner monitoring systems and reports to adopt messages
— Identifies additional content requirements and material development

5.7.3. Information Verification and Clearance/Approval Procedures

— Who absolutely *must* review a new piece of information before it's released from your organisation or incorporated into an overall release from a higher authority?
  – The quickest way to publicly fall flat on your face as an organisation is to be unable to quickly release accurate information. Prioritise what information is needed to know versus want to know and get moving on what must be answered first. If an answer to a "need to know" question is not formulated, give the media and the public information about the process or system to get that answer.
  – Three people should officially clear a document before it's released from the organisation: the communication director responsible for your organisation's reputation, the director whose job is on the line if the information is wrong or counter to policy, and a subject matter expert who is fast and infallible on the subject. Keep legal out of it, unless the subject to be cleared has a legal implication. This doesn't mean that others can't review and comment on the product; they just can't delay its release. Also, don't forget to get clearance from your higher authority as required. As a courtesy, ensure that response partners know which new information you're planning to release. Have the mechanism in place to give a courtesy check to those response agencies with a stake in your release.
  – Clear all information simultaneously and in person, whenever possible. Unless you can get the primary

clearance authorities in one room with the door closed and no phone on the hook, make three copies; take one to each person and stand there while they review and approve the document. Point out any part of the document you believe needs their careful consideration. Ask if they would be comfortable seeing this as the headline of the next day's local paper. Reinforce that the information you've compiled and are attempting to get cleared answers important questions from the public, media, or partners *or* are in response to troubling trends from your own analysis of where the subject is headed.

– It's difficult to delegate clearance. As the communication director, be realistic about the time it will take and build that time into your duties. If the director has designated a surrogate for clearance, go with it. Educate everyone involved in the development and release of information about the steps to clear a document and the expectation for time from development to release. Help responsible authorities understand that no release is worse than an incomplete release. Get "need to know" information out the door fast. Get "want to know" released as soon as possible without straining relationships with authorities who must clear new information.

– The key to this area of emergency response is to have as much information on a topic prepared and pre-cleared as is possible. However, make sure that pre-developed information is sensitive to a crisis situation. When people are sick and dying, the words you choose will naturally have to be more careful—choose them that way from the start.

5.7.4. Agreements on Information Release Authorities

This is the preplanning that saves your job. Get agreements down on paper. Expect them to change. Try to respect everyone in the process. Seldom does an organisation truly own a piece of information exclusively. Typically, many levels of a response command could release information. Learn to work collaboratively. Does it really matter who releases it? What matters is to get information out quickly and accurately. Also, once it's released, you can incorporate the information into products for the public and partners, and meet your audiences' needs.

5.7.5. Regional and Local Media Contact List

Don't rely on scraps of paper. Write the list down. Include e-mail addresses and fax numbers. Because we know that emergencies happen during nonduty hours learn the back-door entries to news directors and editors ahead of time. It shouldn't be difficult to get that information. Test the e-mail addresses or fax numbers periodically to see what happens. The fail rate can be astronomical after only a year. Try to have contacts for all major media outlets.

5.7.6. Coordination with Public Health Organisations

— No man's an island. In a crisis, no communications team goes it alone. Find out how your organisation works during a crisis. Become part of the response team. Have a formal, recognised role. Include an organisational chart in your plan, so you can find people you need quickly. If you don't operate out of an emergency operation centre, find out who is on call. Make sure they know to call you immediately. Let them know that, in some cases, you may be the first person to hear about a public health emergency, often from the media. Make sure that your telephone numbers and after-hours contact information is included in the first emergency notification list. Communication can't afford to be an afterthought. Make sure you respond when you get a call.

— Don't stop with your organisation. Make sure that other response organisations or partners include your contact information in their communication plans. Swap names, numbers, after-duty numbers, and expected roles and responsibilities. Obtain public health organisation emergency response team after-hours contact numbers.

5.7.7. Spokespersons for Public Health Issues

Know who your public health emergency spokespersons will be and designate backups. Don't name someone solely based on his or her position in the organisation. Select people according to their ability and availability. Keep them trained. Spokespersons can get rusty. Understand that even if the Governor will be speaking at the daily press conference, there's plenty of media work or public meeting work to go around. Make a list of names. Be prepared to offer your trained spokespersons to higher authorities if they need them. Know how to reach the designated spokespersons from your organisation. Line up subject matter experts outside your organisation who can perform some of these duties and keep them informed. Media and civic groups will appreciate the offer of an alternative if you're unable to meet their needs.

5.7.8. Procedures to Secure needed Resources

At the local level, a JIC may be the answer to your resource needs. However, some public health emergencies that can tax your organisation may not trigger the operation of an EOC and a JIC. Obtain agreements with other local or nongovernmental organisations for support to your operation if a JIC is not activated.

Most public information officers are accustomed to working with little or no budget. During a crisis, you must be able to get supplies, people, equipment, and space as needed. Based on your needs assessment, identify your needs and the procurement mechanisms. Try to connect with a part of your organisation that has logistical savvy. Take the time to learn to get resources. Put that information in your plan. Don't wait for the emergency to start telling emergency response commanders what you need. Integrate that information into the planning. Make sure that the EOC plans indicate your space, people, telephone lines, etc. needs. Over-plan in this area.

5.7.9. Suggestions about Resources Space

— You need space to operate your communication teams outside the EOC. You need a place to bring media on site (separate from the EOC).

— You need a quiet space to quickly train spokespersons.

— You need space for team meetings.

— You need space for equipment exclusive for your use. You cannot stand in line for the copier when media deadlines loom.

5.7.9.1. People

— You need people designated and trained at a level to either operate a 24/7 public and media information centre or the people needed to support a JIC as part of a local EOC.

— Identity people qualified to take phone inquiries; consider staff from throughout the health department as well as in partner organisations.

— Consider recruiting volunteers from the medical community to help with phones, especially infectious disease specialists.

— You can never have too many support staff. They will save you from your worst mistakes—always! Train them, give them respectful titles, and reward them.

5.7.9.2. Contracts and Memoranda of Agreement

— Consider a contract with a media newswire.

— Consider a contract with a radio newswire.

— Consider contracts with writers or public relations persons who can augment your staff.

— Consider a contract for administrative support.

— Consider a phone system/contractor that can supply a phone menu that directs the type of caller and level of information desired:

- General information about the threat
- Tip line listing particular actions people can take to protect themselves
- Reassurance/counseling
- Referral information for health care/medical facility workers
- Referral information for epidemiologists or others needing to report cases
- Lab/treatment protocols
- Managers looking for policy statements for employees

5.7.9.3. Equipment

You can't wait for a contractor to show up with an extra fax machine. Equipment to support communication to media and partners must be obtained before the crisis. Determine what you may need to augment this equipment if a crisis persists.

- Fax machine (number that's pre-programed for broadcast fax releases to media and partners)
- Web site capability 24/7. Attempt to post information within 2 hours—some say within 10 minutes.
- Computers (on LAN with e-mail list serves designated for partners and media)
- Laptop computers
- Printers for every computer
- Copier machine (and backup)
- Tables—lots of tables
- Cell phones/pagers
- Visible calendars, flow charts, bulletin boards, easels
- Designated personal message board
- Small refrigerator
- Paper
- Color copier
- A/V equipment
- Portable microphones
- Podium
- TVs with cable hookup
- VHS VCR
- CD–ROM
- Paper shredder

5.7.9.4. Supplies

Keep these on hand as "emergency only" to ensure they are there when you need them.

— Copier toner (it always goes out)
— Printer ink
— Paper
— Pens
— Markers
— Highlighters
— Erasable markers
— FedEx and mail supplies
— Sticky notes
— Notebooks
— Poster board
— Standard press kit folders
— Organised B-roll in beta format (keep VHS copies for meetings)
— Formatted computer disks
— Color-coded everything (folders, inks, etc.)
— Baskets (to contain items that you're not ready to throw away)
— Organisers to support your clearance and release system
— Expandable folders (with alphabet or days of the month)
— Staplers (lots of them)
— Paper punch
— Three-ring binders
— Organisation's press kit or its logo on a sticker
— Colored copier paper (for door-to-door flyers)
— Paper clips (all sizes)
— Tape (be creative)

5.7.9.5. Vehicles of Crisis Information Dissemination

Different mechanisms are appropriate at different times and for audiences. The vehicles that can be used to communicate with media, public, and partner are:

— Phone (including hotlines)

— Fax (including broadcast pre-programed fax)
— E-mail (including listserv)
— Partner or other emergency response vehicles (use someone else's mailing list)
— Mail (including special delivery)
— Face-to-face (including town hall meetings or press briefings)
— Partner association to its members
— Web sites
— Contracted press releases wires
— Media—radio, print, Web, TV

5.8. Nine Steps of Crisis Response

5.8.1. Step 1. Verify Situation

— Get the facts.
— Obtain information from additional sources to put the event in perspective.
— Ascertain information origination and determine credibility.
— Did the information come from a formal source, such as HHS or Epi-Aid?
— Did the information come from an informal channel, such as a nongovernment partner?
— Is this a rumor (e.g., an e-mail chain)?
— Review and critically judge all information.
— Determine whether the information is consistent with other sources.
— Determine whether the characterisation of the event is plausible.
— Clarify information through subject matter experts.
— Attempt to verify the event magnitude.
— Begin to identify staffing and resource needs to meet the expected media and public interest.
— Determine who should be notified of this potential crisis.

5.8.2. Step 2. Conduct Notifications

5.8.2.1. Mandatory Notification and Coordination

It is essential for you to carefully think through who should be notified in your chain of command, up to what appropriate level, and within the scope of your organisation.

5.8.2.2. Notification and Coordination

Notification procedures vary by state and local jurisdictions. Know what procedures govern your area of responsibility.

5.8.3. Step 3. Conduct Crisis Assessment

Throughout the event, continue to gather information; try to determine the severity of the situation and the potential impact on communication operations, resources, and staffing. This requires swift and active research.

- Determine the organisation/office/individual in charge of managing the crisis. Ensure direct and frequent contact with the office in charge is possible.
- Continue to gather and check the facts. What happened? What was done to keep this situation from happening? What can be done to keep it from getting worse?
- Determine what your organisation is doing to end this crisis. Is there an investigation? Who's involved in the investigation?
- Determine what other agencies/organisations are doing to solve this crisis.
- Determine who is being affected by this crisis. What are their perceptions? What do they want and need to know?
- Determine what the public should be doing.
- Activate media monitoring.
- Activate internet monitoring.
- Determine what's being said about the event. Is the information accurate?

5.8.4. Step 4. Organise Assignments

5.8.4.1. Initial Organisational Issues

— Determine who is managing the event programmatically/ scientifically.
— How should communication interface with the program staff in charge of managing the crisis? Are there meetings that communication staff should attend?
— Are all crisis communication teams operational (media, public, partner, stakeholder, support)?
— What are our current priorities?
— What resources are needed? Is staffing sufficient?
— Who is the organisation's spokesperson for this event?
— Do we need subject matter experts (SMEs) as additional spokespersons?
— Should communication operate 10, 12, 20 or 24 hours a day?
— Should communication operate 5, 6, or 7 days a week?
— Will communication staff be expected to travel?
— Supplemental funds needed?
— Contractor support needed?
— Determine consistency of information across sources.

5.8.4.2. Ongoing Organisational Issues

— What do investigators say about the potential for the crisis getting worse?
— Could events result in more intense public/media interest?
— What rumors or points of conflict have been identified?
— How should the organisation respond to these issues? Is our response working?
— Should the organisation continue to be a source of information to the media about this crisis, or would some issues be more appropriately addressed by other government entities?

— Are the teams operating with approximately equal intensity? How could we improve efficiency? Would re-assignments help?
— Are resources sufficient?
— Should the organisation reset times for daily updates to media (e.g., set a time for a media update via Web and broadcast fax) or cancel the regular updates?
— Are daily/weekly SME briefings appropriate to reduce the demand for one-on-one interviews with SMEs?
— Should detailed persons be extended or returned to normal duties?
— Should hours of operation be increased or reduced?
— Are supplemental funds needed to meet public/media demand for information?
— What is the organisation learning from the public and media that could be useful to outbreak investigators and policy managers?

5.8.4.3. Partner Involvement

— Are partner organisations concerned about their own reputations?
— Which partners are or should be involved in this crisis?
— How do partners wish to get involved in the organisation's response?
— Have traditional partners been given updates?
— Who are your traditional partners?
  - Other organisations
  - Volunteer organisations
  - Associations
  - Private sector

5.8.5. Step 5. Prepare Information and Obtain Approvals

This function includes all message and materials development activities, the approval process, and the coordination of information within your organisation.

5.8.5.1. Message Development

— Who are our audiences? Who's been affected by this event? Who's upset or concerned? Who needs to be alerted to this situation?
— What are audiences' perceptions and information needs?
— What do media want to know?
— How should your organisation show empathy?
— What are the facts? What happened?
— What is our policy on this issue?
— What is your organisation doing about this issue? How are we solving the problem?
— What can your organisation do to keep this from happening again?
— What other agencies or third parties are involved? What are they saying?
— What should the public be doing?
— What public information is available?
— When will more information be available?

5.8.5.2. Approval Process

The approval process is unique to each organisation.

5.8.6. Step 6. Release Information to Media, Public, and Partners through arranged Channels

5.8.6.1. Likely Media Questions

— Who's in charge?
— What are you doing for the people who got hurt?
— Is the situation under control?
— What can we expect?
— Why did this happen?
— Why wasn't this prevented?
— What else can go wrong?

— When did you begin working on this (were notified of this, determined this)?
— What do these data/information/results mean?
— What bad things aren't you telling us?

5.8.6.2. When talking to the Media

— Provide only information that has been approved by the appropriate managers. Don't speculate.
— Repeat the facts about the event.
— Describe the data collection and investigation process.
— Describe what your organisation is doing about the crisis.
— Describe what other organisations are doing.
— Explain what the public should be doing.
— Describe how to obtain more information about the situation.

5.8.7. Step 7. Obtain Feedback and Conduct Crisis Evaluation

As soon as is feasible following a crisis, conduct an evaluation of the organisation's response.

— Compile and analyse comments and criticisms from the customer base.
— Compile and analyse media coverage.
— Conduct a "hot wash" (an immediate review of what went right and what went wrong) to capture lessons learned.
— Develop a Strengths, Weaknesses, Opportunities, Threats report on the crisis communication operation.
— Report results of content analysis and Strengths, Weaknesses, Opportunities, Threats to leadership.
— Share results within your organisation.
— Consider whether journal articles could be developed from the analyses.
— Determine need for changes to the crisis communication plan.
— Determine need to improve policies and processes.
— Institutionalise changes with appropriate training.

— Revise crisis plan policies and procedures based on lessons learned.

5.8.8. Step 8. Conduct Public Education

Once the crisis has subsided, the organisation may need to carry out additional public education activities.

— Should the organisation be educating the public about public health issues related to this crisis?

— What are the public's perceptions and information needs related to this crisis?

— Does the public understand the organisation's health messages on this issue? Are they taking appropriate actions?

— Should we also consider audiences that were not involved in the crisis for public education?

— Should a public health message related to this crisis event be incorporated into other health communication activities (e.g., Public Health Week or National Infant Immunisation Week)?

— Should we use this event to highlight any related public health messages?

— Should any Web sites be updated as a result of this crisis?

— Should any of the crisis materials be institutionalised?

— Would a series of post-crisis "canned" articles be useful in this situation?

5.8.9. Step 9. Monitor Events

Crisis monitoring protocols include:

— Media monitoring

— Internet monitoring

— Ongoing exchanges of information with yours and other organisations, state health departments, etc.

— Ongoing communication with SMEs and partners

— Monitoring of public opinion data and other research.

References

Dear, M. (1992). Understanding and overcoming the NIMBY syndrome. *Journal of the American Planning Association*, 58, 288-300.

Dietz, T., Stern, P. C., & Rycroft, R. W. (1989). Definitions of conflict and the legitimating of resources: The case of environmental risk. *Sociological Forum*, 4, 47-69.

Douglas, M. (1990). Risk as a forensic resource. *Daedalus, 119*, 1-16.

Edwards, W., & von Winterfeldt, D. (1987). Public values in risk debates. *Risk Analysis*, 7, 141-158.

Fessenden-Raden, J., Fitchen, J. M., & Heath, J. S. (1987). Providing risk information in communities: Factors influencing what is heard and accepted. *Science. Technology, & Human Values, 12* (3-4), 94-101.

Fietkau, H. J. (1990). Accident prevention and risk communication in environmental protection: A sociopsychological perspective. *Industrial Crisis* Quarterly, 4, 277-289.

Fiorino, D. J. (1989). Technical and democratic values in risk analysis. *Risk Analysis*, 9, 293-299.

6

Role of Spokesperson in Risk Communication

In an ideal world, every organisation would clone spokespersons who would all loose charisma, caring, and confidence. In our world, we may have little choice about who ultimately speaks for our organisation. The area of control that must be exerted by the organisation's public information officer is to insist that spokespersons are trained, because we know that few are born. No person should represent the entire organisation unless he or she has invested time and energy in developing the skills of an effective spokesperson. It's not about the color of a tie or scarf one wears on television, but the ability to *effectively* connect with the audience, either through the media or in person.

6.1. Duties of Spokesperson

Your job as a spokesperson in an emergency is to communicate information the public wants or needs to know to reduce the incidence of illness and death. Your job is also vital to reduce the likelihood that:

— Scarce public health and safety resources might be misallocated (through pressures brought forward based on incomplete or misinformation).

— Public health and safety recommendations are ignored or circumvented.

— Unneeded public health and safety response resources are committed (because of public or stakeholder demand based on faulty information or expectations).

Early in an emergency, expect to describe the following:

- — The health and safety risks for individuals and communities—what is the risk?
- — The incident and its magnitude (e.g., who, what, where, when, why, how)
- — What's being done to respond to the incident?

The spokesperson is not solely responsible for the messages to be conveyed; however, he or she must be involved in the development of those messages to ensure that the spokesperson "owns" them. The words and the person must match. Spokespersons don't just read a statement; they *are* the statement. If the spokesperson doesn't fully understand the purpose behind the messages or recommendations, he or she will have difficulty assuming a stance of confidence and conveying believability and trust.

The following basic tenets help to build confidence and trust in the facts and recommendations released. During an emergency, communication to the public is not business as usual. Before one can communicate the facts and recommendations for action, one must reduce the audience's psychological barriers by acknowledging their concerns.

Basic tenets of crisis and emergency risk communication include the following:

- — *Don't over-reassure*. The objective is not to placate but to elicit accurate, calm concern.
- — *Acknowledge uncertainty*. Offer only what you know. Show your distress and acknowledge your audience's distress. "It must be awful to hear that we can't answer that question right now..."
- — *Emphasise that a process is in place to learn more*. Describe that process in simple terms.
- — *Give anticipatory guidance*. If you are aware of future negative outcomes, let people know what to expect. (e.g., side effects of antibiotics).
- — *Be regretful, not defensive*. Say, "We are sorry..." or "We feel terrible that..." when acknowledging misdeeds or failures from the organisation. Don't use "regret," which sounds like you're preparing for a lawsuit.

— *Acknowledge people's fears*. Don't tell people they shouldn't be afraid. They are afraid and they have a right to their fears. Don't disparage fear; acknowledge that it's normal and human to be frightened, (even though...).

— *Acknowledge the shared misery*. Some people will be less frightened than they are miserable, feeling hopeless and defeated. Acknowledge the misery of a catastrophic event, then help move people toward the future through positive actions.

— *Express wishes*. Say, "I wish we knew more," or "I wish our answers were more definitive."

— *Panic is less common than imagined*. Panic doesn't come from bad news, but from mixed messages. If people are faced with conflicting recommendations and expert advice, they are left with no credible source to turn to for help. That level of abandonment opens the door to charlatans and poor judgment. Candor protects your credibility and reduces the possibility of panic, because your messages will ring true.

— *Be willing to address the "what if" questions*. These are the questions that everyone is thinking about and they want expert answers. Although it's often impractical to fuel "what ifs" when the crisis is contained and not likely to affect large numbers of people, it is reasonable to answer "what ifs" if the "what if" could happen and people need to be emotionally prepared for them. If you do not answer the "what if" questions, someone at much less risk regarding the outcome of the response will answer them for you. If you are not prepared to address "what ifs," you lose credibility and the opportunity to frame the "what if" questions with reason and valid recommendations.

— *Give people things to do*. In an emergency, some actions are directed at victims, and those exposed or have the potential to be exposed. However, those who do not need to take immediate action will be engaging in "vicarious rehearsal" regarding those recommendations and may need substitute actions to ensure that they do not prematurely act on recommendations not meant for them. Simple actions in an emergency will give people a sense of control and will help to motivate them to stay tuned to what is happening (versus denial, where they refuse to acknowledge the possible danger to themselves and others) and will prepare them to take action when directed to do so. Give people a choice of actions matched to their level of concern. Give a range of responses: a minimum response, a maximum response, and a recommended middle response.

— *Ask more of people.* Perhaps the most important role of the spokesperson is to ask people to bear the risk and work toward solutions with you. People can tolerate considerable risk, especially voluntary risk. If you acknowledge the risk's severity and complexity, and recognise people's fears, you can then ask the best of them. A spokesperson, especially one who is on the ground and at personal risk, can model the appropriate behavior—not false happiness, but true willingness to go on with life as much as possible and to make reasonable choices. Don't be glib—be stalwart. Your determination to face risk will help others looking for role models. Americans have great heart, a sense of selflessness, and a natural competitiveness. Sparking those inherent attributes will help people cope with uncertainty, fear, and misery.

6.2. Qualities of a Good Spokesperson

It's sometimes difficult to capture the qualities of a good spokesperson and pass them on to others. However, it's not at all difficult to identify the qualities of a poor spokesperson. This section is about what not to do. Nearly all spokesperson training starts or ends with this statement: "Be yourself. Be natural." That may not always be the best advice. The audience can tell when the persona appears stilted or fake. But "be natural" doesn't mean forgetting the seriousness of your role. Perhaps better advice is "Be your organisation. Act like your organisation."

Every organisation has an identity. A spokesperson should try to embody that identity. For example, CDC exists solely to make people safer and healthier. CDC personnel have a history of placing themselves in harm's way to do the detective work needed to stop the spread of illness or death. CDC also is humble in its understanding that it goes where asked. It has partners and relationships that it values and will neither steal the show nor abandon the effort.

A spokesperson must be perceived as trustworthy and credible. Research indicates that being perceived as empathetic and caring provides greater opportunity for your message to be received and acted upon. Express empathy or caring within the first 30 seconds. Besides empathy, credibility is built on expressions of competence and expertise (truly "knowing your stuff"), honesty and openness, and commitment and dedication.

Work with your organisation's public information officer to develop messages, gather facts, and determine what can be released at any given time. Also, be certain that you know when you will be available to the media or the public. Reassure them that you will be back to share updates with them.

Some recommendations for spokespersons in all settings are given below:

— Know your organisation's policies about the release of information.
— Stay within the scope of your responsibilities, unless you are authorised to speak for the entire organisation or a higher headquarters.
— Don't answer questions that are not within the scope of your organisational responsibility.
— Tell the truth. Be as open as possible.
— Follow up on issues.
— Use visuals when possible.
— Illustrate a point through examples, stories, and analogies. Ensure that they help you make your point and do not minimise or exaggerate your message. Try the stories out on a small group first.

6.3. Pitfalls for Spokespersons

— *Remember that jargon obfuscates communication and implies arrogance*. If you have to use a technical term or acronym, define it. If you can define it, do you need to use it? Jargon and euphemisms are security blankets. Try to give yours up.

— *Use humor cautiously*. Humor is a minefield. Soft, self-deprecating humor may be disarming for a hostile audience, but be careful.

— *Refute negative allegations without repeating them*. Don't own the negative by repeating the accusation.

— When possible, *use positive or neutral terms*.

— *Don't assume you've made your point*. Ask whether you've made yourself clear.

— Ultimately, *money will become an issue*. During the early stage of an emergency, don't lead with messages about money.

— At all costs, *avoid one-liners, cliches, and off-the-cuff comments*. Any statement that trivialises the experience of the people involved by saying something such as "there are no guarantees in life" kills your credibility.

— *Discuss what you know, not what you think*.

— *Do not express personal opinions*.

— *Don't show off*. This is not the time to display an impressive vocabulary.

6.4. Emergency Public Meeting

— *Don't show inappropriate hostility*. You can be angry at the organisms, chemicals, or natural disasters causing illness and death. In the case of bioterrorism, you can express outrage at the act and the perpetrators. But don't show outrage or become indignant toward your detractors. Those involved in public health and safety see themselves as the good guys. It hurts when our intentions, abilities, and expertise are criticised. Get over it! Outrage in such cases is natural for many people. As scientists and technical experts, we may be less emotional than others, and that can divide us from the audiences with which we are attempting to communicate. Don't dismiss emotions expressed about the situation or your organisation as hysterical or inappropriate. Those emotions are normal for most people, whether or not they are normal for you. The first step in dealing with the criticism and outrage expressed by your audience is to acknowledge that it exists. Don't "own" their outrage, but don't dismiss it either.

— *Ask for ground rules and have them outlined by a neutral third party.* Acknowledge the anger up front and explain what you hope to accomplish. Refer back to your objectives when the communication deteriorates.

— *Don't react with temper when confronted with accusations.* It's helpful to visualise someone to whom you sincerely hope to communicate what you are doing and talk to that person (e.g., may be your parent, your child, someone you care about and who cares about you). This is a way to continue to reach important audiences by mentally bypassing the reporter or advocate who is trying to cause a negative response.

— *Practice self-management.* Calm yourself, breathe deeply, and remind yourself of your greater purpose. Display confidence and concentration. Visualise a verbal attack and mentally rehearse a temperate response. Don't be caught off guard. Anticipate the attack and practice not feeding the anger. Anger fizzles more quickly if it does not meet an obstruction. Let the person vent, without interruption, for a reasonable amount of time. Ask if he or she has had time to fully express feelings. Don't be insincere. If you can't say it, don't.

— *Engage in active listening.* Listening means being able to express the other person's point of view. Concentrate on what the person is saying. It's hard to do when you're also attempting to form your answer. It's not a race; take the time to listen and frame your response.

— *Don't say, "I know exactly how you feel."* Instead, acknowledge the feeling, and suggest an example of something you've found worked for you and may work for them.

— *Avoid interrupting, but set limits.* If a hostile speaker dominates, appeal to him or her that you want to address the concerns of others in the room.

— *Don't overreact to emotional words.* Remember, you're the professional. Others have a different investment in what's happening. Words that you interpret one way may mean another to others. Give them the benefit of the doubt.

— *Use open body language*. Sit or stand with your arms relaxed by your sides. Do not cross your arms or put your hands on your hips. Make eye contact when possible.

— *Modulate your voice*. Use a slightly lower tone and volume of voice than the angry individual.

— *Don't take personal abuse*. A certain amount of anger and negative emotion directed at you is understandable. If it becomes personal, however, you have a right to express the inappropriateness of that behavior and ask the person to join with you in getting back to the issues. You are your organisation. You are not alone. You are not the true focus of the attack; it's more likely a result of frustration, fear, and a sense of lack of control. Attackers may feel marginalised and feel the need to have their positions validated. Give them the right to feel the way they feel. If you know that the audience will be hostile, bring along a neutral third party who can step in and defuse the situation.

— *State the problem, then the recommendation*. When explaining your position, state the problem before your answer. For example, rather than saying, "Exposed persons should take Cipro for 60 days," say, "To eliminate the risk of respiratory anthrax, CDC recommends that exposed persons take Cipro for 60 days."

— *Commit to a response*. Write down people's concerns and get back to them.

— *Don't promise what you can't deliver*. Explain the limitations of the situation and express that you are doing everything you can to keep the response on track.

— *Look forward, not back*. Acknowledge past mistakes: "I wish we had met with you sooner to hear your concerns." Then talk about where you want to go in resolving problems rather than where you have been. Avoid rehashing old issues.

— *Do not search for a single answer*. One size may not fit all. Consider many possible solutions and do not view a negotiation as an either/or proposition.

6.5. Talking through the Media

The media are important during the first hours or days of an emergency.

They are the fastest and, in some cases, the only way reach the public during an emergency. Media professionals accept their community responsibilities; however, your job is not their job. Respect the differences and look for mutual goals.

— *Go into any media interview with a purpose*. Have a message to deliver. If you don't have a message, you don't have a reason to do the interview.

— *Make sure the reporter gets your name and title right*. Keep your title as short as possible. It's better to make it descriptive of what you do than to give an official position title. For example, medical epidemiologist is better than "acting chief of the XXXXXXXX, section of the XXXX branch," etc.

6.5.1. General Media Interview Pitfalls

— *Don't let a reporter put words in your mouth*. The reporter may use inflammatory or emotionally laden words. Don't repeat them.

— *If the question contains leading or loaded language*, reframe the question to eliminate the language and then answer the questions.

— *Don't assume the reporter has it right* if he or she claims that someone has lodged an allegation. Don't react to new information a reporter gives you. Instead, say, "I have not heard that" or "I would have to verify that before I could respond." Don't let the reporter start a fight.

— *If a reporter leaves a microphone in your face* after you've answered the question, *stop. Do not answer the question again or add to your answer*. Instead, say, "That was my answer. Do you have another question for me to address?" Say it matter of factly, without sarcasm or annoyance.

— *There is no such thing as "off the record."* Background and deep background do not mean you won't be quoted. Do not say anything before, during, or at the conclusion of an interview that you are not prepared to see in print the next day. The interview hasn't ended until the reporter and all equipment is out the door and long gone.

— *Anticipate questions*. Work with your public information officer to anticipate as many expected questions as possible and draft the answers. Nuances count. A word change here or there may make the difference in how well your answer is received. Put the answer on paper (it will usually be too long to give in public) and then find the bottom line—what is the point you want to make? What rings true and doesn't sound evasive? That's your 30-second answer.

— *Make your point first*. Have prepared message points. Try to say it in 30 seconds and in fewer than 90 words.

— *Don't fake it*. If you don't know the answer, say so. If it's not in your area of expertise, say so. Commit to getting the answer.

— *Never speak disparagingly of anyone, not even in jest*. Your mother was right—it's not becoming. Don't assign blame or pass the buck. Stick to what you know and what your organisation is doing. Don't fight your battle through the media. If you don't have something nice to say, don't say anything. Remind reporters that professionals can differ in opinion but that does not mean they should attack each other in the media. There is a peer-review process to discuss differences.

— *Don't buy in to hypothetical questions*. Reframe the question in a way that addresses legitimate concerns of the public without being sensational or "entertainment."

— *Record sensitive interviews*. Be sure the reporter knows you are doing it.

— *Do not ask reporters to review their articles or interviews*. Offer to clarify information for them as they prepare their piece. If a reporter shows you the piece, understand that he or she expects you to correct errors in fact—not viewpoints that may differ from yours.

— *Break down multiple-part questions* and answer each part separately.

— *Don't raise issues* you do not want to see in print or on the news.

— *Don't say "no comment"* to a reporter's question. Instead, state why you can't answer that question. Say that the matter is under investigation, the organisation has not yet made a decision, or simply that you are not the appropriate person to answer that question.

6.5.2. Media Opportunity or Press Conference Tips

— Determine in advance who will answer questions about specific subject matters.
— Keep answers short and focused—no longer than 2 minutes.
— Assume every mic is live—all the time.

6.5.3. In-person Interview Tips

— Know who will be conducting the interview.
— Know the subjects the reporter wants to cover and limit the interview to those subjects.
— Caution the reporter when you are not the right person to answer a question.
— Know the format and duration of the interview. You can set limits.
— Ask who else will be interviewed or has been interviewed.

6.5.3.1. Do not

— Embarrass or argue with a reporter.
— Tell the news organisation which reporter you prefer.
— Demand that your remarks not be edited.
— Insist that an adversary not be interviewed.
— Lie or cloud the truth.
— Demand that an answer you've given not be used.
— State that what you are about to say is off the record or not attributable to you.

6.5.4. Telephone Interview Tips

— Know who is on the other end of the line.
— Ask if you are being recorded.
— Ask when and where the information will be used.
— Obtain the reporter's phone number before the interview begins. You may need to call back if the call is interrupted or if you need to provide updated information.
— Spell out difficult names/technical terms/phrases.

At the outset, limit the time available for the interview. Give yourself an out, such as a pending meeting. You have an obligation to answer important questions from the media, but you do not have an obligation to explore every facet of the incident or to do reporters' homework. Send them to Web-based or print materials to save time. Be certain to ask reporters for feedback to ensure that they understand your points.

— Go to a quiet room.
— Don't allow distractions.
— Stand up. It strengthens your voice and makes you alert.
— Keep key messages at hand. Repeat them often so reporters know these are what you believe are important.

6.5.6. Counters to Electronic Media Interview Techniques

Reporters are not adversaries. They are also not your friends. Some reporters will use well-known techniques to attempt to get a reaction from you. Adjust your interview style accordingly.

— *Sensational or unrelated questions*: Answer the question in as few words as possible without repeating the sensational elements. Then return to your key messages. Here are a few recommended "bridges" back to what you want to say:
  – "What I think you are really asking is..."
  – "The overall issue is..."
  – "What's important to remember is..."
  – "It's our policy to not discuss this issue, but what I can tell you is..."
  – "What I'm really here to discuss..."
  – "Your readers/viewers need to know..."
— *Character attack*: Don't lock horns with an adversary during an interview. Do question the science, issues, or goals, but not someone's character. "I can't speak for Dr. X. You'll have to ask him or her, but what I can address is..."
— *Machine-gun questioning*: Reporter fires rapid questions at you. Pacing is quick. Reporter interrupts your response. You respond, "Please let me answer this question." Control the pace. Take time to think.

— *Mic feeding and pausing*: You've given a good answer on a controversial issue. The reporter pauses and the camera continues to roll. Stay on your agenda. Be aware of nonverbal cues (deer in the headlights look, fidgeting). Don't sweat. It's the reporter's job to fill the air time. Dead air doesn't make scintillating viewing—unless you're reacting nonverbally. Relax.

— *Hot mic*. It's always on. Always—including during "testing."

— *Sensational question with an A or B dilemma*. Use positive words, correct the inaccuracies without repeating the negative, and reject A or B if neither are valid. Explain, "There's actually another alternative you may not have considered," and give your message point.

— *Surprise prop*. The reporter attempts to hand you a report or supposedly contaminated item. Don't take it. If you take it, you own it. React by saying, "I'm familiar with that report, and what I can say is" or "I'm not familiar with that report, but what is important is," and then go to your key message.

6.5.7. Radio Interview Tips

A live interview is very different from a taped interview. Be sure you know whether it's live, live to tape, or taped. If the interview is live, determine whether callers will be permitted to ask questions. Try to avoid answering caller questions seldom is that an effective means to provide information.

— Speak in normal tones.

— Watch out for "uh," "um," and "you know." You do not own the air time. It's not your responsibility to fill the space. Take the time you need to form your thoughts and answer.

— Use notes, but don't rustle your papers.

— Radio interviews will not be as in-depth as print. Get your key messages out quickly and succinctly.

— Don't offer lengthy scientific explanations. Remember that your audience has very little scientific background. Tell them what it means to them. Take on your audience's point of view.

— Reporters may ask the same question multiple times in an attempt to elicit a different answer from you *or* to get you to answer the question with fewer words.

— Be careful *not* to repeat the negatives in a reporter's question. Typically, radio interviews do not include the questions from the reporter. Therefore, if the reporter says, "Some say you blew it when you failed to...," do not respond: "We didn't blow it." Instead, start with what you *did* do and what you want the audience to know you did.

— Assume the mic is always live.

6.5.8. Television Interview Tips

Do not make broad unnatural gestures or move around in your chair. Ask for a chair that does not swivel.

— *Practice, practice, practice*: Spokespersons must take the time to prepare for an appearance. With the help of your public information officer, practice answering questions, especially aggressive, rapid-fire questions. Ideas, facts, and anecdotes must be part of your thinking so you can discuss them easily and naturally. Memorised answers might sound as if you are reciting the material by rote. Practice answering questions in 10–20 second phrases. If a question calls for a longer answer, pause every 20 seconds. This will make it easier for the host to break in for a commercial interruption. Practice stopping the minute you are directed to; hard breaks in mid-sentence at commercial look unprofessional and desperate.

— *Slow down*. Microphones tend to make people talk faster. Slow down and deliberately pause between sentences to appear in control.

— *Drive out monotone*. Practice raising and lowering the pitch of your voice, not the volume. Natural animation helps increase credibility. Monotone may be due to fear. The more practice, the less fear— and the greater the animation in the voice.

— *Don't look at yourself on the TV monitor*. It is distracting to the viewer.

— *Look at the reporter*, not the camera, unless directed otherwise.

— *Ensure that your earphone fits securely* and that you know what to do if it pops out of your ear. Ask the producer or sound/camera technician for help if needed.

— *Sit comfortably upright*. Do not slouch.

— *In taped interviews, ask to repeat your response if you believe the first attempt was not your best. In live interviews, correct misstatements as* quickly as possible.

6.5.9. What to Wear on Television

Wear clothes appropriate to the situation. If you're in a field situation, a suit may not be appropriate. Do not wear medical clothes or a lab coat unless you would be wearing them for your job.

6.5.9.1. Men

— Avoid patterned suits, stripes, and checks. The camera will make them wavy and distracting to the viewer.

— Button double-breasted suits. You may unbutton single-breasted suits. If possible, sit on your coattails, to avoid bunching around your neck and shoulders.

— White shirts are considered the most conservative. Also consider wearing light blue or grey. Bottom line: in an emergency, you should look conservative, not stylish or flashy.

— Neckties should be somber. Do not "advertise" a product or point of view on your tie.

— Wear knee-length socks darker than your suit. Your credibility can plummet if your socks end at your ankles and viewers get a "skin shot" when your pant legs creep up.

— Be clean-shaven.

6.5.9.2. Women

— Tailored clothes work best.

— Short skirts kill credibility as quickly as short socks on men.

— Neutral colors and muted patterns work best. Most set backdrops are blue or purple. Consider taking along a contrasting shawl or scarf to ensure that you do not blend into the background if your suit matches the set color.

— Wear dark shoes.

— Avoid distracting or shiny jewellery and any accessory that jangles or needs constant adjusting.

— Wear everyday make-up. Avoid loud fingernail color. Lipstick should be a neutral/natural shade; lip liner helps define the lips. Women who never wear make-up should consider color on the lips. The lighting for TV is not natural, and you'll look years older and less energetic without the lipstick color. Wear pink or coral or berry red seldom looks good. Avoid the trend toward dramatic dark colors on the lips and eyes and heavy lip liner. You'll look ghoulish, not reassuring.

6.5.9.3. Men and Women

— Neat, trimmed hair is best.

— If your skin is shiny under the lights, ask for powder. Bald men should powder the tops of their heads.

— If you can take off the glasses without squinting, do so. Consider nonglare glasses if you must wear them. Never wear tinted lenses or sunglasses. If the light hurts your eyes, ask that it be adjusted.

6.6. Assessing Your Communication Skills

In his book *The Art of Talking So That People Will Listen*, Paul W. Swets lists a number of causes of communication breakdown.

— *Fear*: Fear of being judged negatively, fear of appearing stupid, and fear of expressing or not controlling emotion can all cause roadblocks.

— *Assumptions*: We are often not aware that we select one meaning out of a number of possibilities when we make inferences. A study of the 500 most common English words produced an average of 28 dictionary definitions per word. We must be careful not to assume we know the meaning intended by the communicator.

— *Insensitivity*: Failing to care about the feelings of others may stem from preoccupation or an unwillingness to care about another.

— *Labeling*: Once we've assigned a negative label to another person or group, it is very difficult to overcome that belief and attempt empathy.

— *Uncertainty*: The uncertain person is often silent, tense, and afraid. Uncertainty is normal at times, but not all the time.

— *Resentment*: Resentment (a feeling of indignant displeasure for some perceived injustice) will cloud one's ability to perceive another's intent or gestures as sincere or neutral.

— *Egotism*: Egotism conveys lack of respect for another person and lack of genuine interest in hearing the other person's point of view. The listener will feel used as if the speaker's words serve only an ulterior motive.

Swets recommends the following communication-builders:

— *Self-awareness*: You can help develop self-awareness in a situation by asking yourself, "What do I really think about this issue and why do I hold that view?"

— *Understanding*: Repeat what you've heard and ask for clarification to correct misunderstandings and avoid wrong assumptions.

— *Care for others*: When people sense that a speaker does not really care about them, they stop listening. If you can empathise with your audience, they will listen.

— *Control of emotions*: Some believe that they are helpless against such emotions as anger, frustration, envy, resentment, and jealousy. These are, in fact, habits that we can choose to control. These are habits, but also a choice. We must believe we can control our emotions before we can motivate ourselves to change.

6.6.1. Assess Your Communication Habits

— Write down the problems you can identify about your communication habits.

— Consider recording some of your conversations to look for negative communication patterns.

— Ask for feedback on the strengths or weaknesses in your communication patterns. Try not to be defensive.

6.6.2. Choose to Listen

Research has found three barriers to effective listening:

— *Stress*: High stress, when our minds may be going in a million different directions, makes it very difficult to pay full attention to another person unless we make a choice to listen.

— *"Me syndrome."* Some social analysts call this the "new narcissism," in which our world view is centred on the self, with happiness and personal survival as its sole goal. A person affected by the "me syndrome" doesn't seem to care about others and can't see the legitimacy of any point of view but his or her own. He/she hears only what he/she wants to hear.

— *Brain speed.* While an average speech rate for many people is about 200 words per minute, most of us can think about 4 times that speed. With all that extra "think time," ineffective listeners let their minds wander.

Passive listening engages only part of the brain; in active listening, the brain is fully engaged. To actively listen, concentrate on what is being said and provide empathetic feedback. This encourages the speaker to continue. This is a language of acceptance, an unmistakable message that, regardless of whether you agree with what is said, the person is important and his or her thoughts matter.

Listen for ideas and feelings. Facts generally deal with external events. Thoughts represent our interpretation of events or facts. Feelings can be divided into two categories: feelings about external events and feelings about ourselves. Both types of feelings can be very intense.

6.6.2.1. As a Listener You Can

— Refuse to evaluate or judge the speaker.

— Aim for understanding and cooperation, not manipulation and control. Openly clarify your motives.

— Don't be afraid of deep feelings. Feelings change, sometimes in a moment. The release of deep feelings is therapeutic and enables one to return to a truer representation of self.

6.6.3. Facial Expressions

— *Positive*: smile, laughter, empathic face, head nod, eye contact

— *Negative*: frown, sneer, cry, glare, mocking laughter, smirk, angry face, disgust

6.6.4. Voice Cues

— *Positive*: caring, warm, relieved, concerned, cheerful, laughing
— *Negative*: cold, tense, scared, impatient, hard, clipped, staccato, whining, blaming, sarcastic, angry, blaring, accusing, depressed

6.6.5. Body Positions and Movements

— *Positive*: touching, reduced distance, open arms, relaxation, forward lean
— *Negative*: neck or hand tension, rude gestures, raising hands in disgust, point, jab, inattention

6.6.6. Effective Nonverbal Communication

— Maintain eye contact.
— Maintain an open posture.
— Do not retreat behind physical barriers such as podiums or tables.
— Do not frown or show anger or disbelief through facial expressions.
— Do not dress in a way that emphasises the differences between you and your audience

References

Ice, R. (1991). Corporate publics and rhetorical strategies: The case of Union Carbide's Bhopal Crisis. *Management Communication Quarterly*, 4, 341-362. (*)

Jasanoff, S. (1987). EPA's regulation of daminozide: Unscrambling the messages of risk. *Science Technology. & Human Values*, 12 (3-4), 116-124.

Johnson, B. B. (1987). Accounting for the social context of risk communication. *Science and Technology Studies*, 5, 103-111. Johnson, B. B. (1987). Public concerns and the public role in siting nuclear and chemical waste facilities. *Environmental Management*, 11, 571-586.

Kasperson, R. E. (1986). Six propositions on public participation and their relevance for risk communication. *Risk Analysis*, 6, 275-281.

7

Role of Media in Risk Communication

Today, India does not have a self-contained method to instantly communicate with its citizens, such as an emergency broadcast system that would reach everyone who may need important emergency information about what actions to take. The private media serve as an emergency broadcast system during a crisis and do it very well. If you ask someone where they go to get up-to-date information during an emergency, they will mention radio, TV, and, today, Web sites. Communities around the nation are served by professional media representatives that recognise their role in public safety.

The disconnect for public health and safety professionals about the media's role is that they would like to turn media demand on and off at whim. It doesn't work that way. The media are not an adjunct to public emergency response, they have their own place in a free society and their own obligations to the public. Public emergency planners should acknowledge the media's role in a crisis and plan to meet reasonable media requirements during the crisis. Few reporters, editors, directors, or producers will abandon their effort to obtain information and provide perspective on a crisis just because, as an emergency response person, you don't want them involved.

It's imperative that emergency operation centres (EOCs) and all government and nongovernmental organisations involved in crisis response understand the legitimate needs of the media and how to fulfil those needs as an ongoing and well-thought-out part of the response plan.

To add a little perspective, emergency response would be considerably hampered if media were not involved—the absence of mass media would make it nearly impossible for EOC and public officials to communicate the nature of the crisis and the appropriate actions citizens should take to mitigate morbidity and mortality. Granted, in some disasters, response officials find themselves in trucks with bullhorns moving through neighborhoods telling people where to find shelter or not to drink the water from their facets without purifying it. However, for most public health emergencies involving infectious diseases, including bioterrorism, the expectation is that the community infrastructure will be in place, electricity will continue to flow, buildings will stand, and roads will be clear. Therefore, the media will be an excellent vehicle to quickly communicate to the public. It is important to understand that the media will not allow you to spoon-feed them headlines. They will decide what to tell their viewers or listeners about what is occurring. Don't treat them like a member of your staff; suggest, do not dictate, and the relationship will move smoothly forward.

As the event unfolds, expect a widening gap between what you believe the media should be concentrating on (or not) and what they want to know. Also, remember that it's their job to look for alternate perspectives on what is happening. Make your points clearly and consistently, and you will have done your job. If incorrect factual information that could harm the public is presented by the media, it's imperative that you correct the facts. Expect only limited success in influencing, especially in the 24-hour news arena, that part of the crisis coverage devoted to debate, discussion, and speculation. Remember that what seems like facts to you may not seem so black and white to reporters and commentators.

7.1. Role of Media

The quickest way to destroy your relationship with the media is to ignore the finite aspects of their job—they have space and time to fill and deadlines to meet. Know those deadlines and work to accommodate them. During a crisis, be available—if necessary, around the clock—to help reporters get the facts and get them right, before deadline. Attempt to give media a reasonable expectation of when new information will be provided and, as quickly as possible, establish a schedule for information releases. Everyone involved will appreciate some ground rules. Those ground rules will depend on the type and phase of the crisis.

Today, even print media face short deadlines because of their online Web editions. In the past, response to media could be prioritised by their deadlines. Today, everyone seems to have the same deadlines, and this requires a revamping of the way emergency information is provided to the media.

The most ethical way for a public agency to approach this responsibility is to provide all media with the same access at the same time. As technology progresses this becomes easier to do. Through the use of pre-agreed-upon e-mail addresses, fax numbers, and onsite media opportunities (including tele-conferencing, so media away from the event can attend), you can be the pillar of fairness. In the first critical hours or days of an emergency, do not play favorites; equal access to information is imperative. If you have a message to communicate that is essential to the well-being or safety of the public, it's not up to you to decide where they get that information. Give the same information to all media all the time.

7.1.1. Local Media

Don't ignore local media in favor of the national media and the well-known names. National media have contacts outside the local area to fill in much of what they need. They won't be shortchanged. Local media are counting on local response officials to work with them, and you should. If you are the public information official at the local level, think local media. If you are at the state level, think regional media or border media, and at the national level, think national media. The key is to have consistent information flowing back and forth between the official response levels.

If the content of the message is consistent, we can begin to fulfil the needs of reporters at all levels. Following the H5N1 influenza outbreak in the late 1990s, national and local reporters on a panel at the first Emerging Infectious Disease Conference, held in Atlanta, praised the public information response because "everywhere we turned the facts were the same. When the Hong Kong Health Department released something, that same information appeared on the CDC Web site." Like the public, the media are looking for consistent information.

Things change, no doubt, but as the information moves along it should be the same quality and content at all levels.

7.2. Role of Reporters

An age-old question. They want answers to their questions, access to experts, and visuals to support their coverage. That stands true during an emergency, only they all want it NOW.

Questions at the top of the list in an emergency include the following:

— Who is in charge here?
— How are those who got hurt getting help?
— Is this thing being contained?
— What can we expect?
— What should we do?
— Why did this happen? (Don't speculate. Repeat the facts of the event, describe the data collection effort, and describe treatment from fact sheets.)
— Did you have forewarning this might happen?
— Why wasn't this kept from happening (again)?
— What else can go wrong?
— When did you begin working on this (e.g., were notified of this, determined this...)?
— What does this data/information/results mean?
— What bad things aren't you telling us? (Don't forget the good.)

The more you can prepare to anticipate the needs of the media, the more completely you will accomplish your goals: inform the public, help the public understand public health actions or recommendations, and gain public acceptance for public health activities during the response and recovery of a major public health emergency. Background information—the information that will not change during a crisis—such as a description of the organism involved, its incubation period, methods of treatment, etc., should be in place as soon as possible and easily retrievable. The CDC and other federal agencies work together to develop most of this background information. It will continue to be available to local and state public health officials through the CDC

Web site. You may want to check there when faced with a infectious disease or chemical event.

7.3. Media Operations in a Crisis

Just as a public health emergency is not business as usual for your agency, it's not for the media either. Media outlets have plans to cover major breaking news, and it's worthwhile to know what those plans are. During non-emergency times, EOC managers should invite local media into the operations centre to explain how it will work, the agencies that will be involved in the response, and where media will be accommodated when the EOC is operating. There should be a designated media room, outside the command centre but adjacent to it. This could be used for media opportunities and, when agreed to, to conduct individual interviews.

The media onslaught could start in a matter of minutes, depending on the type of public health emergency. The natural public curiosity feeds the media frensy, along with pressure to fill 24-hour news outlets. Media are most apt to exert pressure en masse—they are all looking for answers to the same questions at the same time. It's imperative that the EOC or the public health department leading the response be ready for that pack of journalists. If official channels cannot meet the media's needs, experts and outside authorities on a subject will almost instantly be speculating to the media about what officials are or should be doing. This won't be "Monday morning quarterbacks" talking—the second-guessing will begin immediately.

During an unfolding emergency, media may not behave as they usually do, so you must expect the possibility of the following from media during the early moments of a crisis:

— *Diminished information verification.* Tentative information, sometimes incorrect, will be broadcast.

— *Diminished adversarial role* (media are people, too). They will have genuine concern about what is occurring and will want to help by providing important messages. Don't expect the media to be this accommodating throughout the entire crisis, but in the beginning, the "them" versus "us" ratio diminishes and media contribute in their way to public safety.

— *For major crises, expect the national media to dominate.* Most people will be getting their news from the national media. Local media will be feeding information to the national media that will be on the air, coordinating the coverage. Messages meant for local audiences will have to compete for airtime with the national coverage. Respect local media deadlines and keep the information flowing to help disseminate local public health messages.

— *Media will expect an EOC*, where they can consolidate information to deliver to their viewers and listeners. Initially, the media will accept that much of their information must come from the command post. Within hours or days, depending on the crisis, media will be looking for other perspectives and other places from which to broadcast. If you want the media to use official releases of information, you'll have to ensure that the information is timely, fresh, and easy to access. Reporters have options about where to get information, and there are plenty of people inside and outside official channels who are willing to talk. A well-functioning media command centre within the EOC that gives the most, the most accurate, and the freshest information will rule.

— *Inadequate scientific expertise.* The other reality during a public health emergency, especially those involving infectious disease issues, is that many media will not have the technical or scientific background to quickly grasp new information or the nuances of that information. Prepare to fill in the blanks, without being condescending. Remember not to assume that everyone knows the technical jargon. Talking plainly to the media is a good way to practice talking plainly to the public during the emergency. Some people do not understand the difference between bacteria and viruses. Start with the basics and bring your reporters along. They will appreciate not being made to feel stupid, and you'll appreciate that the reports are accurate.

7.4. Getting Emergency Information to Media

Media releases: In an emergency, print information must move electronically to the media or be given as handouts to media at the site of the incident. If it's important enough to put down on paper (the information will remain current for at least a 12-hour cycle), get it done.

7.4.1. Pluses

- Ensures consistent information to all media.
- Provides an historical record.
- Allows for background information and direction to other sources of information.
- Gives media, who like paper, something in their hands from which to work.
- Releases that are fill-in-the-blank will guide you to answer the questions at the top of reporters' minds—keeps you organised in the early hours.
- Creates expectation for releases within the media and the public.
- Allows for the same releases to be posted on your own Web site.

7.4.2. Minuses

- They take considerable time to write and information may be changing in that time.
- They may be difficult to clear through all layers of official command.
- If the release is not coming from the EOC (if it's involved), it could start a turf war.
- Reporters will expect more where that came from—be prepared to consistently release information this way.
- If the release of information is not organised through a command post, competing press releases could be frustrating for media, especially if press releases cover information that spans across response areas, and are unclear about who is responsible for collecting and releasing what information.

7.5. Press Conference or Media Opportunity

A public health emergency is an appropriate time to consider holding a press conference. Though, in truth, the term press conference implies an event that is scheduled in advance, sometimes weeks, includes a press kit, and is designed to allow media to ask questions of the featured experts. A media opportunity is more appropriate for the early phases of a crisis. One can be arranged at the site of the crisis and allow for information to be released to all media, even without press kits or a question and answer opportunity.

7.5.1. Pluses

— If media are at the site of an event, it's an effective way to conduct media interview requests in one shot and control their access to the site.
— It helps ensure consistency in the information released.
— It can introduce your spokesperson and subject matter experts (SMEs) to the public, allow them to express their feelings and begin to build their credibility with the public.
— It allows the response organisations to show very early on that there is a process in place to respond to the crisis and that, although the event is unfolding, someone is ready to help with response and recovery.
— Strict rules about questions from the media can be imposed.
— If information is changing rapidly or not enough is known to issue a press release, it fulfils the immediate need of electronic media to fill space and time.
— Elected officials have a forum to present a united front.

7.5.2. Minuses

— It is sometimes difficult to get the right people in front of the media to give updates (planning helps).
— Information may be sketchy and response officials may balk at meeting with the media when they do not have the answers (training helps).
— If media cannot be at the site, they will not have the information they want or need.
— You can't do this just once—media will expect periodic opportunities.
— If coordination isn't solid, you could find competing media opportunities occurring. Local, state, and federal officials, and people across levels of other organisations, need to have a plan and agree to the timing of media opportunities.

— Early media intensity will push the limits of any rules set about the length of the availability and the no-questions policy. (There must be an escape route for speakers out of the media area).

— Media will want to follow up on individual interviews. Set the ground rules and be consistent.

7.6. Satellite Media Tours

At the national or regional level, or at the local level if media in other cities are pushing for access, a satellite media tour may be appropriate. Although a satellite media tour can be arranged in a matter of hours during a crisis, it may not be an efficient tool early in the emergency. It may be an effective tool for communities to talk to each other through the media—offering support, ideas, and lessons learned. Think creatively about these. Satellite media tours are usually conducted by a single spokesperson or SME and are meant to allow local media to interview the SME directly. To avoid confusion, be sure that the SME has a Teleprompter® identifying the speaker and the name and city of the reporter. Be alert for earphones that pop out. These interviews are typically live-to-tape. Correct misinformation on the spot. This concept will work well when the satellite trucks are parked outside your door, and it won't cost you a dime.

7.6.1. Pluses

— Allows media unable to be onsite or are prevented by the nature of the public health emergency (e.g., the area becomes restricted) to be given access to the centre of action and response officials

— Provides a way for local or regional media to speak in depth to SMEs and ask questions specific to the region or population

— Increases the chances that media in other local or regional areas get it right—right from the horse's mouth, so to speak, instead of translated through national media back to them at the local level

7.6.2. Minuses

— Expensive

— Not easily arranged in a crisis, unless resources and agreements are in place in advance

— Limited reach, right for only very specific situations
— After a round-robin of similar interviews, spokespersons can burn out.
— Time-consuming

7.7. Telephone News Conferences/Web Casts

Computer and phone technology now allow the public information officer to set up a toll-free telephone number that media can call at a specified time and listen to updates from response officials. Participating spokespersons need not be co-located. It would be possible to conduct a local, state, or federal press opportunity by phone, even if spokespersons were working from many locations. In addition, the technology is interactive and can allow media to ask questions.

7.7.1. Pluses

— Reaches far more media than just those at the site of the incident
— Multiple-community and national involvement give local and national media access to response officials
— Easy to arrange
— Moderate cost
— Allows for the number of telephone lines to be adjusted according to rising or falling interest from the media
— Officials are comfortable with this format
— Great flexibility in when and where
— Allows control by public information official about who has the toll-free number
— Can be regularly scheduled to mollify media by assuring them of regular updates
— Format allows for last-minute changes in spokesperson (e.g., a new development requires a new expert to appear or a spokesperson is called away for unavoidable reasons; it's easier to get a substitute)
— Allows time for questions and the questioner's name to be announced by the call moderator (phone operator)

— List of all participants, even those not asking a question, is provided by phone operator, making news monitoring and analysis easier
— Can be archived and made available to media after the fact
— Can be recorded so transcripts can be supplied on request

7.7.2. Minuses

— Requires a funding source or advance contract
— Cost can add up over time
— Difficult to wean media from this format; regular calls should not be stopped abruptly
— Does not fulfil the visual needs of TV news; favors print and Web media

7.8. Commercial Press Release Services

These services (e.g., PR Newswire, US Newswire, etc.) give organisations access to national, regional, or specialised media using media lists and fax numbers. Many of these services are available 24 hours a day.

7.8.1. Pluses

— Eliminates the need to maintain up-to-date specialised media lists or those outside the local area
— Press releases move very rapidly to newsrooms
— A list of media outlets that received the release is available
— A way to reach media that may not be on your core media list but have an interest in what is occurring

7.8.2. Minuses

— Funding source must be in place in advance.
— Releases through a newswire may appear less than official for some types of emergency information that, perhaps, should come directly from the response organisation to the newsroom.

— It may not be necessary when media are actively engaged and could waste resources—appropriate at less intense times during the emergency response.

7.9. E-mail Listservs and Broadcast Faxes

Many media are prepared to receive information from organisations through e-mail or by fax.

7.9.1. Pluses

— You can almost instantly disseminate information to media on your e-mail listserv at an imperceptible cost.

— Corrections are easy to make.

— The organisation gets credit for having contacted reporters or outlets by name.

— Provide an open channel that, until they yell "stop!" allows you to feed information to the media at will.

7.9.2. Minuses

— Lists require regular updating and maintenance—media move around often.

— Provide a passive way to give the media information; some may not get to your e-mail or broadcast fax until it's too late for them or you.

— Not highly personal. They may still want a return phone call.

— Require cleared print information, which is time-intensive for the public information office and could slow information flow to the media.

7.10. Websites/video Streaming

Anyone who can afford the monthly cost can have a Web site. The Internet-connected public and media expect to go to the Web for information. Official Web sites can be a media-response tool.

7.10.1. Pluses

— Serve as a rapid way to update all media simultaneously

— Become transparent since the public and media will see the same information on the site
— Organise the documents and creates a historical record for media and the organisation
— Permit links to help media collect background information
— Allow rumors, myths, and misinformation to be addressed without drawing undue attention
— Allow official video or pictures to be available to media digitally
— Permit FAQs on the page to do double duty for media and public, providing a user-friendly way to educate both during a crisis
— An inexpensive communication tool

7.10.2. Minuses

— Not available to all public or media.
— May frustrate media if too much information is provided or if the site's organisation is not clear; they want it easy and immediate (you may have to walk some of them through the site the first time).
— Require the continual availability of a Web master who is willing to post updates on the Web within the 2-hour window that should be maintained between release of information and its appearance on the Web.
— Technology dependent—may be vulnerable to glitches or interruption by hackers, etc.

7.11. Response to Media Calls

The bread and butter of the relationship between public information officials and the media is the simple calls from media requesting specific information or an interview. In a public health emergency, the manner in which an organisation responds to these calls may make a difference in the way the organisation's responsiveness or professionalism is portrayed to the public. The fact is that if the media don't believe you're responding well, they aren't going to believe that you're responding in good faith. Resources allocated to media response are well invested and will provide long-term returns. Every organisation must establish a workable plan to respond to the surge of media calls. This aspect of working with the media is not an option, but a must. Training, planning, and coordination will make the difference. Media should know ahead of time how the flow of information will work, how to get their requests answered, and what you can or can't do. If your phone lines overload, what's your back up plan?

7.11.1. Pluses

— Media can provide information you may not be aware of (e.g., a neighborhood leader who is complaining that the response resources are not being fairly distributed. It's a fact that some disgruntled people will call the media for resolution before they will call the responsible official organisation).

— Media inquiries may reflect the public's level of interest. The number of calls and frequency of subjects raised can give the response community a sense of what is important to the public and where more information resources may need to be directed.

— One-on-one contact with the media allows opportunities to emphasise key message points, direct media to upcoming issues, and correct misinformation.

7.11..2. Minuses

— Returning calls take a lot of time.

— Potential exists for inconsistent or premature release of information, unless press officers and spokespersons are well trained and the release is coordinated.

— Follow-up calls may be required if information changes before the media/reporter releases it—or you'll be guilty of not giving them the right information.

— Phone Tag is the name of the game.

— Massive prioritisation is required, and the media will know if they're not at the top of the list.

— You can become the public library or return calls on subjects not in your area of responsibility unless the screening of calls is very well done.

7.12. Writing for the Media during a Crisis

The rules of journalism apply even during a crisis. The pressure, however, is to move the process along at a pace that reasonable media and people will perceive as responsive and credible. Research has shown that the public's belief that an emergency response was effective correlates with how much access to information they had during the crisis. The challenge is speed versus accuracy. Both are important. If information is accurate and released after the public has moved on to another issue, it has no value. If it's out fast but is inaccurate, the best-case scenario is to admit it and move on; the worst case is that the inaccuracy causes harm to the public.

Public information officials must stabilise that pendulum and push the responding officials toward releasing accurate but incomplete information as quickly as possible. It's like cooking a turkey when people are starving: if the wings are done, break them off and start chewing; keep cooking the turkey but don't let people starve waiting for it.

So what can you get on paper first? Start with what you can verify, and be careful to alert the media and the public that more will come as more becomes available. If decisions are not finalised, then explain that the process to reach decisions is ongoing. If laboratory tests are not completed, explain the testing process. You can keep the media and the public engaged and feeling involved and important even if you don't have the answers to the hard questions.

7.12.1. Standard Press Releases

During the early phases of an emergency, you'll be writing standard press releases. As the crisis evolves, you may follow up with feature releases about individuals or units involved in the response or outcomes and their successes, or personal stories of those helped during the crisis.

An emergency press release should be limited to one page. Practice, and you'll be amased how quickly you'll be able to determine what information belongs in the factsheet and what belongs in the press release. Think of press releases, from the very start, as press updates. The press release should answer, the who, what, when, where, why, and how of the ongoing event. Additional information should go into an attached factsheet or backgrounder. This method will speed up the clearance process for the press release, reduce the opportunity to introduce errors into the release, and help the media quickly determine what is news and what is background.

— At the top of the release, include the following information: your organisation's name, address, and telephone number, and contact name(s).
— In an emergency, it's critical to give the media a 24-hour contact number.
— If you have a toll-free number for media, include that, too, and tell media it's for them, not for the public.
— Include the date or the date and time if more than one release is issued during a 24-hour period. Give your press release a headline; it's a way for media to identify quickly what they're calling back about. Create headlines in an active voice and summarise the core information in a few words. Never reuse a headline during the crisis.
— Some organisations employ a press release number. That's fine, but don't let it take the place of unique headlines.
— Put "for immediate release" at the top under your contact information—don't make reporters or editors guess.
— Write in the inverted pyramid style—most important information first.
— Press releases do not have strong concluding paragraphs.
— If you're providing a *new* telephone information number or Web site address, introduce it higher in the press release. Don't assume the editor will notice it in the last paragraph.
— Limit the length of sentences (rarely more than 20 words) and paragraphs. A one-sentence paragraph is acceptable in a press release.
— Remember, the more syllables per 100 words, the more difficult text is to understand.
— Explain scientific or technical terms. Don't assume your audience knows what you're talking about.

— Make every effort to eliminate adjectives or emotionally laden words.

— A well-written press release reads like a news story.

— Check your facts, especially after including revisions from subject matter experts.

— Do a security check—some information is classified.

— Do a privacy check—some information may violate the privacy of victims and their families. If names have unusual spellings, mark an OK note next to the name, so editors know that you've not made a mistake.

— If a name has an unusual pronunciation, include the phonetic pronunciation so radio and TV reporters will get it right. This is good for the reporter and good for the person being mentioned.

— If you detect an error in a press release that has already been distributed and there's time to fix it before it's used, make the effort to reach everyone who has it. Reporters don't like taking the blame for your mistake. Don't just correct it on your Web site and leave the media hanging. If it's too late, and it has appeared, apologise.

7.12.2. Press Statements are not Press Releases

— Statements typically are not news; they may be an official position or perspective of the organisation.

— They normally contain only a few paragraphs.

— They are usually attributed to a high-ranking official in the organisation.

— They may be used to counter a contrary view about an important subject related to the emergency (e.g., why the organisation is choosing one treatment recommendation over another).

— They should not be used to generate a peer-review debate.

— They are a means for an official to be quoted as having responded to an issue without the need for a media opportunity.

— They can be used to offer words of encouragement to victims, responders, and employees.

— They should be posed with press releases on the Web site.
— They need a contact number from the press office.
— Use them sparingly for best impact.
— Take the high road; no whining!
— Don't state the negative that's being countered; state the organisation's position only—don't validate the contrary point of view.
— Get these cleared up, down, and sideways.

7.12.3. Media Factsheets

— These should be attached to a one-page press release.
— Both can run for several pages.
— They should define scientific and technical terms.
— Factsheets should be in a bullet format with a logical progression from the broad to the specific about a single subject.
— Backgrounders may be in paragraph form and typically give historical information and information too in-depth for a bulleted factsheet.
— They are excellent sources of information for the media.
— FAQs can serve as both factsheets and backgrounders, but depending on the subject, may be annoying to seasoned reporters.
— Expect to see them on media Web sites, so get them right.
— Avoid including information in factsheets and backgrounders that will be changing. Press releases are the place for updates on the ongoing situation. Factsheets and backgrounders give just that—facts— and background or history.
— Don't include quotes from officials or SMEs.
— Both are official documents released from the organisation or the EOC.
— Coordinate information to ensure that all parties agree on what's fact and what's background.
— Prepare these in advance, when no emergencies are in sight. Check in at state or local levels to see if the work has been done.

7.12.4. Visuals, Video Press Releases, and B-roll

More people are getting their news information from TV or Web sites than ever before. News outlets are hungry for visuals to support their reporting—talking heads get boring. Digital technology makes it easier and less expensive for official response organisations to provide some visual support for the media covering the emergency.

— Consider 10–20-second sound bites from response officials and SMEs that can be edited into local newscasts.

— Get your key messages on tape.

— Video press releases (VNRs) quickly become dated and may be too time-consuming to produce in the early phases of an emergency.

— B-roll (silent, background video) is easier to produce, and news directors prefer it because they can build their own stories around it.

— Prepare B-roll in advance, if possible, and get a security check to ensure that classified information is not being released.

— Write the sound bites for your spokesperson. Spokespersons do not have time to pare points down to 20 seconds, so do it for them.

— Make sure each sound bite stands alone so it won't confuse a viewer who may see only one of five possible sound bites.

— Don't raise a subject in a B-roll if you do not want to promote it.

— Give the VNR or B-roll a paper and on-tape index of who is talking or what is being shown (e.g., SL2 bacterial lab technician preparing samples for testing).

— Determine your distribution methods: scheduled satellite feed following a media advisory or beta copies of the B-roll that can be picked up by media, dropped off for media, fed from a local network affiliate to national network satellite for feed to other locals, or via overnight mail, with the request that the hard copy be returned to you.

— VNRs and B-rolls must be professionally produced to fulfil the needs of media. Some in-house digital video can be used on your Web site.

7.13. Media Opportunity during a Public Health Emergency

Ask yourself one more time, "Is this the right way to release my information?" If you've coordinated with other responding organisations or you've been directed to hold a press conference, the answer may be an easy yes.

7.13.1. Where to Hold the Press Conference

Press conferences are best held:

— On the site of the emergency, if it lends itself to a media event (e.g., it's safe for the media to be there, it won't interfere with recovery efforts, or would not violate the privacy of victims of the emergency)

— Hold the press conference at the EOC, if room has been set aside that is separate from the operations centre. You don't want media moving in and out of the operations centre. If the conference is held in a restricted building, try to streamline the media's screening and access to the site, even if it requires volunteer escorts for each reporter.

— At a separate official location, such as the town hall, the health department headquarters, or the governor's office.

— At a hotel meeting room convenient to the officials involved and the media who are likely to attend.

— Somewhere with sound equipment either available or in place, with electrical outlets (if not on the street) and other specialised equipment needed by media.

7.13.2. Whom to Invite

Before you announce a media opportunity, guarantee that your spokespersons or officials are available. Have backups on standby.

— Invite print and electronic media, and don't forget radio stations. If the EOC is hosting a press room, be sure to post a notice in that room too.

— Attempt to limit the number of emergency response officials attending who will not have a speaking role. It's disconcerting to media to see a pack of people in the back of the room, possibly wearing response uniforms or credentials, who are never identified. Also, expect that anyone in the room from the response team could be approached by the media for comment, not to mention that information not yet ready for release could be the topic of conversation among the pack in the back of the room. "By invitation only" holds true for response personnel, too.

7.13.3. How and When to Invite the Media

— Give the media as much advance notice as possible, but not so early that the event is cancelled because it's overcome by events. An hour is the absolute least amount of time from notice to the event, unless media are all standing by waiting for a comment.

— If the emergency has gone on for some time, schedule a regular time for media opportunities and stick to it to eliminate the need to contact the media each time.

— If you have something really important to release and media may not be aware of what's coming, use the resources necessary to call reporters or their news directors/editors and tell them why they need to be there.

Send a brief media advisory about the opportunity. It should be only a-half page long and give the following information: the nature of the event (media opportunity or press conference beware of the differences); date, time, place, contact person, who is scheduled to appear (by name and title, or by position and subject matter expertise), and the topics that will be covered. Keep the advisory short you'll get it cleared more quickly and have greater flexibility if you want to adjust messages or add topics. Be specific enough that the media understand the urgency (easy early in the emergency, but may be more difficult in later phases of the crisis).

7.13.4. How to Conduct the Media Opportunity

Keep the speakers out of the room until the event begins—you don't want the negotiations about logistics and who speaks when being worked out in public. Do that in private. The instant that the principals are visible to the media, their demeanor and behavior is a matter of public record. It's natural to blow off a little steam, joke around, even during the heat of a crisis. Your officials need to be able to do that away from the cameras. Respect that need.

Whether the speakers sit or stand depends on the room, the length of the event, and whether they are all speaking and all taking questions. There are pluses and minuses to each. Remember, if they all stand, you get a "herd" effect that makes the group seem more active, as if there is more urgency to the situation. That's good if that's what you want to convey because you're about to ask the public to move immediately on the information you're about to release; it's bad if you're attempting to present a calm, reasoned response to an emergency.

You can choose to have a press officer moderate the event or allow the lead official to do so. Accommodate the preferences of the official but be available on the side if they decide to go it alone.

Unless the officials are nationally known faces and names, ask speakers to introduce themselves by name, title, and organisation. They should repeat their names and organisations if they step forward to answer a late question.

It's appropriate to alert the media ahead of time whether questions will be addressed from the podium or if only statements of information from organisation officials will be made. Caution: media do not like to be restricted from asking questions, but they'll accept it if the information is real news and they are given access to the officials at other times to get answers. Taking questions means giving some control of the content over to the media. In the early phases, it may not be necessary to take questions.

If you plan to take questions, decide who will select reporters to ask questions (e.g., the lead official or a press officer moderating the event). Decide the time limit of the event, including questions and answers, and let the media know there will be a limit. If you're moderating controversial issues surrounding the emergency that should not be addressed by your officials, let the media know that questions should be limited to the topic at hand.

Have a backup plan for such glitches as the loss of sound equipment.

Tell the media, either before the officials enter the room if you're not moderating, or at the end of the event, how to get more information and answers to questions.

Decide ahead of time whether officials are going to do standup media interviews for individual reporters following the event. It's fine to do this if the official has the time, won't go off-message (because they've received good training in advance), and there's an exit plan to end the interview (e.g., official is pressed for time and has only 5 minutes before his car leaves for another appointment).

Expect radio and print media to surround the TV reporter conducting the interview or vice versa. It's really like another small, informal press conference. Keep control of the officials and the media by assigning a press officer to each official. You need to know if something has been said to which you'll have to react. It happens.

7.13.5. Using Visuals

It may be too much to ask of the officials to manage charts, PowerPoint presentations, or slides during the briefing. If there's a way to position a communications expert to manage the visuals, do that.

Media will want copies of any slides, graphs, or visuals you introduce. Caution: if an official waves a document or report or refers to it during the media opportunity, reporters will be asking for that, too. Try to agree on what will be mentioned and what will be available, and prepare the visuals ahead of time. You can reduce reporters' angst if you tell them ahead of time that they will get copies of what is being shown.

7.13.6. Handouts

If possible, have copies of the presentations, useful fact sheets, and backgrounders available. Media like to use them to write their pieces, even if they have it all on tape.

Don't forget background information on you organisation, simple mission statement, and facts.

If speakers are not well known, attempt to have brief biographies of the speakers. This helps build their credibility to reporters and the public who may read about them. You want your subject matter experts publicly accepted as such.

Following your press conference, immediately assess:

— Were key messages delivered?
— Were similar questions asked repeatedly?
— Spokesperson's delivery (e.g., tone, body language, clarity, etc.)?
— Any "next day" issues to prepare for?
— Any need to follow up with specific media, based on their questions, to clarify issues?
— What can you do next time to improve the media opportunity?

7.14. Responding to Media

You're ready to throw your remote through your big-screen TV, or rip your daily paper to shreds—it must mean someone is reporting negative stories about your organisation! If that is the case—what next?

7.14.1. Tip 1: First, Calm Down

Remember: when you talk to the media, you are speaking for your agency or organisation. No matter how angry you are, you cannot react thoughtlessly and attack the reporter. Doing so will reflect negatively on you and your organisation, and will detract from your mission to communicate accurate health information to the public. Some reporters believe that only sensational, negative stories are news. "If it's good news it's no news" and "if it bleeds it leads" are two quotes frequently uttered by this type of reporter. Also, reporters do not always have time to get all the facts before their deadline pressure becomes a job-retention factor. If they continue with research, a competing reporter may release the story first. Reporters are just trying to do their job, so don't take the negativity personally. Always try to think in terms of educating the media and, thereby, building bridges to promote accurate stories in the future. After all, the media are an important communication link to the audiences you are charged to serve. To do this, you need a strategy.

7.14.2. Tip 2: Analyse the Situation

Is the publication, television, or radio program credible? Have you worked with the offending reporter previously? After a negative news report is not the best time to make a "cold call"—to speak to reporters or work with media outlets for the first time. Expressing your complaint to someone who knows you, and knows you are credible, is easier and more productive. If the media outlet is unwilling to hear your position, you may consider trying to get your point across to your audience through an alternative source. Try to understand the reporters' point of view, and that they do not serve as your public relations firm. Reporters have no obligation to report only positive stories for you although they do have a responsibility to present their audience with accurate information. You can and should appeal to their sense of community service if the stories they are running are not in the public's best interest. Also, remember who you are trying to reach. You are not trying to win a contest with media representatives. You are trying to serve the public interest by disseminating accurate information to promote public health. No matter the response from reporters, keep your anger in check.

To reporters, a balanced piece is one that examines opposing sides of a story. Whether one point of view is an extreme position and the other generally accepted does not matter. As long as reporters attempt to present both sides, they consider this fair reporting.

Correcting a factual error is relatively simple and straightforward. Reporters and media outlets want to do their jobs well, and, like you, no one wants to make a mistake. However, a difference of opinion about a subject is not as easy to counter. Statements you may perceive as biased, uninformed, or sensational reporting will not be viewed by reporters as an error on their part. You can still respond to the piece; however, your strategy will be different from that required to simply correct a factual error.

Obviously, you would prefer that only positive stories about your mission appear in the media. That is not always possible. There will be times when you will not have a response to counter a bad news story. There is an old saying that in order to prevent the perception of covering up bad news, we must get the good news out fast, and get the bad news out faster. When there is bad news to report, your job is not to withhold or counter the information. It is to reassure the public that no matter what the issue, positive or negative, you are open and responsive to the public's need for accurate information. Remember, you are not attempting to win a contest with the media, or a popularity contest with the public. Your mission is to communicate accurate health information to the public. This event may be simply your time to "take it on the chin" to satisfy your critics who are also served by the media. If the facts are reasonably true, and any mistakes made by the reporter are minor, you may want to let the story run without comment. Quibbling with a reporter over a minor point when a news item is otherwise accurate will not help you build bridges for future positive stories. You may want to contact the reporter to establish a dialogue for future, more positive stories.

7.14.3. Tip 3: Know What to ask For

Once you have analysed the situation and decided that action is necessary, know your options. There are only a few possibilities available for a reporter to respond to your complaint.

Decide ahead of time your ideal, as well as your minimal, solution. Think of this as a negotiation. Here are some actions you may request:

— A retraction is reasonable when an egregious error has been made—if the facts are clearly on your side and you have supporting material to refute statements originally reported. Ask for a correction immediately, and request that it be run as prominently as the original piece. Although this is not likely to happen, you may be able to discourage the editor from burying the retraction.

— A followup response is a reasonable request if your point of view was completely ignored or misrepresented in the original report. The best way to get a report redone is to provide reporters another angle for the story. Reporters are not likely to present a followup piece that simply contradicts a story they have recently run. They will not want to lose credibility. If you give them a fresh perspective, a new angle, or supply some new information (and give them a way to maintain credibility), they are more likely to work with you.

— Sometimes reporters make unintentional mistakes. If the errors are not endangering a person's life or reputation, perhaps an acknowledgment of the mistake over the phone by the reporter is enough. If this is the case, you may use this as an opportunity to establish yourself as a source for this reporter and develop rapport that could lead to accurate, more positive stories in the future. The reporter may call you to check the accuracy of a forthcoming story before running it. This would give you the opportunity to avert future inaccuracies in that reporter's stories and would provide forewarning if another bad news story is about to run.

— Ask the reporter or editor to file a written correction with the original piece in the permanent record. If the mistake is a factual one, you do not want to see it repeated (even if a correction is made). Ask the reporter or editor to officially tie the correction to the original report. Reporters often go back to do research, and they may report the mistaken information again if they do not realise that a correction was made.

— If you have an important message concerning the issue reported, a letter to the editor may be the right choice. Letters to the editor are widely read, and publications are usually quite willing to print opposing views. Keep in mind that your message must be concise, or your opportunity to correct an error could be lost in editing. Make your strongest points early in the letter and keep the letter short and to the point. Editors who are rushing to meet a deadline tend to simply cut the end of written material when trying to fit text into a specific space. Be sure to seek concurrence from SMEs within your organisation before releasing your letter. Be sure to coordinate with public affairs.

7.14.4. Tip 4. Know Who to Contact

Media outlets have a chain of command. Starting at the top is not usually the best approach. Follow the chain of command when contacting the media to respond to an article or broadcast piece.

7.14.4.1. Talk to the Reporter First

Always give the reporter the first opportunity to respond to your concerns. Perhaps the reporter is frustrated because an editor changed a piece without the reporter's knowledge. Perhaps the producer who put together the nightly news teaser misunderstood the reporter's message, or sensationalised an originally balanced report. Let the reporter have an opportunity to respond and explain. Know the reporter's position before taking any action.

7.14.4.2. If the Reporter can't be Convinced...

Ask to speak to the news editor or producer. Keep moving up the chain until you are satisfied, or until you are convinced that you will not get satisfaction.

7.14.4.3. If You have Doubts about the Integrity of the Media...

If the reporter or media outlet that presented the negative or inaccurate report is known to have no journalistic integrity, consider going to an alternative media outlet. Of course, go to them with a great story idea, not just a complaint about the other media outlet.

7.14.4.4. Consider reaching Your Public through Alternative Outlets

If all else fails in your efforts to set the record straight with the offending media outlet, redouble your efforts to get your message to the public through alternative means. For example, set up a public forum, make your presence known on the Internet, and invite partners to write letters or make phone calls. Offer articles for community newsletters. Work to establish contacts in competing media outlets.

7.14.5. Tip 5: Know What You Want to Communicate

When you decide to counter the bad news article, you must thoughtfully develop the message you want to communicate. Know your audience and the message you want your audience to receive.

— Develop your message and have it screened by advisors and SMEs. Remember, an organisation should speak with one voice to maintain credibility. To do so, we must confer with interested parties within the organisation to ensure that we are not working at cross purposes with colleagues who have more information or a different perspective.

— Make sure to frame the message in a positive way.

— Include a call to action, if appropriate.

— Focus on your audience the public and your purpose: to promote public health.

— Keep your anger at your critics or the media out of the message. The media are neither the message nor the audience.

If you want to convince a reporter or producer to give your message an airing, you must be prepared to communicate that message without delay.

7.14.6. Tip 6: Have a Plan before You need it

7.14.6.1. If an Objection is to be Effectively Heard, You must express it as soon as Possible

You know the important issues within your organisation and the basic arguments of your critics. Prepare messages on the various issues ahead of time, especially when an issue is controversial. Draft letters to the editor that could be altered slightly and submitted within hours of the appearance of the offending piece. You may wish to release articles on these issues before reporters have the opportunity to run inaccurate or negative stories.

7.14.6.2. Put the Media on Notice that You are paying Attention

You are part of the media's audience. They have a stake in responding to your needs, too. Let them know you watch or read their stories. Maintain regular contact. You may call a reporter to praise a good story. Remember to build bridges with media at every opportunity. They are an important communication link to our public, as they can facilitate our efforts to promote public health.

7.14.6.3. Let the Media know that You're a Potential Source for the Future

Don't just ask for an immediate airing on the subject: invite reporters to call on you for interviews in the future. Make sure you are available to give credible and constructive interviews. You may also want to develop internal sources of interview candidates that you can offer to media when issues surface. Be willing to deal with tough subjects. Don't minimise the arguments of your critics. Remember to focus on getting your message to your audience.

References

Coleman, C. L. (1993). The influence of mass media and interpersonal communication on societal and personal risk judgments. *Communication* Research, 20, 611- 628.

Fischer, Henry, W., III. (1998). *Response to Disaster.* Lanham, Md.: University Press of America.

Hornig, S. (1993). Reading risk: Public response to print media accounts of technological risk. *Public Understanding of Science,* 2, 95- 109.

Mazur, A. (1981). Media coverage and public opinion on scientific controversies. *Journal of Communication*, 31.

Yale, David, R. (1991). *The Publicity Handbook.* Chicago: NTC Business Books.

Ury, William. (1993). *Getting Past No: Negotiating your way from confrontation to cooperation*. New York: Bantam Books.

8

Role of Stakeholders in Risk Communication

In crisis communication planning, the first step in responding to stakeholders is to identify them. Stakeholders may vary according to the emergency, but core stakeholders will be interested in every public health emergency your organisation becomes involved in and will expect a response from your organisation.

Not all stakeholders are supporters of your organisation; nonetheless, it is critical to identify unsupportive stakeholders and be prepared to respond to them appropriately. In fact, stakeholders will fall into three categories based on their responses to you in a crisis: advocates, adversaries, and ambivalents. Your response to stakeholders will depend on which of the three groups to which a stakeholder belongs. The point is to anticipate stakeholders' reactions based on their affinity for the organisation and the way that similar groups have reacted in the past when this type of crisis has occurred.

Why expend energy on stakeholders during an emergency? The effort secures input from people who have information you need. They represent points of view that are vital to understanding the perceptions of various groups of your organisation's response to the incident. Involving stakeholders gives people a chance to tell you what they feel you need to know. It also ensures that everyone is aware that they are welcome to get involved and that they are valued.

An emergency or crisis may be an opportunity to strengthen your partner and stakeholder relationships as they see you in action. A positive response will enhance the organisation's credibility. Don't forget to consider existing stakeholder controversies or concerns and how the ongoing relationship will color their attitude during this incident.

Following are the five most serious mistakes an organisation can make in communicating with stakeholders:

— Inadequate accessibility

— Lack of understandability

— Dullness, lack of energy in the response

— Problems with timeliness (e.g., too little, too late)

— Perceptions of arrogance (e.g., stakeholders are not valued).

You must provide timely, accurate information to audiences and key stakeholders, both internal and external:

— Use audience assessment tools to ensure that appropriate messages are tailored to specific audiences.

— Concentrate on those stakeholders who can have the most impact on your ability to conduct public health business.

— Focus on the common concerns and reactions that will have to be addressed.

Develop strategies to minimise negative reactions by considering the following:

— *Emphasise factors that inspire trust*, such as expressing empathy, showing competence in the area of expertise needed to respond to the incident, encouraging stakeholder feedback, honesty and sincerity in your communication and actions, and committing to the long term by maintaining a visible presence even after the news cameras have left.

Trust is usually endowed early in a crisis. However, that trust may quickly erode if information is inaccurate, inconsistent, or overly optimistic. If the estimate of risk turns out to be "more serious than we thought," your trustworthiness is greatly damaged. The damage is much less if you overestimated the degree of risk. People would much rather hear "the incident is much less serious than we thought."

— *Pay attention to organisational process* and, whenever possible, involve the affected community in determining recommendations for action.

— *Explain organisational procedures*. Be prepared to describe your organisation's mission, the tools and methods used to provide its service, and the expected outcome—that which makes your response a success (e.g., fewer deaths, decreased infection rates, systems in place to detect secondary outbreaks).

— *Promise only what you can deliver, then follow through.* Under the pressure of scrutiny and the desire to "fix" problems, one may be tempted to guarantee outcomes. Don't. Make every effort to get back to people to ensure that the promises you make are being kept.

Be forthcoming with information; focus on building trust as well as providing good technical information. After identifying key stakeholders, determine their interests. Provide information that meets people's needs.

Try to gain trust and convey consistent themes and messages with empathy. Can you satisfy stakeholders' needs with blasts of e-mailed or faxed messages or will you need to make phone calls or hold special meetings to ensure continued understanding and support?

Before reaching out to stakeholders, be certain you've coordinated with other responding organisations to ensure that your message is consistent, you can accomplish what you intend to offer, and you don't send mixed messages. Remember, your stakeholder may also be a stakeholder of another responding organisation. Power struggles or visible confusion among your organisation and other organisations will reduce credibility of all of the players and further frustrate your stakeholders.

Methods to communicate to stakeholders include:

— Designated Web page for partners

— Telephone call from management or management representative

— Specific backgrounders and periodic updates.

8.1. Stakeholder Reaction Assessment

Define the advocates, adversaries, and ambivalents who are likely to be interested, and wish to be involved in this crisis.

— Note what will they want to know and likely reactions.

— Project the impact and/or financial effect of their reactions.

— Identify stakeholders whose reactions will have the greatest impact if the crisis escalates.

— Forecast the involvement of top management.

— Develop a reaction management strategy for key stakeholders' likely reactions. These reactions will vary based on the disruption and how the perception affects them. Identify:

— Stakeholders who can have the greatest impact

— Common concerns and reactions to address

— Strategies to minimise negative reactions

— Actions and communication to inform and develop trust

— Consistent themes and messages to convey with empathy

— Preemptive communication strategies

— Concern for less important stakeholders

— Loyalty of your advocates, discouraging your adversaries, and keeping your ambivalents neutral.

8.2. Responding to Stakeholders

Develop a reaction plan to determine the factors that would trigger the plan's implementation and to minimise disruptions from important stakeholder groups.

— Advocates maintain their loyalty and support.

— Adversaries discourage them from getting involved.

— Ambivalents stay on the sidelines and/or provide tacit support.

Estimate the management time and resources based on what had to be done and who is responsible for each action item.

8.2.1. Stakeholders to Consider

— Employees

— Families

— Retirees

— Board members

— External advisors

— Your organisations' clients/consumers
— Local residents
— Business and community leaders
— Elected officials
— Consumer action groups
— Union or labor organisations
— Competitors
— Legal advocates
— Media
— Public
— Others

Consider plans to provide advance notice to important audiences. Prioritise stakeholders according to the type of emergency.

8.3. Partnership Development

A partner may be defined as anyone with a role in aiding in the response. Partner relationships should be developed in advance of the crisis. One of the best methods of building partnerships is to start building relationships informally through community and social networks. Strong, collegial relationships can be very helpful when emergency coordination is required. Partnerships should be based on the partners' common purpose of serving the community.

Each potential partner should play a specific role during a crisis, and this role should be determined and agreed upon before a crisis situation occurs (or at the very least, in the first few hours of a crisis event). It is helpful to assess what each partner brings to the table, including strengths, weaknesses, and unique abilities.

The partner organisation will most likely choose its representative. That representative should be someone who will be able to execute the partner's role and has the organisation's authority to make decisions and speak on its behalf. Usually this person is not the head of the organisation, but typically will keep the leader of the organisation informed.

Tips for developing partnerships:

— Design a plan for building relationships before the crisis.

— Create a partner contact sheet with every available phone number and e-mail address (e.g., work, home, cell, etc.), Obtain permission to contact the people by any means necessary in an emergency.

— Draft a plan for partner communication during a crisis (e.g., e-mail alerts, twice-daily faxes, conference calls) to which everyone agrees.

8.4. Community Relations

Research indicates that community leaders and institutions (e.g., schools, employers, community organisations, churches/religious institutions, and major employers) can be valuable partners in gaining support for public health actions, distributing information, or countering rumors surrounding an emergency event. These partners may be familiar, trusted, and influential with your target audience, and may be more likely than media alone to motivate the public to take recommended actions. Also, the partners can reach groups of people in a familiar setting.

In pre-event planning, make an effort to reach out to these groups. Consider memoranda of understanding with partners to engage them as information disseminators during a public health emergency. Consider supplying them with background information before or soon after an emergency occurs. Develop fast and reliable channels of communication directly to these community leaders so that they will have the facts when their constituencies begin to ask questions. Invite them to tour emergency facilities. Brief them on such issues as the national pharmaceutical stockpile or public health emergency laws.

8.4.1. Strategies to Navigate a Process for Consensus Building

Don't leave it to the media to negotiate public controversies during an emergency response effort. Instead, consider engaging a neutral party to speak for the diverse group of stakeholders to help resolve differences. The neutral party can speak to the media on behalf of all involved or facilitate a face-to-face meeting. The neutral party can express both consistent and inconsistent points of view from the entire group in an effort to find consensus.

8.4.2. Convening a Citizens' Forum

A professional facilitator, comfortable with the culture of the community, who is perceived by all sides as neutral, should convene the public forum. Conduct a needs assessment to determine the stakeholders in this issue. Representatives from all elements of the community must be considered, not just those from a vocal advocacy group.

8.4.2.1. Empower Group Decisionmaking with the following Steps

- Identify the options and discuss the pros and cons of each alternative.
- Analyse the costs and benefits, weaknesses and strengths of each.
- Present all known scientific or technical information about the alternatives.
- Choose the "must" versus "want" criteria for the decision.
- Be able to express why one alternative was chosen over the others (e.g., the highest number of people will be helped with a minimum disruption to self-reliance and community sovereignty).
- Reach a clear, justifiable decision.

8.4.2.2. Quality Listening

Asking questions shows that you care. The first step in solving problems is to know what's really going on. Questions can do that. Good listeners are perceived as more intelligent. Listening actively reduces mistakes— like believing you understand what is being asked of you, only to discover later that you are mistaken.

- Listen for intent (feeling).
- Listen for content (facts).
- Listen for who is speaking.
    - Is this person qualified to give expert opinions on this subject?

- Does this person have underlying motives?
- Does this person have prejudices or beliefs that will compromise objectivity?

8.4.2.3. Dealing with An Angry Public

When risks are uncertain, because science has not reached an answer or a consensus answer, controversies will arise. Add the need to make decisions under the enormous time pressure of a crisis, and the uncertainty may seem unbearable to both response officials and the public. When science cannot lead to a clear path, decision-makers must make choices about what is and is not acceptable. In non-pressure environments, the public may turn to the courts to settle differences about the amount of acceptable or perceived risk.

In a crisis, as in the emergency room, where imperfect decisions must be made in minutes, not months, the fallout can be incredibly harsh, especially after the crisis is resolved and the decisions are reviewed with the omniscient power of hindsight. With the strongly held sense of self-determination among Americans, the struggle of imposing some risk on individuals or suspending some civil liberties to protect communities may be great. Great, unless, even in the crisis situation, response officials make an effort to empower the public.

At the community level, that may mean a face-to-face meeting. Involving stakeholders and building consensus is the most powerful way to advance compliance with public safety requirements before and during an emergency. Anything less will invite civil unrest and greater mistrust of the institutions or government responding to the crisis. These public forums sooth tempers and help the community to work toward a mutually agreeable solution to the common problem.

Communication experts and psychologists agree that anger is a defensive response to pain or the threat of pain. Experts identify three basic circumstances where anger is likely to arise:

- When people have been hurt
- When they feel threatened by risks not of their own making
- When they believe that their fundamental beliefs are being challenged.

The intensity of that anger can be confounded by related factors. For example, when people feel weak in the face of others who are more powerful, their anger is increased. When people feel that they have not been treated fairly or with respect, their anger multiplies. If they have been manipulated, trivialised, ignored—or worse still, lied to—anger and a sense of unfairness will build. However, don't forget that displays of anger may be a form of manipulation by another party, especially in public, to bully others into accepting their demands. Of course, more than one anger-causing element can be involved in a single situation.

Don't make the error of defining anger as either rational or irrational. That's judgmental, counterproductive, and truly in the eye of the beholder. It's dangerous to label others as irrational because you may then feel justified in dismissing them, which will only heighten their sense of injustice.

8.4.3. Let the Audience Discover the Answer

No one willingly accepts a lecture, and seldom have lectures changed anyone's mind or behavior. Lecturing is easy—the lecturer gets to vent his or her emotions and doesn't have to take others' points of view into account. That which makes it easy also makes it ineffective. A lecture does not engage the audience. Telling is easy, asking is tougher. Asking questions is a deliberate action. It forces the process to slow down and forces everyone to stop and think before replying.

Instead of attempting to persuade an individual or community group to take an action, allow them to persuade themselves through a self-discovery process. The key is to not give the solution, but help your audience to discover its own solution.

How do you help an audience discover its own answers? By asking the right questions.

Using feedback as your tool, you can ask the audience questions that will create awareness about the situation in such a way as to empower them to make a difficult choice. As many therapists will attest, a person who comes up with his own answer and says something in his own voice will take ownership of that idea. It's better for you to ask a leading question than to make an interpretation. The right questions can help an audience to make the necessary connections.

This strengthens the audience's tendency to claim ownership for the insight.

For example, were a severe communicable disease outbreak to occur, a challenge for officials in emergency response and public health is the possibility that civil rights may need to be temporarily suspended to control the spread of disease. A extreme case would be the need to quarantine individuals or communities. It makes sense that a population that understands the need to quarantine will be more likely to uphold the curfews or quarantine requirements.

8.4.3.1. Questions to Help People persuade Themselves

— Start with broad, open-ended questions.

— Then, ask questions to discover the explicit wants, needs, and desires of your audience.

— Follow with questions that are more specific to the situation now being faced by the audience.

— Then, ask questions that encourage audience members to state the benefits they would like to see result from a course of action.

— Once the audience sees and expresses the benefits, it will be much easier to demonstrate how your strategy can solve the problem.

Allowing people to persuade themselves is not an easy process. Done poorly, it can seem condescending or manipulative. It takes practice and a great deal of empathy. However, it's worth the effort, because it is truly the most effective way to gain acceptance in thought and behavior.

8.4.3.2. How to De-escalate the Conflict

Start by trying to agree on issues that may not be core to the conflict—not the hot button issue that no one is willing to concede. Agree whenever you can. It is hard to attack someone who agrees with you. You don't have to concede a thing. Find the elements that bring some agreement among both groups. Set up guidelines for interaction and make an effort to "humanise" each side for the other.

— At all times, seek common principles on which to base a common dialogue.

— Remain open to reason and allow yourself to consider that you might be wrong.
— Strive for fairness in the process, especially where a real or perceived inequity has occurred.
— Work to get input from all stakeholders.
— Leave the community or population better off than how you found it.
— Decision makers in the community should have access to open and complete scientific information.

Try to get as many "yeses" as you can. If someone says, "Your proposal is totally unrealistic," try this response: "Are you saying that you don't see how my proposal can (respect citizens' rights and stop the spread of disease)?" When person says "yes," this transforms the relationship. Each question you offer that allows a "yes" answer from the other side further reduces the tension.

8.4.3.2.1. Don't say "but"—say "yes, and."

Typically, people express their differences by prefacing their responses with, "but." The other group will be more receptive if you first acknowledge their views with a "yes" and then preface your view with an "and." Example: "Yes, we want to protect people's rights and we want to keep them alive to enjoy those rights."

References

Bord, R. J., & O'Connor, R. E. (1990). Risk communication, knowledge, and attitudes: Explaining reactions to a technology perceived as risky. *Risk Analysis*, 10, 499506.

Borman, Ernest G. (1975). *Discussion and Group Methods. Second Edition.* New York: Harper and Row Publishers, Inc.

Covello, V. T. (1991). Risk comparisons and risk communication: Issues and problems in comparing health and environmental risks. In R. E. Kasperson & P. M. Stallen (Eds.), *Communicating risk to the public* (pp. 79124).

Leeds, Dorothy. (2000). *The 7 Powers of Questions*. New York: Berkley Publishing Group.

Smith, Larry. (2001). *The ICM Crisis Management Certification Course.* Louisville, Kentucky: Institute for Crisis Management.

9

Choosing Communication Channels

In the initial relief phase of an emergency you must find ways to reach as many affected people as fast as possible with your messages. During this phase, communications systems may be temporarily out of commission. Low cost and low-tech communications systems are often the most practical and effective during such difficult circumstances. Megaphones, car battery-operated public address systems, community radio (also powered by battery or generators) are good ways to quickly disseminate messages to affected families and communities. Properly organised public gatherings and community or camp meetings provide further opportunities to quickly share information.

Choose more than one communication channel to help reinforce the information. Beyond using mass and small media, interpersonal and participatory community based media are indispensable channels to lead communication efforts aimed at improving or changing behaviours and in sustaining such behaviours. To choose the right mix of channels in the different phases of an emergency response, consider the following:

— How do affected families and communities seek information?

— How do affected families and communities share information?

— Who are trusted and respected spokespeople in the community or relief camp?

— Which groups have access to generators, mobile phones, megaphones, public address systems, radio or TV?

— Which groups among the affected population do not have access to any media?
— What traditional, telecommunications and mass communication channels are available?
— If available, using these in an emergency is often easier and more efficient than setting up new ones.
— Which groups can you reach via community-based group channels such as social or religious functions?

9.1. Mass Media

The mass media include print, radio, television and cinema. When operating during an emergency, these media can reach large numbers of people in a short time. The mass media are most effective when coupled with other communication approaches through which the affected community can talk about the new information with someone whom they trust, such as community opinion leaders. Consider these points when you use mass media in an emergency:

— Depending on the consequences of an emergency, the mass media can reach a substantial number of people.
— Enjoys credibility.
— Can be important channel for advocacy as it can reach and get the attention of policy-makers, senior officials and community leaders.
— Not participatory in nature.
— Messages may tend to be for general consumption, not taking into account the unique needs of the affected community.
— Might reinforce gender based stereotypes (e.g. portraying women as helpless victims)
— The affected population may not have access to radio or TV.

9.2. Small Format Community Media

Small format community media are often the most practical, useful and effective in reaching affected people during an emergency. These media include community radio (generator or battery-powered FM transmitters), community bulletins or flyers, and loudspeakers or megaphones - stationary (e.g., those in mosques) or itinerant (connected to vehicles). In an emergency, you can use these types of small community media to quickly disseminate information to a camp or affected community. With community coordination and support, you can plan, conceptualise, produce and disseminate messages with affected community members.

— Points to consider in using small format media in an emergency:
— Participatory in nature, involving all possible community groups.
— Requires how-to knowledge, therefore you need to engage participants in basic training
— Easy to set up.
— Needs oversight to make sure it is not abused or exploited by political factions.

9.3. Interpersonal Communication Channels

Interpersonal communication (IPC) refers to face-to-face communication. IPC can either be one-to-one or in a small group. IPC makes it possible for people to exchange information, express their feelings and obtain immediate feedback, respond to questions and doubts, convince and motivate others to adopt certain behavioural practices. IPC requires listening skills, the ability to empathise and be supportive. IPC in a crisis situation is particularly useful in counselling approaches such as through hotlines, clinic consultations, in training service providers and community volunteers as peer educators, through pep talks by specialists, and for facilitating group meetings where the affected community can share and discuss the issues at hand.

9.4. Peer Educators

Peers are persons who belong to the same age group and social cultural background. In addition to promoting healthy behaviours, we can build local capacity by training peer educators in effective communication and participatory approaches. Even after the end of a emergency communication initiative, these individuals can continue to pass on messages through casual conversations with friends, family members and their wider peer group.

Points to consider in tapping peer educators in an emergency:

— They can be easily organised in emergencies but you must invest in training which takes time.

— They need supportive supervision.

— Affected individuals can both give and receive information.

— Does not need to be costly.

— If planned and supported well, can be an effective way to motivate people. Affected people may not have a lot of time in an emergency to participate in meetings.

— Sharing personal information may not be culturally acceptable in some affected communities and will require time to establish trust.

— Messages spread via word-of-mouth may diminish message accuracy.

9.5. Participatory Drama

Participatory drama is an important aspect in the preparedness and recovery phases. This type of communication method allows the affected community to be directly involved in the drama itself. This gives individuals greater control, and helps them to explore issues and possible solutions. Participatory performance emphasises working with and from the affected community's own reality, and choosing their own modes of expression. Local people replace outside scriptwriters, illustrators, editors, directors and actors and become actively involved in creating and exploring solutions to a real life situation. Through participatory drama, you can encourage participation in the decision-making, implementation, monitoring and evaluation phases of relief and recovery projects.

— Points to consider when using participatory drama in an emergency:

— Stimulates critical thinking, stresses process rather than outcomes.

— Community can prioritise their needs.

— Develops a sense of community ownership.

— Offers a creative approach to deal with distress and trauma and thus supports healing among affected community members.

— Can be time consuming for the initial emergency response because of need to raise consciousness through IPC and relationship-building while it promotes sustainability.

— Castes, class, gender and other social variables can create different realities for some members of the affected community.

— Be sensitive to the cultural and gender-based specifics and act accordingly, by resorting to locally appropriate and innovative means of achieving equal participation.

— Community members may lack the commitment to the process if there are no perceived benefits.

9.6. Local Folk Media

Local folk media can include music, local art forms, local theatre, puppetry, drawing or dance. Many affected communities have their own traditional media forms to express themselves. Local ways of communicating are powerful avenues to stimulate psychosocial healing, return to normalcy and motivate affected families and communities to practice healthy behaviours.

Points to consider for an emergency:

— Information can be presented in the most culturally appropriate forms. Messages can be adapted to suit the needs of the affected community by local as well as imported experienced performers.

— Most folk media are entertaining and hold the attention of the audience, allowing them to be temporarily distracted from the realities at hand. It takes time to research on which folk media are acceptable to the affected community.

— Local participants need to be identified and trained on the messages to be shared.

— Technical information can be difficult to communicate. The actors may not be able to ad-lib or be spontaneous in acting out the local art forms.

9.7. Information, Education and Communication (IEC) Materials

IEC materials with prepared messages can be conceptualised as part of a communication preparedness plan before a disaster strikes. You can easily adapt and produce these as part of your BCC programme provided messages, design and presentation are duly pre-tested with the intended audience groups. Once a disaster strikes, producing and disseminating IEC materials can be a quick way to reach a large number of affected people. This form of communication typically leads to 'awareness raising' of an issue, and serves to reinforce existing knowledge and practices, such as the importance of hand washing, but this may not necessarily lead to changes in behaviour.

IEC materials include radio public service announcements in print form, posters, leaflets, brochures, videos, flip charts, banners, and promotional items like T-shirts and badges.

Points to consider when using IEC materials in an emergency:

— Generic messages addressed to and pre-tested with specific audience groups, for example, on hygiene, can be conceptualised. researched, tested and printed before a disaster strikes.

— Easy to do in initial response.

— Good way to get information out fast.

— Awareness of message does not equal action.

— Messages disseminated can easily be ignored, forgotten or cause confusion.

— Each message needs repetition and reinforcement through other communication channels.

When you decide on the communication channels to use in an emergency situation, keep in mind to mix media and interpersonal communication channels based on audience realities to achieve better results.

Numerous communication research studies have documented that individuals are particularly influenced to adopt new or improved practices through interpersonal communication with their peers or with opinion leaders. The studies have shown that using communication materials tend to reinforce the effectiveness of interpersonal communication.

9.8. Public Telephone and E-mail Services

Consider the following when planning for toll-free number services (or building capacity inhouse).

— Decide between rapid expansion of an existing phone number or a "new" toll-free number generated specifically for the emergency.

— The service must be expandable in terms of number of calls managed per hour or day and the hours of operation.

— The toll-free number must be answered by trained people who can reassure callers, provide requested information, and/or refer callers as needed.

— Precleared materials on multiple subjects should be easily accessable during an emergency. The following are concerns about predeveloped materials:

  – Materials must be specific to the emergency and the community impact.
  – They must be easy to read and understand.
  – They must be available in multiple languages based on community needs.
  – They must be field tested for cultural sensitivity and preferences.

— Standards of performance and evaluation should be considered: customer satisfaction, response capacity, accuracy, etc.

— Call managers must be able to quickly integrate new information into their emergency responses.

These issues must be considered for your public e-mail response service. State up front how long it will be before the public gets a response to an e-mail (2 hours, 24 hours, same week) and provide a way to reach your organisation if the need is more urgent. Be sure to advise people to seek out their health care providers or 911 for a personal medical emergency.

The CDC Public Response Service (PRS) began in October 2001, and is available free-of-charge to local and state health departments. PRS provides a rapid, turnkey toll-free hotline and interactive e-mail service that will provide both local information specific to the emergency (e.g., where to get shots in your community) and CDC-approved background health and medical information. This service is available to help a community or state manage its public information requirements during a public health emergency.

The service works with the general public, public health professionals, and emergency response teams. Service is available for Spanish and English speakers and the deaf and hearing impaired.

9.8.1. Achieving Effective Communication

Achieving effective communication with your audiences depends on selecting methods of communication that will reach them. This is especially important in health risk communication, where the audience participants can become disenfranchised quickly if they do not feel they are getting information.

Message delivery channels include:

— *Face-to-face* (e.g., health care professional to patient, or your organisation's staff member to state partner organisation or individuals in the community)

— *Group delivery* (e.g., small group or public meetings)

— *Organisational* (e.g., constituents of influential community organisations)

— *Mass media* (e.g., radio, television, newspaper, or direct mail)

— *Community* (e.g., employers, schools, malls, health groups, or local government agencies)

— *Combination of any or all of these* (i.e., most likely to work best).

9.8.2. Questions to Ask

— Which channels are most appropriate for the health risk problem/ issue and messages?

— Which channels will the target audience find credible and accessible?

— Which channels fit the program purpose (e.g., inform, influence, allay fears, influence attitudes, or change behavior)?

— Which channels and how many channels are feasible, considering your schedule and budget?

9.8.3. Identifying Specific Communication Tools

The tools you will use depend on your audience, how participants prefer to receive information, and the information you need to communicate. Possible tools include:

9.8.4. Briefings

A briefing is a session with key state and local officials, media representatives, and community leaders. Agency staff conduct sessions in person. Briefings help to notify key state and local officials, media representatives, and community leaders of developments at the site, such as results of studies or actions that should be taken to protect health. A briefing can be used to introduce your organisation and explain its role and work process. Briefings are not usually open to the general public.

9.8.4.1. Conducting a Briefing

— Schedule the briefing in a small public room, such as a hotel meeting room or a conference room.

— Hold the briefing in a neutral location, particularly when dealing with an antagonistic situation.

— Prepare a factsheet or question and answer sheet.

— Present a short, official statement about the agency's findings, health concerns, or recent developments.

— Use simple language.

— Avoid jargon, acronyms, and overly technical terms.

— Answer questions about the statement.

— Work with your organisation to coordinate briefings.

9.8.4.2. Benefits of a Briefing

— Allows state and local officials, the media, and citizens to question your organisation directly about any activity before the public release of information

— Prepares officials and citizen leaders to answer questions from their constituents when the information becomes public

— Allows for the exchange of information and concerns.

9.8.4.3. Limitations of a Briefing

— Although briefings can be effective, they could become the only means of communicating with site communities. Briefings should always be complemented by activities to inform the general public, such as small group or public meetings.

— Negative feelings or bad publicity could result if some people believe that they should be invited to the briefing and are not. Be sure not to exclude such persons or convey favoritism toward certain parties.

9.8.5. Community Mailings

A community mailing sends information to key contacts and concerned or involved members of the community. It disseminates information quickly and easily in writing, and it is particularly useful when you have updates for the community.

If the updates are straightforward, noncontroversial, and easy to understand, the mailing can stand on its own. However, if the updates are more complicated and require discussion or further explanation, the mailing should augment a public meeting or small group meetings. The community mailing can announce upcoming meetings and provide advance information or serve as a followup for people who did not attend previous meetings.

9.8.5.1. Developing a Community Mailing

Compile a mailing list and include:

— State and local officials (check with city clerk for assistance)

— Community leaders (check with local chamber of commerce)

— Local residents of the site area (check with city clerk for assistance)

— Community members who have signed up to receive information.

9.8.5.2. Creating Mailing Materials

Include:

— A cover letter that introduces you, briefly explains the purpose of the mailing, and provides contact information for comments or questions
— A factsheet, newsletter, report, or other documents
— First-class postage to deliver the mailing quickly.

9.8.5.3. Benefits of a Community Mailing

— Enables you to deliver information quickly and may require less planning time than conducting a meeting

9.8.5.4. Limitations of a Community Mailing

— Allows no interaction or opportunity for community members to ask questions

9.8.6. Exhibits

Exhibits are visual displays of maps, charts, diagrams, or photographs, and can help illustrate health issues and proposed actions in a creative and informative display. Effective exhibits can make technical information accessible and understandable.

9.8.6.1. Creating an Exhibit

— Determine where it will be placed, preferably in a highly visible location—a public library, convention hall, or shopping centre—especially if your target audience is the citizens of the town.
— Set up a temporary exhibit at a public meeting if a segment of concerned community members is the target audience.
— Design it according to the message to be transmitted.
— Include photos or illustrations. Use text sparingly.
— Keep it simple and visual. A bulletin board could suffice, if appropriate.
— Staff the exhibit with someone to answer questions, guide people through complicated issues, and gain informal feedback.

9.8.6.2. Benefits of an Exhibit

— Stimulates public interest and understanding

— Creates visual impact and leaves a lasting impression

9.8.6.3. Limitations of an Exhibit

— Exhibits are a one-way communication tool and do not provide an opportunity for community feedback.

9.8.7. Flyers

A flyer is a brief report summarising current or proposed activities. Flyers are appropriate whenever new information is available.

Flyers can be useful for:

— Introducing your organisation and explaining its role

— Explaining associated health risks

— Guiding community members in precautionary health actions

— Announcing new findings

— Dissemination at public meetings or community gatherings.

9.8.7.1. Types of Information in a Flyer

— Explanation of the triggering event that caused the health risk situation

— Timetable for the proposed actions

— Description of the health issues or problems

— Description of the health acticns necessary

— Description of public participation opportunities

— Name, address, and phone number of your organisation's contact person who can provide additional information on request

9.8.7.2. Presenting the Information

— Select a simple format.

— Be concise avoid jargon, acronyms, or highly technical language.

— Provide written information (a press release summarising your announcement, factsheets, copies of your prepared statement, and biographies of your speakers).

— Open the conference to questions for organisation officials, local officials, and technical staff.

9.8.7.3. Benefits of a Flyer

— Effective in briefly summarising facts and issues
— Provides background for information discussed during a meeting

9.8.7.4. Limitations of a Flyer

— Is a one-way communication tool
— Requires careful writing and coordination between making technical information easy to understand and message delivery

9.8.8. Newsletters

A newsletter is a publication that informs community members about activities, findings, health precautions, and other information concerning a health assessment.

9.8.8.1. Newsletter Topic Areas

— Overview of your organisation and background of its involvement at the site
— Plans for your organisation's onsite work and findings, if available
— Health guidelines, if applicable
— Upcoming activities and previous organisation activities, if any, that have taken place in the community
— Frequently asked questions and answers
— Contact information for your organisation

9.8.8.2. Newsletter Design

— Use simple, understandable language with headlines, boxes, lines, type variations, and other effects to make the newsletter attractive and easy to read.
— Establish a 4-page limit (an 11-by-17-inch sheet of paper folded in half makes a good 4-page newsletter).
— Ask someone not involved in the project to test-read the newsletter and provide feedback on message clarity.
— Use two colors if resources allow.

— Photocopy or print the newsletter.

Mail the newsletter to your mailing list and/or distribute it at public or small group meetings. If there is a central gathering place in the community, ask to leave copies there for community members.

9.8.8.3. Benefits of a Newsletter

- — Explains your work and findings to the community
- — Allows you to deliver a written document that community members can keep and refer to later

9.8.8.4. Limitations of a Newsletter

- — Can backfire if community members do not understand or are angered by what you have written
- — Does not give community members the opportunity to ask questions. (Always include contact information in your newsletter so people have a way to ask questions.)

9.8.9. Open Houses/ Availability Sessions/ Poster Sessions

An open house or availability session is an informal meeting where community members can talk to agency staff one-on-one. It is most appropriate when key milestones or major decisions have been reached.

9.8.9.1. Conducting an Open House/Availability Session

- — Determine community interest in the site before planning an open house.
- — Select a date, time, and location for the open house. To encourage attendance, choose evening hours or weekends at an easily accessible building familiar to residents (e.g., a public library or local meeting room).
- — Anticipate the number of attendees and plan accordingly. Consider holding two open houses if necessary to enable staff to greet and talk with each attendee. One staff member per 15–20 attendees generally fosters an informal atmosphere for conversation and avoids the situation where a staff member must speak to a crowd.

— Publicise the open house at least 2 weeks before the event. Send announcements to newspapers, television and radio stations, citizens on the mailing list, and any interested community organisations that publish newsletters.
— Create exhibits and factsheets to provide background information that enables citizens to ask more informed questions about the site during the open house.
— Include staff who are prepared to discuss technical information in an easy-to-understand manner.

9.8.9.2. Benefits

— Allows for one-on-one conversation
— Helps build trust and establishes a rapport between community members and agency staff

9.8.9.3. Limitations

— Can require significant staff time for planning and conducting an open house. A low turnout may not justify the effort.

9.8.10. Presentations

A presentation can be a speech to a club, civic or church organisation, school class, or similar local audience. Presentations are more effective if they focus on such major milestones as research findings or health recommendations.

9.8.10.1. Developing

— Describe the health risk situation.
— Describe how the health risk affects the community.
— Discuss what your organisation is doing to alleviate the health risk situation.
— Discuss how citizens can assist your organisation and obtain additional information.
— Select materials to support the presentation, such as slides, graphics, and exhibits, that will hold the audience's attention.

— Conduct a trial presentation in front of colleagues and rehearse the presentation as much as possible.

9.8.10.2. Benefits

— Offers the audience a chance to ask questions so the agency can gauge community concerns

— Reaches many people simultaneously, reducing individual inquiries

9.8.10.3. Limitations

— If poorly presented, can distort community members' view of the situation.

— Can only address individual community concerns during a question-and-answer period following the rehearsed presentation; could try people's patience.

— The presenter may face difficult or argumentative questions from community members.

9.8.11. Public Meetings

A public meeting is a large meeting open to the public, where experts present information and answer questions, and community members ask questions and offer comments.

9.8.11.1. Arranging a Public Meeting

— Create an agenda. Involve citizens in developing the agenda.

— Hold the meeting in a public, comfortable setting that is easily accessible, well lit, and has adequate parking and seating, especially for persons with disabilities.

— Be sensitive to special needs of community members. Consider translations for non-English speakers or sign language for hearing-impaired participants.

— Announce the meeting in local media 2 weeks in advance if possible. Distribute flyers to community members and groups interested in attending. Clarify that the meeting is not a formal public hearing, but rather, a place to exchange information and comments.

— Follow up with media closer to the meeting time to encourage them to attend. Send a "media alert," which contains brief information about the meeting date, time, and topic, and/or make phone calls to key contacts.

9.8.11.2. Conducting the Meeting

— State the purpose of the meeting, then outline the agenda and the procedures for making statements.

— Present preliminary findings and proposed courses of action.

— Distribute materials, including factsheets and other materials, for participants to take home.

— Prepare a transcript of the meeting, make the transcript publicly available, and announce how it can be obtained.

— Allow time for citizens' comments. Include a question-and-answer session. Meetings should last from 1 to 3 hours.

— Consider audio- or videotaping the meeting as a record so you can refer to it to refresh your memory on community concerns, if necessary.

9.8.11.3. Benefits

— Allows the community to express concerns and the agency to present information

9.8.11.4. Limitations

— Can intensify conflicts rather than resolve controversies. If public meetings have failed in the past, use an alternative method (e.g., small group meetings or a formal public hearing) to transmit information and obtain feedback.

9.8.12. Small Group (or focus group) Meetings

At a small group meeting, agency staff share information with interested community members and state and local officials. It is especially useful for informing and keeping in touch with community concerns, answering questions, and clearing up any misconceptions or misunderstandings.

9.8.12.1. Preparing for a Small Group Meeting

— Identify interested citizens and officials. Contact each citizen, group, or local organisation that is directly affected by site activities. Offer to discuss health issues at a convenient time.
— Limit attendance to 5–20 people. If more community members and officials are interested, schedule additional small meetings.
— Decide whether to invite the media. Media presence may intimidate the community. You may want to hold a similar meeting for media only.
— Select a meeting place conducive to two-way interaction. Place chairs in a circle or other informal arrangement.
— Select a date and time that allows for maximum participation. Make sure that the date and time do not conflict with other public meetings, holidays, or other special occasions.

9.8.12.2. Conducting the Meeting

— Ask people to provide contact information so you have a record of who attended.
— Begin with an overview of current and future health-related activities and findings.
— Encourage citizen participation.
— Distribute factsheets and other written information for attendees to take home.
— Follow up on major concerns. Stay in touch with the group and contact newly formed groups.

9.8.12.3. Benefits

— Allows two-way interaction with the community

9.8.12.4. Limitations

— May require a day or more of staff time to reach only a few citizens.
— May be perceived by community groups as an effort to limit attendance or a tactic to prevent large groups from exerting influence. (Hold additional small group meetings with

organisations that express concern about being left out of the process.)

— Irate groups or individuals may accuse your organisation's staff of giving different information to different groups. (Avoid criticism by inviting a cross-section of community representatives to each small group meeting and by keeping a written record.)

9.8.13. Telephone Contacts

Telephone contacts are calls to state and local officials and concerned community members, informing them of your organisation's activities, finding out who is involved, and gathering information about the event. After this initial contact is made, you may make calls to inform these individuals and monitor the extent of community concerns.

Know exactly what information to request (e.g., additional references, site specifics, or background information) and tailor questions accordingly. Information to solicit from these contacts might include:

— Background on the problem and recovery process

— Recent government activities

— Nature and extent of citizen involvement

— Names, addresses, and telephone numbers of other possible contacts.

Always test your messages with a small group before public release to ensure that the meaning is clear.

References

Chess, C., Saville, A., Tamuz, M., & Greenberg, M. (1992). The organizational links between risk communication and risk management: The case of Sybron Chemicals Inc. *Risk* analysis, 12, 431-438.

Kasperson, R. E., & Stallen, P. M. (Eds.). (1991). *Communicating risk to the public: International perspectives.* Dordrecht: Kluwer Academic Press.

Covello, V. T., Sandman, P. M., & Slovic, P. (1988). *Risk* communication, risk statistics and risk comparisons: A manual for *plant managers.* Washington DC: Chemical Manufacturers Association.

10

Terrorism and Risk Communication

The release of health-related information during a terrorist attack is a critical part of the national response to the event, and government officials and state and local health departments are aware that the quality, timeliness, and credibility of our messages and messengers may make the difference between people staying safe or becoming vulnerable to health risks presented by the emergency. Government officials have learned, sometimes the hard way, that institutional pressures and deeply rooted processes can get in the way of effective communication during an emergency. They are also learning that the public receives information and makes decisions about how it will respond differently during emergencies than during nonemergency times.

Terrorist attacks and public health emergencies present different situational characteristics and different emotional and psychological dynamics in the general public that affect how we deliver information. Some of the most significant emotions expressed include fear and anxiety (This is horrifying. Where can we turn? What awful things are ahead?! What do I do now?); anger (How could they?!); misery, depression, and empathy (poor victims); hurtfulness (Why do they hate us so?); and guilt (How come I survived and they didn't? How dare I still care about day-to-day trivia?).

As with many public health issues or natural disasters, information has the power to save lives—possibly many, many lives. People require information to find out what is actually happening and also what they must do to safeguard their own and their family's personal safety. But strong emotional responses to the event—fear, misery, concern, guilt, anger—make understanding and acting upon that information more difficult.

There is great uncertainty. Almost every instance of terrorism would present a profoundly new and previously unknown set of circumstances—to government officials working to manage the situation and to the public at large. Many pathogens considered to be potential weapons are almost never seen in the United States. Even though a lot is known about these agents and how they might present themselves, in reality not everything is known, as one would like it to be, in the event of a terrorist attack. Individuals and communities will be trying to cope with the situation and take necessary actions to protect their health and safety, while what is known and believed is unfolding with the constantly evolving story.

Individual and community levels of distress peak. Fear and uncertainty lead to unusually high levels of distress. Because of the psychological impact of acts of terrorism—and of many public health emergencies—it is not enough for the officials to give the facts of the situation and tell the public what to do, and expect that people will actually take these protective actions. High distress levels can keep individuals and communities from engaging in protective behaviors. However, how public health officials communicate can actually help channel this distress into productive and protective behaviors instead of destructive ones. Distress, if not excessive, leads to information-seeking and precautionary behavior.

The psychology of response to a terrorist attack is different from that of response to other types of emergencies. Current knowledge and widely accepted theories of disaster psychology suggest that there are many aspects of a terrorist attack, biological or other, that have an impact on how the public thinks, feels, and responds to information. This will have implications for how the health and human services communicates with the public. Some of these psychological aspects include:

— The intentional nature of the assault (as opposed to hurricanes and floods, for example)

— Unfamiliar agents or pathogens (as opposed to typical strains of influenza, which cause many deaths each year but are not so greatly feared as anthrax, which has caused relatively few deaths)

— The random nature of the attacks and the fact that they are largely outside our (Americans', the officials', the media's, etc.) control
— The potential for permanent and catastrophic harm and loss
— The involuntary nature of exposure (as opposed to smoking, for example, which causes smokers to suffer health and social consequences because of their voluntary exposure to tobacco and smoke)

Given these aspects of terrorism, it is known that people react and respond to information differently in times of attack from the way they do in ordinary times.

10.1. People's Reaction to Terrorism

Based on experience from past emergencies, many public health experts believe that an individual's decisionmaking process changes during a catastrophic emergency related to terrorism. The natural reactions people have in other emergencies may become even more exaggerated. Examples include:

— People simplify. Individuals' ability to comprehend numerous levels of detail decreases early in their response to an emergency. This means that people will generally miss nuances that help define the situation early. Public health guidance, including the protective actions individuals need to take, should be stated clearly, simply, and repeatedly.
— People become much more vigilant in a crisis. They check out their neighbors for signs of terrorism, surf the Internet for background information, and become glued to the media for news and context. This hypervigilance can have negative emotional consequences (added trauma from additional exposure to a traumatic event, for example), but is also useful as it helps people collect and assess the information they are getting. Is it consistent? What do people they respect think about it?
— People maintain their current beliefs. People are adept at maintaining faith in their current beliefs during a crisis. They tend to avoid contradictory or conflicting information. This means that if a new situation challenges conventionally held beliefs or views, it may be difficult to convince people that there is a new truth. Resistance to change in beliefs increases.

— People rely on past experiences. Whether or not past experiences are relevant, people use them to help define new ones. People remember what they see. They tend to believe what they have experienced in their own lives. However, faced with a terrorism emergency, they will have to rely on experts. But even reputable experts may disagree about the level of threat, the risks, and the appropriate recommendations. In nonemergency times, there is a natural give and take among experts that is expected and helps shape scientific debate. However, in times of crisis, this lack of agreement may leave the public with increased uncertainty and fear. According to some risk communication experts, the first message to reach listeners may often be the most accepted message, even if more accurate information surfaces later.

10.2. Objectives of Public in a Public Health Emergency

Most citizens share five main objectives during public health emergencies, including those caused by acts of terrorism:

— Protect themselves and loved ones

— Get the facts they want and need to protect themselves

— Be able to make choices and take action

— Be involved in the response

— Stabilize and normalize their lives

There are many ways people's feelings can affect their responses. Some examples include:

— *Fear*. Fear is one of the single most powerful emotions present during a terrorism emergency. It has the capacity to propel community members to action. Whether that action is helpful or harmful to the community depends on whether the individual can hear, understand, and act on sound guidance from public health authorities. Public health officials have the capacity to help individuals channel their fear and distress into protective actions, rather than irrational behaviors. Interestingly, in the aftermath of past emergencies, it has been observed that people seldom panic. People act. Effective communication can help people take the most appropriate actions to support the public health response.

— *Denial.* No doubt, some members of the community will be in denial. They may choose not to hear or heed warnings or recommended actions. They may become confused by the recommendations or simply not believe that the threat is real or that it is an actual personal threat. In such cases, people will not act on even the best advice. Denial, in fact, is one of the reasons why panic is rarer than we realize. People go into denial as a coping mechanism when the fear is too great. But there are several important antidotes to denial. The two key ones are: first, the legitimization of fear—people who feel entitled to be afraid don't have to go into denial; and second, action—people with something to do have more capacity to tolerate their fear and, therefore, are less vulnerable to denial.

— *Hopelessness, helplessness.* Some people can accept that the threat is real, but it looms so large that they believe the situation is hopeless and so they feel helpless to protect themselves. The resulting withdrawal and paralysis can impair their ability to take appropriate protective action in a public health emergency. People who feel powerless to affect the outcome are more likely to retreat to denial and the resulting hopelessness and helplessness that lead to inaction. Therefore, self-efficacy is important. Hopelessness, helplessness, and denial are all reduced by messages of self-efficacy and empowerment.

— *Stigmatization.* Some members of the community may suffer even greater effects from the attack if the rest of the community stigmatizes them. Fear or isolation of a group may occur if the community perceives it as contaminated or "risky." For example, in some cities, residents avoided "Chinatown" and Chinese restaurants out of fear of exposure to SARS. This type of stigmatization can hamper community recovery and affect evacuation, relocation, or, when necessary, quarantine efforts. In addition, groups people perceive as related to those who are "to blame," such as Arab-American communities following September 11, can become targets of local violence, even though they are as much victims of the terrorist attack as their neighbors.

— *Vicarious rehearsal.* Interestingly, experience has shown that people farther away (by distance or relationship) may react as strongly as those who are more directly impacted. Today's communication environment allows people to participate vicariously in a crisis in which they are not in immediate danger. This psychologically normal response to new risky situations results in people mentally rehearsing the crisis as if they were experiencing it and asking themselves, "What would I do?" In their minds, they imagine that the risk is here (instead of there), now (instead of soon), and definite (instead of maybe). They may believe that they, too, are at immediate risk and demand unnecessary services; as a result, they may go to the emergency room or take medications they do not need. Their stress reactions will be immediate danger, often resulting in some of the health consequences of stress. Further, because many of the agents are invisible and difficult todetect, we may not always be able to tell a community with certainty that it has not been exposed. This imaginative leap from there/soon/maybe to here/ now/definitely can be beneficial if it is acknowledged and the opportunity is taken to prepare, emotionally and logistically, for a real crisis.

10.3. Public Information Agencies

It's imperative that public health communicators understand the information release challenges faced when responding to a terrorist event. First and foremost, the Federal Bureau of Investigation (FBI) must have final authority over the release of information about the incident. The Department of Justice (DOJ) and the FBI have committed to ensuring that health information regarding a terrorist or suspected terrorist incident will be immediately released to protect the public's health and safety. However, information that, in the normal course of a disease outbreak would be considered just "filler information," may be withheld to protect the integrity of the criminal investigation. The response to a terrorist threat or incident within the United States will entail a highly coordinated, multiagency local, state, and federal response. The primary federal agencies that provide the core federal response are:

— DOJ/FBI
— Federal Emergency Management Agency (FEMA)
— Department of Defense (DoD)

— Department of Energy (DOE)
— Environmental Protection Agency (EPA)
— Department of Health and Human Services (DHHS).

The FBI is the lead agency for crisis management. FEMA is the lead agency for consequence management. As the lead agency for crisis management, the FBI will implement a federal crisis management response and designate a federal on-scene commander to ensure appropriate coordination of the overall response with federal, state, and local authorities. The Attorney General may, at some point, transfer the overall lead role to FEMA for consequence management, although both may be ongoing from the start.

DHHS serves as a support agency to the FBI for technical operations and to FEMA for consequence management. DHHS provides technical personnel and supporting equipment to the lead federal agency during all aspects of a terrorist incident. DHHS can also provide regulatory followup when an incident involves a product regulated by the Food and Drug Administration (FDA). DHHS assistance supports threat assessment, epidemiological investigation, and technical advice. Technical assistance to the FBI may include identification of agents, sample collection and analysis, onsite safety and protection activities, and medical management planning. Operational support to FEMA may include mass immunisation, mass prophylaxis, mass fatality management, pharmaceutical support operations (The National Pharmaceutical Stockpile [NPS]), contingency medical records, patient tracking, patient evacuation, and definitive medical care provided through the National Disaster Medical System.

As in all incidents, weapons of mass destruction (WMD) incidents may involve mass casualties and damage to buildings or other types of property. There are, however, several factors in WMD incidents that are unlike any other type of incidents and must be taken into consideration when planning a response. First-responders' ability to identify aspects of the incident (e.g., signs and symptoms exhibited by victims) and report them accurately will be key to maximising the use of critical local resources and for triggering a federal response.

— There will be a stronger public reaction to WMD incidents than to other types of incidents. The thought of exposure to a chemical or biological agent or radiation evokes terror in most people. The fear of the unknown also makes the public's response more severe.

— The situation may not be recognisable until there are multiple casualties. Most chemical and biological agents are not detectable by methods used for explosives and firearms. Most agents can be carried in containers that resemble everyday items.

— There may be multiple events (e.g., one event in an attempt to influence another event's outcome).

— Responders are at a higher risk of becoming casualties. Because chemical and biological agents are not readily identifiable, responders may become contaminated before recognising the agent involved. First responders may, in addition, be targets for secondary releases or explosions.

— The location of the incident will be treated as a crime scene. As such, preservation and collection of evidence is critical. Therefore, it is important to ensure that on-scene actions are coordinated between response organisations to minimise any conflicts between law enforcement authorities, who view the incident as a crime scene, and other responders, who view it as a hazardous materials or disaster scene.

— Contamination of critical facilities and large geographic areas may result. Victims may unknowingly carry an agent to public transportation facilities, businesses, residences, doctors' offices, walk-in medical clinics, or emergency rooms because they don't realise that they are contaminated.

— First-responders may carry the agent to fire or precinct houses, hospitals, or to the locations of subsequent calls.

— Time works against responders. The incident can expand geometrically and very quickly. This may affect mutual aid jurisdictions.

— Airborne agents flow with the air current and may spread via ventilation systems, carrying the agents far from the initial source. In addition, the effects of some chemicals and biological agents worsen over time.

— Such support facilities as utility stations and 911 centres, along with critical infrastructures, are at risk as targets.

— Specialised state and local response capabilities may be overwhelmed.

10.3.1 Joint Information Centre

The FBI is responsible for coordinating information dissemination to the White House, Congress, and other federal, state, and local government officials. In fulfilling this responsibility, the lead federal agency ensures that the release of public information is coordinated between crisis and consequence management response entities. The Joint Information Centre (JIC) is established by the lead federal agency, under the operational control of the FBI or FEMA public information officer, as a focal point for the coordination and provision of information to the public and media about the federal response to the emergency. The JIC may be established at the same location as the FBI Joint Operations Centre (JOC) or may be located at an on-scene location in coordination with state and local agencies.

The following elements should be represented at the JIC:

— FBI public information officer and staff

— FEMA public information officer and staff

— Other federal agency public information officers, as needed

— State and local public information officers.

10.3.2. State and Local Response Agencies

Throughout the management of the terrorist incident, crisis and consequence management components will operate concurrently tc ensure multiagency coordination and a tailored, time-phased deployment of specialised federal assets. It is critical that all participating federal, state, and local agencies interact seamlessly.

Once an incident has occurred, local government emergency response organisations will report to the incident scene and make appropriate notifications to local, state, and federal authorities. Control of this incident scene will be established by local response authorities (likely a senior fire or law enforcement official). Command and control of the incident scene is vested with the Incident

Commander/Unified Command (IC/UC). Operational control of assets at the scene is retained by the designated officials representing the agency (local, state, or federal) providing the assets. These officials manage tactical operations at the scene in coordination with the UC as directed by agency counterparts at field-level operational centres, if used.

10.3.3. Terrorist Explosion

The United States is not immune to covert biological terrorist incidents. The traditional tools of public health officials would likely be the first to detect an infectious agent released to harm Americans. The role of public health is to recognise (detect), investigate, and work with responders to reduce the impact of a bioterrorist event. This is most important with biological agents, which, after a silent release, may first present as unidentified illnesses.

Expect a delay between the covert release of a biological agent in a public place and the onset of illness. Doctors or emergency rooms may be the first to identify the initial casualties. By then, the terrorist(s) may be far away. With some infectious diseases, only a short window of opportunity will exist between the time that the first cases are identified and the second wave of the population becomes ill. During that brief time, public health officials must determine that an attack has occurred, identify the organism, and prevent more casualties.

Early detection and response are crucial, and require a level of knowledge among medical caregivers about possible biological terrorist agents. These individuals must possess this knowledge because they are in the best position to report suspicious illnesses. Early detection requires access to a communication system between doctors and public health officials.

10.4. Preparing Public Health Agencies

Disease detectives are being trained to detect and respond to biological attacks in order to speed detection and response. Increased laboratory capacity—well-trained lab workers and needed supplies—will speed diagnoses. The implementation of such secure, reliable, and swift communication channels as the national Health Alert Network (HAN) ensures early detection and rapid response.

Medical providers and public health officials are "going back to school" to become familiar with symptoms and signs of diseases rarely or never seen in the United States that could be used as biological weapons. The nation has strategically stockpiled drugs, medical supplies, and vaccines needed to supplement local supplies that could be quickly overburdened by a large-scale biological or chemical event.

10.4.1. Emerging Infectious Disease

Because the intentional release of a biological organism could mimic a naturally occurring outbreak, recognition and response to an undeclared terrorist use of an infectious disease agent will be much more difficult to detect than an announced biological release, a chemical release, or terrorist bombing.

Health investigators may not immediately recognise that an infectious disease outbreak is the result of an intentional release of germs. CDC has long recognised that the following selected illnesses may result from nature or from bioterrorism: encephalitis; hemorrhagic mediastinitis; pneumonia with abnormal liver function tests; papulopustular rash (e.g., as smallpox); hemorrhagic fever; descending paralysis; and nausea, vomiting, and diarrhoea.

The following list of epidemiological attributes summarises some characteristics of outbreaks that should suggest the possibility of intentional use of an infectious agent:

— Outbreak of a rare disease
— Outbreak of a disease in an area that normally does not experience the disease
— Occurrence of a seasonal disease at an inappropriate time of year
— Unusual age distribution of people involved in the outbreak
— Unusual epidemiologic features of an outbreak (e.g., a typical pathogen transmitted solely by food ingestion now found to be transmitted from person to person)
— Unusual clinical symptoms not typically seen with a known pathogen (especially respiratory symptoms)

In approximately the last 30 years, the CDC has been involved in the discovery of 30 emerging infectious diseases, either in the United States or around the world. Beware, however, that many past outbreaks, now known to be only nature at work, could have been mistaken for terrorism. The following are examples:

- — *Legionnaires' Disease outbreak*, Philadelphia, 1976, was characterised by a severe pneumonia of unknown origin. The discovery of the cause of the pneumonia took many months.
- — *Hantavirus Pulmonary Syndrome*, United States, 1993, consisted of an outbreak of severe pneumonia of unknown origin affecting healthy young adults. This virus had never before been recognised in the United States.
- — *Food-borne crytosporidiosis*, Minnesota, 1995, investigators determined that a common organism previously associated with drinking contaminated recreational water, exposure to animals, or person-to-person contact, was, in this outbreak, found to be associated with contaminated chicken salad.
- — *Antibiotic-resistant strain of plague*, Madagascar, 1995, could have been attributed to genetic engineering for bioterrorism purposes, although it was found to be a naturally occurring strain.
- — *Ebola virus infection*, Saire, 1995, was found to be a 99 percent genetic match to an Ebola virus that caused the 1976 outbreak. This finding raised the possibility of intentional reintroduction from a strain kept in a laboratory. (Most virus mutate over time, causing a greater gap in genetic matching to strains from previous outbreaks.)
- — *Nipah virus encephalitis*, Malaysia and Singapore, 1998–1999, was an outbreak by a previously unrecognised virus that caused illness in pigs with transmission to humans. The outbreak raised questions about whether pigs were targeted to introduce a bioterrorism strain of virus to humans.

Whether epidemics result from terrorism or natural factors, the public health community must detect and quickly investigate outbreaks, here and around the world. Because new disease agents could simply be nature at work, however, the past is a cautionary tale that we should not prematurely assume that bioterrorism is the cause of an emerging infectious disease outbreak.

In fall 1999, West Nile virus made its western hemisphere debut in the media capital of the world, New York City, and hasn't disappeared from headlines since. In the last 30 years, disease detectives from the CDC, have discovered—in places around the world—a new infectious disease in each of those 30 years. But the West Nile virus has rivalled such killers as plague, Ebola, and hantavirus for its continuing notoriety. Why?

Perhaps because this killer with a checkered past was now on a rampage in our own backyard. Unfortunately for public health communicators, the number of questions about when, where, and how it would strike was much greater than the answers about this unwelcome visitor.

Concerns about the "whys" and "hows" of this unusual infectious disease outbreak conflicted with media theories of domestic bioterrorism. Some experts believe that, if not for the mature emerging disease and bioterrorism plans and training of New York City public health and medical professionals, the initial cluster of illness may not have been brought to public health officials' attention as quickly as it was. Infectious disease experts are taught: "when you hear hoof beats think horses, not sebras." On the lookout for a bioterrorist act, they must think horses and sebras. That distinction is vital in early responses to disease outbreaks regardless of whether the virus is supplied by nature or by the hand of a human.

A New Yorker article released in October—after most of the first wave of questions about the new virus had been answered—led to a potential media frensy about West Nile and bioterrorism. However, the day that advance news releases about the article went to national media, the CDC issued a statement reassuring New Yorkers that, as awful as West Nile was, it still appeared to be nature at work. Working closely with the CDC, local media officials also minimised the plausibility of bioterrorism theories. Within 24 hours of the CDC statement, the media frensy waned and the investigation continued.

Consider this: Formulate your policy on commenting about bioterrorism aspects of your outbreak investigation now, because it's no longer "business as usual" in public health disease investigations. The increasing concern about bioterrorism and the likelihood that a bioterrorist act could be initially identified as a naturally occurring disease outbreak make law enforcement a real potential partner during a disease investigation. Since those of us involved in public health know first-hand that outbreaks often initially generate more questions than answers, the likelihood of the media raising the "bio-T question" is very high.

By stating officially to the media that West Nile was believed to be nothing more than nature at work, the CDC set a challenging precedent. For example, what if, in the course of the next outbreak, early suspicions about bioterrorism are raised? Do we confirm those suspicions? CDC experts can easily name 20 past outbreaks with characteristics that could have been believed at first to be the work of terrorists. Of course, none was. So plan your response before you're asked. CDC proposes that health officials give media the following response to the future "bio-T question" during the early stages of an ongoing infectious disease outbreak investigation:

> "We're all understandably concerned about the uncertainty surrounding this outbreak and we wish we could easily answer that question today. For the sake of those who are ill or may become ill, our medical epidemiologists (professional disease detectives) are going to first try to answer the following critical questions: (1) who is becoming ill? (2) what organism is causing the illness? (3) how should it be treated? And, (4) how can it be controlled to stop it from spreading?
>
> "A question that disease investigators routinely ask is: 'could this outbreak have been caused intentionally?' (Your organisation name) must keep an open mind as data in this investigation are collected and analysed.
>
> "With public safety in mind, we should not speculate on the organism's route of introduction until we have enough data to formulate a theory. We must consider the possibility that we may never have the data to answer this important question, based on epidemiology alone.
>
> "Any specific questions about the FBI's involvement in this outbreak investigation should be referred to them. However, the FBI and (your organisation) have a strong partnership in the investigation of unusual disease outbreaks and have worked comfortably together in past parallel investigations."

The following are federal authorities on terrorism response:

— Presidential Decision Directive 39, including the domestic guidelines

- — Presidential Decision Directive 62
- — Robert T. Stafford Disaster Relief and Emergency Assistance act
- — Other plans and directives
- — Federal Response Plan, including the Terrorism Incident annex
- — Federal Radiological Emergency Response Plan
- — National Oil and Hazardous Substances Pollution Contingency Plan
- — DHHS Health and Medical Services Support Plan for the Federal Response to Assets of Chemical/Biological Terrorism
- — Chairman of the Joint Chiefs of Staff CONPLAN 0300/0400
- — DODD 3025.15 Military Assistance to Civil Authorities
- — Other Department of Defense directives

10.5. Psychological Responses to Terrorism

1. Never lose sight of the fact that a terrorist act is intended to create feelings of psychological uncertainty, personal vulnerability, fear, and terror.
2. Once a terrorist act has occurred, the target population's state of mind and leadership serve to support or oppose the intent of the terrorist. Restoring a sense of community is critical.
3. Consider preincident psychological resiliency training, as well as ongoing psychological support for response personnel during and after the terrorist attack.
4. Collaborate with media to provide ongoing information to all involved and affected populations. Credible information contradicts the sense of chaos. Information combats destructive rumors.
5. Take whatever steps seem necessary to re-establish the public's sense of physical safety. Widely publicise these efforts to the degree that security considerations allow, and make special consideration for children, the elderly, and infirm.
6. Enlist the support of local political, educational, medical, business, and religious leaders to add to communication that calms fears, provides personal crisis intervention, and instills hope.

7. Re-establish normal communication, transportation, school, and work schedules as soon as possible.
8. Symbols (e.g., flags, bumper stickers, signs, and billboards) can help re-establish community cohesion.
9. Initiate rituals to honor the survivors, the rescuers, and the dead. Provide opportunities for others not directly affected to assist those who are directly affected, such as providing donations of blood, food, clothing, and money. Communicate to all the concept that an effective way to honor the dead is to carry on and succeed. To do otherwise is to allow the terrorists to succeed.
10. Be careful not to interfere prematurely with psychological support, which could undermine that support.

10.5.1. US Pharmaceutical Stockpile Program

Managed by the Centres for Disease Control and Prevention (CDC), the National Pharmaceutical Stockpile (NPS) program is composed of skilled, highly motivated people and large quantities of medical materiel and equipment. NPS exists to help states and communities respond to the medical consequences of terrorist attacks, natural disasters, and technological accidents.

During an emergency, NPS ships drugs, vaccines, medical supplies, and medical equipment to states and communities—the first within 12 hours of the federal decision to deploy—and to continue to deliver materiel for as long as it is needed. NPS experts also will assist states and communities with receiving, storage, staging, distribution, and dispensing NPS materials.

NPS is not one package, but multiple, comprehensive packages of drugs, vaccines, medical supplies, and medical equipment that can be used to augment depleted state and local resources for responding to terrorist attacks and other emergencies. The packages are stored in strategic locations around the United States to ensure their rapid delivery anywhere in the country. The NPS typically will arrive by air or ground in two shipment phases. The first phase is called a 12-hour Push Package. "12-hour" refers to the package's transit time: 12 hours or less after the federal decision to deploy. "Push" is so named because a state need only ask for help—not for specific items—and NPS will "push" or ship virtually everything a state needs to respond to a broad range of threats in the early hours of an event, when people are sick or dying from an ill-defined threat.

Second-phase shipments normally begin within 24–36 hours after a state identifies a threat. These shipments contain large quantities of specific items designed to deal with a specific threat. These shipments are referred to as vendor managed inventory (VMI), because major pharmaceutical vendors will store this materiel until it's shipped.

A 12-hour Push Package typically will arrive in more than 100 specialised cargo containers via a wide-body jet (e.g., a 747 or 767) or on seven 48-foot tractor-trailers. The package weighs approximately 50 tons and occupies 5,000 square feet when off-loaded. The 12-hour Push Package includes large quantities of medicines, antidotes, medical supplies, and medical equipment that states and communities will need in order to respond to such nerve agents as sarin; and biological agents, such as anthrax, plague, and tularemia. The package will enable state and local authorities to immediately treat thousands of symptomatic individuals and protect hundreds of thousands more who may have been exposed.

CDC scientists work closely with the intelligence community to assess the probability of different biological and chemical threats. Once the scientists identify the threats, they create protocols for therapeutic treatment and prophylaxis. The protocols determine which drugs and other supplies are in the NPS. Because threat assessments, treatment protocols, and other factors change over time, the items in the 12-hour Push Packages may also change.

10.5.2. Vital Communication Concerns

In your crisis communication plan, special consideration should be taken regarding NPS issues. During a large-scale emergency, public fear and anxiety could impair your ability to distribute and dispense prophylaxis to those who need it. An effective public information plan, using sound emergency risk communication principles that inform and reassure the public, will earn public confidence and cooperation.

Precrisis planning is critical. The plans should consider language barriers, cultural sensitivities, hearing and sight impairment, and the means by which population groups get their information (e.g., television, radio, church) to plan and create messages and information that effectively inform the public.

In your planning, consider the following:

— Are disease and drug information prepared in all of the languages spoken by your community members?

— Are messages and information threat- and incident-specific? Threat-specific messages give specific information about the disease, the protective drug regimens that public health agencies will provide, and the routine that people should expect at a dispensing site.

— Are processes in place to create incident-specific messages for people who are potentially exposed where they must go for prophylactic medications if they are well, and where they need to go if they are sick? The number of dispensing and treatment locations, for instance, will depend on the scale and type of threat.

A large-scale threat will require more dispensing sites, but if contagion is a concern, the number of treatment centres may be limited to avoid spreading the disease. Public information officers will need to know where the active dispensing and treatment locations are before they can effectively inform the public.

Public information officers also need to work with the media before an event to discuss the dissemination of information and messages. In addition to the important task of broadcasting health messages to the public, the media should be able to suggest ways to effectively present and deliver the information to target population groups.

Your plan should include the following:

— Multilanguage text of all documents used to inform the public during an emergency. These include television and radio public information announcements and the informational materials, forms, scripts, and video-tapes that dispensing sites use to issue prophylaxis to the public

— Storage location of all informational material (including electronic versions)

— Methods for reproducing and disseminating informational materials during an emergency

— Specific communication channels, partnerships, and staffing pools that support public information release, reproduction, and dissemination. Dissemination channels should include volunteers or contract professionals to serve as onsite interpreters for people who do not speak English; are hearing impaired; and assist with public information campaigns, printing needs, and onsite public information assistance.

— To determine how much NPS materiel and information you will need to provide to site locations, consider the following:

— Is the agent contagious?

— Who should be concerned about exposure?

— Who should seek preventive treatment at dispensing sites and who should seek symptomatic treatment at treatment centres?

— Directions to and information about dispensing and treatment locations. This information will affect the use of specific locations, the amount of NPS materiel, and the number of deliveries of that materiel that you make to specific locations. The information should answer these questions:

 - When will the dispensing operation start and what hours will it operate?
 - Where is the nearest dispensing site?
 - What is the best street access to each dispensing site?
 - If driving, where should the public park at each dispensing site?
 - What is the best transportation mode to the dispensing site (e.g., walk, use public transportation, drive)?
 - What is the dispensing process?
 - What form(s) of identification are needed?
 - What information must someone present when picking up medications for family members?

— Children: weight, age, health information, drug allergies, current medications.

— Adults: health information, drug allergies, current medications.

10.5.3. Information about Drugs

The information should include the following:

— Reason(s) for using specific drugs or changing drug regimens. The cultural and ethnic sensitivity with which you provide the latter information is important to ensure that residents of a neighborhood do not think that others are getting preferential treatment because they receive different drugs. This information will affect the quantities of specific drugs that you provide to dispensing and treatment locations. It will also affect the public's acceptance of those drugs.

— Information about importance of taking the medication. This information must stress the importance of taking all of a prescribed regimen (e.g., 60 days of doxycycline for anthrax). This information affects the demand for NPS resources and minimises the likelihood of additional people becoming symptomatic.

Adherence is a well-known problem and will be especially challenging during an emergency if the treatment regimen is long, the prescribed drugs cause unpleasant side effects, and/or disease outbreaks stop before the public finishes the regimen.

After anthrax attacks in fall 2001, CDC surveyed those who received prophylactic drugs. Despite initial counseling and strong local appeals that encouraged individuals to finish the 60-day regimen, CDC found that only 45 percent adhered to the regimen. Reasons for sporadic or discontinued use included drug side effects and the perception that they were no longer at risk for anthrax.

Be aware of the danger of overmedicating. Focus on dispelling the erroneous notion that if 2 doses per day are good, 4 or 6 must be better. The goal is to reduce the demand for NPS materiel by discouraging individuals from acquiring drugs from multiple dispensing sites. A secondary goal is to minimise the possibility that some individuals will take more of a drug than is safe.

Recently, CDC awarded cooperative agreement funds to 62 project areas for bioterrorism response. Some of those funds support the improvement of health communication during emergencies. As a state or local public health communicator, you should contact the state official managing NPS planning under the cooperative agreement to coordinate health communication needs.

Checklist 9-1. National Pharmaceutical Stockpile Communication Needs Assessment

As a state or local public health communicator, you should contact the project area official managing NPS planning under the cooperative agreement to coordinate health communications needs.

10.5.4. Pre-event Planning

— Is the disease and drug information prepared in the multiple languages spoken by your community?
— Are processes in place to create incident-specific messages that tell people who are potentially exposed where they must go for prophylactic medications if they are well, and where they need to go if they are sick?
— Are processes in place to ensure that public information officers know which dispensing and treatment locations are active?
— Are media aware—before an event—of the need to disseminate NPS-related information and messages?

Your plan should include the following:

— Multilanguage text of all documents used to inform the public during an emergency
— Storage location(s) of all informational material (including electronic versions)
— Methods for reproducing and disseminating informational materials during an emergency
— Specific communication channels, partnerships, and staffing pools that support public information release, reproduction, and dissemination

To determine how much NPS-related information you will need to provide to site locations, consider the following:

— Is the agent contagious?
— Who should be concerned about exposure?
— Who should seek preventive treatment at dispensing sites and who should seek symptomatic treatment at treatment centres?

— Directions to and information about dispensing and treatment locations.
— When will the dispensing operation start and what hours will it be open?
— Where is the nearest dispensing site?
— What is the best street access to each dispensing site?
— Where should those who drive park at each dispensing site?
— What is the best way to get to the dispensing site (e.g., walk, use public transportation, drive)?
— What is the dispensing process?
— What forms of identification are needed?
— What information must someone have in order to pick up medications for family members? Children: weight, age, health information, drug allergies, current medications Adults: health information, drug allergies, current medications.

References

Atman, C.J., Bostrom, A., Fischhoff, B. & Morgan, M.G.. (1994). Designing risk communications: Completing and correcting mental models of hazardous processes, Part 1. *Risk Analysis, 14*, 779-788.

Eggers, S.L., & Fischhoff, B. (2004). A defensible claim? Behaviorally realistic evaluation standards. *Journal of Public Policy and Marketing, 23*, 14-27.

Morgan, M.G., Fischhoff, B., Bostrom, A., Lave, L., & Atman, C.J. (1992). Communicating risk to the public. *Environmental Science and Technology, 26*, 2048-2056.

Fischhoff, B. (2002). Assessing and communicating the risks of terrorism. In A.H. Teich, S.D. Nelson, & S.J. Lita (Eds.), *Science and technology in a vulnerable world* (pp. 51-64). Washington, DC: AAAS.

Riley, D.M., Fischhoff, B., & Small, M., & Fischbeck, P. Behaviorally realistic regulation. (2001). In P.S. Fischbeck & S. Farrow (Eds.), *Improving regulation: Cases in environment, health, and safety* (pp. 145-164). Washington, DC: Resources for the Future.

11

Human Resource in Risk Communication

Part of health and well-being is good preparation and planning so that people understand their roles and can maximise efficiency while minimising unnecessary frustration. Crises bring enough unavoidable challenges without adding disorganisation to the list.

Public health officials and the communication professionals who support them are responders who need to pay attention to their preparation, as well as their physical and emotional needs, as a crisis continues. The following describes important steps that should be taken to assure that they, like all who are serving the public good, can do so most effectively.

11.1. Planning for Human Resources

Train communicators for designated emergency response jobs and refresh that training periodically (e.g., at minimum, require them to read and initial the crisis communication plan and discuss their roles).

Consider creating training drills (possibly unannounced) to see how quickly you can get your crisis communication operations up and running. Are phone numbers up to date in your plan? Do people respond within 45 minutes after being paged? Are backups ready if primary responders are away and out of reach? Can you assemble and make mock assignments within hours of the launch of the operation? Can your early skeletal staff produce, clear, and release a press update within 2 hours of obtaining information? Are the initial steps being considered (e.g., verification, notification, coordination, etc.)?

11.1.1. Acknowledge Levels of Experience

Develop an expertise ranking system and "promote" your team members as they gain more skills and experience in responding during an emergency. For example, the American Red Cross ranks responders, from technician to specialist to coordinator and then assistant officer and officer. They offer two tracks, one for subject matter expertise and another for leadership. Not everyone with specialised skills wants to lead, yet, their level of emergency response expertise should be recognised.

11.1.2. Maintain a Registry of Communication Professionals

Identify your human assets, especially those who volunteer to participate at the headquarters or to be deployed as part of an emergency public health response. Keep a database and continually reach out to find and add new volunteers within your organisation. Make sure that their supervisors are in agreement and willing to sacrifice those staffers to the emergency response. Register communicators by specialty areas, level of experience and willingness to work in the headquarters, be deployed to a JIC, sent overseas, etc. The more "truly available" persons on your list, the more likely your operation can be maintained and, ultimately, go the distance. Ask people annually to recommit; this will ensure that you have a list representing a true inventory of your human assets.

Divide your registry according to the types of jobs that your organisation's crisis communication plan has identified to be executed internally. If your plan indicates that your Web or 24-hour phone operations support will come from another organisation, there's no need to keep those assignments active on your registry. Find out now if nonpaid, trained volunteers are permitted to augment your operations. Indicate on the registry who is eligible, based on your criteria, for management or leadership positions during an emergency response.

11.1.3. Execute your Crisis Communication Plan

As an initial step in crisis response, you will be making decisions about your communication operations, especially about daily hours of operation the number of days per week, and, at some point, the expected duration of the response. Re-assessments, of course, will be needed as the nature of the crisis is more clearly understood. Apply your risk assessment tools to help you make these decisions. Remember to stagger work hours to ensure continuity in your operation. You don't want an uninformed fresh crew to come in—at various times in the operational day, you'll want new workers to relieve members of a core group. For example, stagger shifts in a 24-hour period so that some are working 7 a.m. to 7 p.m., others come in at 4 p.m. and work until 4 a.m., and still others are arriving at noon and working until midnight.

Don't forget relief for leadership. Workers deserve clear and competent leadership—it's the duty of all involved to take occaisional breaks to keep them functioning at the high level required in an emergency.

The following are tried and true guidelines for establishing staff working hours during a crisis from the American Red Cross—an organisation that has deployed millions of volunteers domestically and around the world for more than a hundred years. It's worth trying their formula.

11.1.3.1. Initial Phase

— Hours worked per person per day: reasonably 12, but never more than 16

— Days worked per person per week during a 3-week deployment: the first 7 to 10 days with no days off if the emergency is very intense

11.1.3.2. Maintenance Phase

If the emergency is less intense, staff should normally be directed to take one 24-hour period off after 7 days of work, with the expectation of 2 days off within 3 weeks. Typically, an assignment is for 3 weeks. However, if someone continues to be physically and mentally fit, the Red Cross may extend an assignment for another 3 weeks, with further reassessment for a final 3 weeks. However, the Red Cross expects that the volunteer, if deployed far from home, will return home for a brief stay before redeploying for each of the 3-week assignments.

11.1.3.3. Resolution Phase

Before volunteers return home or to their normal jobs, the American Red Cross either requires or encourages a visit to a mental health counsellor. The organisation also believes that there is value in debriefing participants. The Red Cross also provides support and educational materials to family members of persons deployed away from home.

11.1.4. Public and Media Response

How much can one communication "super-hero" accomplish in a day? There's a great deal of variation; however, there is reasonable consensus about the following rules:

Taking repetitive information calls from the public working from a script and requiring no analysis, a motivated worker may manage between 30 and 40 repetitive calls requesting information per hour. However, no one should be expected to do an 8-hour shift of this type of calltaking; 6 hours is more reasonable. Reduce that by two-thirds if calls require reassurance, referral, or recommendation. That degree of interaction would make for an overly intense 6-hour shift on the phones.

11.1.4.1. Media Response Needs

Press assistants who take media calls can manage at least twice as many calls than can media information officers who provide more indepth assistance. However, the work of a press assistant can range from taking a message (not always an easy task), to directing the media representative to an alternate source. The people answering media calls provide your organisations' first impression—ensure that you assign enough people to this task. Also, make sure you have enough incoming phone lines, lest your press assistants endure a lot of grousing. When possible, create a frequently asked questions (FAQ) document containing all of the known facts that is available to reporters by fax, Web, and e-mail. This will reduce the amount of human power you'll need to get through the emergency operation.

Public information officers have been known to manage 100 calls in a day (but that could be a "fish" story) when the facts are straightforward. However, quantity must be tempered by quality. A tough day of media calls on a single but complex subject could mean between 40 and 50 for one press officer. Someone working with "issues" and not just providing information, won't be able to field as many calls. Someone acting as a spokesperson for the agency—doing radio or print interviews—will field even fewer calls. There's an obvious correlation between the intensity of the work and the amount of analysis and judgment needed in the response, and the reduction in the number of calls handled in a day.

11.1.4.2. Spokesperson Assignments

If the media interest is intense or enduring—what you'd expect in a crisis—stagger your spokespersons, too. Fatigue creates mistakes. Attempt to arrange interviews when your spokesperson is most fresh (e.g., not at the end of a shift). Reduce stress with lots of support from the public information officer.

Top leaders should expect no more 4 TV interviews in a day, along with 2 or 3 telephone interviews if they're not too indepth. That pace, however, can not be sustained day after day, and an organisation director or hands-on leader of the response can't afford to do continuous interviews. Save the big guns for important moments when the public expects to hear from a real policy-maker or decisionmaker. If possible, substitute lower-level organisation leaders or subject matter experts for more routine interview requests. The director should be reserved for the greatest possible reach and for pivotal moments. Overexposure of the top director may lead to accusations of grandstanding or perceived power struggles.

A spokesperson or subject matter expert assigned solely to provide media and public information response (a luxury rarely afforded) can keep pace with a top public information officer and should be able to do six or more short on-camera interviews, interspersed with print and radio interviews, each day. However, if that number of requests remains constant over time, be sure to capitalise on regular press availabilities and open more channels of communication to the public and media. The media would love unlimited access to exclusive in-person interviews. Use your assets wisely and save your human resources for the times that they're really needed.

11.2. Emotional Issues

According to the Red Cross, those who respond to a crisis have the potential to become "secondary victims," as they work long, intensive hours often under poor conditions. In some cases, physical dangers exist for responders. For those deployed away from home, personal support systems are left behind. Supervisory styles vary from person to person; and administrative organisation and regulations often must change with little warning, adding additional stressors.

Most people who willingly respond to a crisis are dedicated individuals who also tend to be perfectionists. As such, they are at risk of pushing themselves too hard and of not being satisfied with what they have accomplished. With so much yet to do, they often fail to take credit for the amount of work completed and their contribution to the operation.

Frustration is common, and one's usual sense of humor is often stretched beyond its limits. Workers become exhausted, and anger easily surfaces. The anger of others—workers, victims, media—becomes difficult to deal with, and may be experienced as a personal attack on the worker rather than as a normal response to exhaustion. Survivor guilt may emerge as workers see what others have lost.

11.2.1. Coping

Remember that your response efforts are a gift of yourself—your time and your caring—that you couldn't give if you, too, were a victim.

Few of us have experience with mass death or destruction. Workers need to understand and appreciate the intensity of their emotions, and others talk about their feelings.

Although workers may function in superhuman ways during a disaster operation, the stress associated with this work takes its toll. Workers get tired, confused, hurt, and scared. It is critical for both the workers and those they are trying to help them understand the effects of stress and make an effort to deal with it.

Stress-relieving activities are not as difficult or time-consuming as we may think. A 15-minute walk, talking to someone, taking a "brain break" by going out to dinner or a movie, or just using deep breathing exercises, can significantly reduce stress.

During the operation, it's important to eat nutritional foods, avoid drinking large amounts of caffeine and alcohol, get some exercise whenever possible, and get as much sleep as possible.

Supervisors will attempt to juggle schedules so workers can have time off to sleep, read or sit in the sun. If workers need such time before they're scheduled, they should request it. If they need a change of assignment or setting, they should ask for that, too. And, as difficult as it may be to turn over duties to someone else, when a shift is over, workers must leave and take the time to recharge.

11.2.2. Personal Coping

— Recognise that emotions will be high in this abnormal setting and talk about it.

— Eat nutritious food (e.g., fruit versus donuts, or peanuts versus chips).

— Take mental breaks.

— Avoid lots of caffeine or alcohol.

— Leave when your shift is over.

— Exercise.

— Remind workers about the value of their effort.

— Insist that scheduled meal breaks be taken.

— Make nutritious foods and drinks available.

— Expect high emotions and provide someone for workers to talk to.

— Respond to even timid requests for relief or reassignment.

— Encourage exercise and personal grooming time.

— Accept non-offensive "silliness" that some use to let off steam.

— Despite what they say, insist that workers take time to sleep.

11.2.3. Coping with Disasters for Family Members of Workers

Someone very important to you and your family has just left on an emergency response assignment. It is natural for you to be worried about the experiences and potential hardships he or she may face on assignment.

Your family member has probably given you all of the information available at the time of the assignment. It may seem very scanty to you. That's because in the beginning stages of any operation, we don't really know much about where the need is greatest and where we will require your family member's particular skills. We often don't know that accommodations are available or even whether phone service is in place.

For the emergency response member, the beginning of any operation is a process of reporting as quickly as possible to a command centre (which may change location), to perform a function that may change as the needs of the operation change. The staff member may be reassigned once or many times to different locations during the assignment. It is a time of great confusion and considerable frustration, as we begin to meet the needs of victims and affected communities. But we can guarantee that this is an opportunity unlike any other for emergency response workers to experience the satisfaction that accompanies helping others and stretching their own limits and potential.

We know that you will keep in touch with your deployed family member as often as possible, and continue to make him or her feel like part of the family. Friendships are quickly formed on assignments and workers look out for each other's welfare as if they had been lifelong friends. But even this sense of camaraderie is not a substitute for news and expressions of caring from home.

Deployed staff usually work long hours with little time off. They are constantly exposed to scenes of suffering, possible destruction, and the strong emotions of victims. The fast pace of the response operation is intended to quickly help the largest number of people to resume a normal, although changed, life.

When your family member returns home, he or she may need some additional time to adjust to the "normal" pace of everyday life, and may require a few days of rest before resuming previously normal responsibilities. It will be important for your family member to be able to talk to you about what happened and the emotions that accompanied the work. He or she may be proud, frustrated, angry, sad, tearful, and happy all at the same time. It will take some time to sort out these conflicting emotions.

He or she may seem preoccupied with the disaster experience, and may not seem to share your excitement, disappointment, or frustration about events at home. Be assured that what has happened at home is as important as it always was; your family member has been through an experience that tends to overshadow everyday events and puts them in a different perspective when viewed against the enormity of the situation he or she just left.

All emergency response workers return home with a conscious or unconscious need to reassure themselves of the safety of their environment. And virtually all workers feel that they left something undone on the operation. It is important that you greet your family member with the love and understanding that made you the type of family he or she could feel comfortable leaving in order to help others.

References

Allen, F. W. (1987). Towards a holistic appreciation of risk: The challenge for communicators and policy makers. *Science, Technology & Human Values*, 12 (3-4), 138-143.

Baird, B. R. N. (1986). Tolerance for environmental health risks: The influence of knowledge benefits, voluntariness, and environmental attitudes. *Risk analysis* 6, 425-435.

Sandman, P. M., & Miller, P. M. (1991). *Outrage and technical detail: The impact of agency behavior on community risk perception*. Final report to the New Jersey Department of Environmental Protection, Division of Science and Research. Brunswick NJ: Rutgers University Environmental Communication Program.

Schwarz, M., & Thompson, M. (1990). *Divided we stand: Redefininq politics technology and social choice*. Philadelphia: Univ. of Pennsylvania Press.

Slovic, P., Fischhoff, B., & Lichtenstein, S. (1981). *The assessment and perception of risk*. London: The Royal Society.

12

Tips for Effective Risk Communication

Communicating in a crisis is different. In a serious crisis, all affected people take in information differently, process information differently, and act on information differently. A well-prepared organisation will have communication plans and resources in place to help minimise the number of decisions about communication that must be made in the moment. We can predict both the types of disasters our communities face and the questions the public will have during a disaster. Plan now. Plan with your communication and public information professionals. Plan with your disaster-response partners.

12.1. Reasons of Communication Failure

Communication experts and leaders who've faced disasters can tell others what is going to cripple or even destroy the success of their disaster response operation:

— Mixed messages from multiple experts

— Information released late

— Paternalistic attitudes

— Not countering rumors and myths in real time

— Public power struggles and confusion

12.1.1. Mixed Messages

The public doesn't want to have to "select" one of many messages to believe and act on. During the mid-1990s the Midwestern United States suffered a spring of great floods. Response officials determined that the water treatment facilities in some communities were compromised and that a "boil water" directive should be issued. The problem developed when multiple response organisations, government and nongovernment, issued directions for boiling water and each of them was different. The fact is, in the United States, we turn on the facet and clean water comes out. Few of us know the "recipe" to boil water because we've never had to.

So, what's the big deal? Just pick one and get to it. Not so fast! Consider this: I'm a young mother with an infant son and I need to mix his cereal with water. I'm a middle-aged son caring for his mother who is currently immune-compromised because of cancer chemotherapy. I'm the sister living down the street from my HIV-positive brother whose T-cell count is back on the way down. Or, just maybe, I'm an average person who doesn't like the thought of gambling on a bad case of diarrhoea if I don't pick the right boil-water instructions.

In a crisis, people don't want to "just pick one" of many messages; they want the best one or the right one to follow. When faced with a new threat,

people want a consistent and simple recommendation to follow. They want to hear absolute agreement about what they should do from multiple experts through multiple sources. Messages do not have to be wrong to be damaging. If they are inconsistent the public will lose trust in the response officials and begin to question every recommendation. Local, state, regional, and national response officials and their partners must work together to ensure messages are consistent, especially when the information is new to the public.

12.1.2. Information Released Late

Following the September 11, 2001 terrorist attacks, many people wanted advice on whether or not to buy a gas mask. These calls found their way to CDC. Three weeks after the attack, CDC had an answer on its web site. During the 3 weeks CDC took to develop and vet its answer, a number of experts were willing to give an answer—unfortunately it wasn't the right one. When CDC issued advice to the public not to buy gas masks, the "gas-mask" aisles at the local Army-Navy surplus stores were already empty. In all fairness, few of us could contemplate the consequences of a 9-11 type attack—but all of us can now create a process to quickly react to the information needs of the public. If we can not give people what they need when they need it, others will. And those "others" may not have the best interest of the public in mind when they're offering advice.

If the public expects an answer from your organisation on something that is answerable and you won't provide it or direct them to someone who can, they will be open to being taken advantage of by unscrupulous or fraudulent opportunists.

12.1.3. Paternalistic Attitudes

Putting on a John Wayne swagger and ostensibly answering the public's concerns with a "Don't worry little lady, we got ya covered" doesn't work in the information age. People want and expect information to allow them to come to their own conclusion. As a leader, it's not enough to satisfy your own worries with copious bits of information and then turn around and state a bottom-line unsupported with the facts you know. As difficult as it may be, help the public to reach the same conclusion you did by sharing with them what you learned to reach that conclusion. What did you learn that made you believe the situation wasn't worrisome? Share that.

Treat the public like intelligent adults and they will act like intelligent adults. Treat them any other way and they will either turn on you or behave in ways that seem illogical to you. You are a leader for the public; you are not their parent. Never tell people "Don't worry." Tell people what they need to know so they can reach the decision that they do not need to worry. Engage the public in the process and they will follow your lead.

12.1.4. Not Countering Rumours in Real-Time

During a pneumonic plague outbreak, how successful will your drug distribution program be if a rumor starts that there aren't enough drugs for everyone? What is your system to monitor what is being said by the public and the media? What is your system to react to false information? Don't spread a rumor by holding press conferences every time you hear a rumor, unless it has been widely published already. If the rumor is circulating on the Internet, have a response on the Internet and with your telephone information service ready to deal with the rumor. The media will report rumors or hoaxes unless you can answer quickly why it's false. Have an open, quick channel to communicate to the media if your monitoring system picks up a troublesome rumor. Don't think, "This is preposterous; no one will believe it." In a crisis the improbable seems more possible. Squash rumors fast, with facts.

12.1.5. Public Power Struggles or Confusion

Did you hear about the governor who held a press conference about a public safety crisis at the same time the mayor of the city was holding one on the other side of town? It really happened and it set the tone for a lot of speculation about who was in charge and what was or was not true.

In this information age, it's easy to see how this could happen. Sometimes there may be a power struggle over jurisdictions or other issues. The important thing is to make sure these are worked out quickly and confidentially. It's naturally disconcerting to the public to think that the people responsible for helping them are not getting along. All partners need to have clearly defined roles and responsibilities. When they overlap, and they do, make sure you can settle concerns without causing headlines about power struggles or, worse, confused response officials. When all else fails, stay in the scope of your responsibility and refrain from declaring "I'm in charge" without being certain that you are.

Even if everyone shows up at the same press conference, the officials could send the wrong message to the public. If people are jockeying for the microphone or looking back and forth at each other hoping someone will answer a question posed by a reporter, the public will be left with the impression that there are power struggles or confusion going on.

Early in the sniper shooting incident in metro Washington, DC, Montgomery County Police Chief Charles Moose had to formally request involvement by the F.B.I. Although there were natural concerns about what that might mean to local law enforcement, the chief chose to involve the F.B.I. and did it quietly and what appeared seamlessly to the public. At no time did the public perceive a power struggle among the response agencies. This, however, was a community that had previously survived a terrorist attack at the

Pentagon and an anthrax attack at the Capitol. They had learned the value of a united front with multiple jurisdictions working cooperatively for the good of their community. Turf wars need to end at the moment the crisis begins. A good plan can help avoid turf wars from the start.

12.2. Five Steps for Success

Could it be as simple as five steps to communication success in a disaster? Yes and no. These five steps are the keys to success, but each step is a challenge in itself. However, every bit of research in the area of successful communication, especially in a crisis, unanimously agrees you can't skip any one of these and expect to be successful. Remember, the reason you as a leader are focused on better communication is because most of this burden will fall to you, according to peers who've been there before you.

The following are the five steps to communication success:

— Execute a solid communication plan.

— Be the first source for information.

— Express empathy early.

— Show competence and expertise.

— Remain honest and open.

12.2.1. Execute a Solid Communication Plan

Working from a communication plan is as important in a crisis as working from a logistics plan— stuff won't get where it needs to go when it needs to be there without a good plan. As a leader, you need to know that the public judges the success of your operation, in great part, by the success of your communication.

Consider what CDC experienced during the 2001 anthrax incident and then in the 2003 SARS outbreak. A full year after the 2001 anthrax incident, national media were still criticising CDC's anthrax operation. However, the theme of the criticism was consistently about its inability to effectively communicate to its partners, important stakeholders, and the media. In 2001, CDC did not have a crisis communication plan and adequate resources dedicated to the effort.

A lot changed at CDC following the anthrax incident, especially in the area of crisis communication. Then in late 2002, people started dying from an emerging disease around the world, SARS. While the SARS outbreak was still unfolding, and there was great uncertainty about the magnitude of the outbreak, national media were praising CDC for its effective operational response. The change the media perceived was not in the operational functions, because both in anthrax and in SARS CDC had smart, dedicated people responding. The difference perceived by media, stakeholders, and partners was the speed and consistency of its communication. CDC had a plan, the plan was executed, and the plan made a huge difference in the public's perception of its ability to do the job.

12.2.2. Be the First Sources of Information

There are two important reasons to strive to be the first source of information in a crisis. The public uses the speed of information flow in a crisis as a marker for your preparedness. No matter that the HASMAT team showed up in 2 minutes, evacuated the scene, and determined that the fire at the chemical plant should be allowed to burn out instead of putting water on it which could spread hazardous chemicals into the water table. The operational response was perfect. Yet, when this happened recently in Atlanta, the local news coverage was filled with angry families who saw the black smoke and wanted to know if they should evacuate but weren't able to find out as quickly as they wanted. Parents, gripping the hands of their small children, castigated the people who knew but didn't tell them that they were safe. Living in the information age means being expected to not only save lives, but also to be able to tell people while it's happening that you are saving lives.

The second reason is a psychological reality. When people are seeking information about something they do not know; the first message they receive carries more weight. The tendency is for people to typically accept the information and then if they hear a second message that conflicts with the first, they start to weigh them against each other. This is especially dangerous if the first message is incorrect but it sounds logical.For example, the news media reports that health officials are swabbing the noses of congressional staffers for anthrax spores to see if they need to take antibiotics. So, Mr. Public is exposed to a white substance in the breakroom of his factory, and he thinks he should get a nose swab too. In fact, a positive or negative nose swab for anthrax spores is not a reliable way to determine if someone should be given antibiotics. That determination is made with other data such as proximity to the exposure site and ventilation systems. Even so, reasonable people who had heard about the nasal swabs and were incorrectly told they help in a medical diagnosis would be expected to clamor for the same kind of care.

So, by putting energy into getting the right message out first means that later incorrect messages will have to bounce up against the right message. That's better than having not only to get out the right message, but also having to spend considerable effort discounting the incorrect first message.

12.2.3. Express Empathy Early

If a leader takes only one concept from this book, this may be the most important and, for some, the most challenging. Your peers who have experienced a leader's role in a public safety crisis and academic experts from around the country agree on this point: A sincere expression of empathy is as essential to your ability to lead the public in a crisis as the right key is to opening a lock. You can stick other keys or bent paper clips or tiny screwdrivers into the lock, but it won't open until you insert the key with the right grooves and edges. So it is with your message: The public won't be open to you until you express empathy.

So what's empathy? Empathy is the ability to understand what another human being is feeling. Empathy does not require you to feel what that person is feeling. Empathy does not require you to agree that what the person is feeling is appropriate. Empathy is the ability to at the very least describe your understanding of what they are feeling. In its best form, empathy is talking from the heart and relating to fellow human beings as fellow human beings—not victims, not casualties, not evacuees, or refugees, or the public—but as people who, in a crisis, are hurting physically, perhaps, but especially emotionally.

Research shows that an expression of empathy should be given in the first 30 seconds of starting your message. To do otherwise is to waste your time because the public will be waiting to hear whether or not "you get it." Your audience is wondering whether you understand they are frightened, anxious, confused? If you don't articulate what they are feeling in the moment, your audience's minds will be consumed with the question of "Do they get it?" And not hear a thing you are saying. A sincere expression of empathy early in your communication will allow people to settle down the noise in their minds and actually hear what you have to say.

12.2.4. Show Competence and Expertise

If you have a title and are part of the official response to a crisis, the public will assume you are competent until you prove otherwise. It's not necessary to recite your entire resume or Curriculum Vitae at the start of a crisis response. According to the research, most people believe that a person holds a professional position because he or she is experienced and competent.

12.2.5. Remain Honest and Open

If you are a government official, there is a healthy belief in your community that the government withholds information, according to research done as recently as 2003 (CDC, unpublished). So, before you even begin to communicate with the public, they already assume you are holding back information. In criminal investigations that may be true. In all cases, treat people like you would like to be treated yourself. The danger comes from assuming you are protecting people or avoiding a bigger problem by keeping information away from the public. The motives may be noble, but the outcome could be the opposite. CDC and five universities did a series of 55 focus groups. Among the findings, three points were clear themes from the participants: (1) Any information is empowering. (2) Uncertainty is more difficult to deal with than knowing a bad thing. (3) Participants are prepared to go to multiple sources for information.

Here's where the idea of holding back information as a way to "manage" the crisis breaks down. We live in the information age. It's going to get out either in an upfront way or a backdoor way. Assume that if someone other than you knows the fact, everyone knows the fact. Do you want to present the facts in context or do you want to try to clean up a mess of someone else's making?

Bad news does not get better over time. There is absolute consensus among professionals that the faster you give up bad news the better, because holding back implies guilt and arrogance.

Do we choose to withhold frightening information because we don't want people "to panic?" Do we withhold the information because we think it will cut down the number of phone calls from the public and media requests from reporters? Not knowing is worse than knowing. People can cope with bad news and the anticipation of bad things to come. During a summit at Johns Hopkins University in 2003, one participant made the following point: "Do you know what the definition of panic is from the perspective of public officials? It's when the public does anything they don't want them to do."

Without question, for very good reasons some information must be withheld. When that is the case, respectfully tell the public you are withholding information and why. If the answer is "because we don't want you to panic," then there is no reason to withhold the information.

Sometimes the public will see on the TV what you can't officially confirm. To be honest would be to say, "I know what is being reported, but this instant I'm going to let our official channels work. I want you to know the steps we take to make sure what is officially reported is as accurate as possible. Like you, I want information as fast as possible and like you I'd prefer it also to be right. We will definitely tell you what we can confirm and will update you as we learn more. In the meantime, let me remind the community to (action step)."

Former mayor Rudolph Giuliani experienced pressure like that regarding the casualty numbers in the days following the terrorist attack in New York City. He said, "There was tremendous pressure to place a figure on the casualties. The media demanded an official estimate. I decided right away not to play the guessing games with lost lives. I told the truth: 'When we get the final number, it will be more than we can bear'". The mayor was honest and open, and did not violate the city's operational plan for release of casualty numbers in a crisis.

12.3. Overcoming Psychological Barriers

People are feeling a lot of different emotions. Each person may or may not feel any or all of a range of emotions. However, patterns do emerge in a crisis and a leader needs to expect these and understand that is why communicating in a crisis is different. A number of psychological barriers that could interfere with the cooperation and response from the public. Many of them can be mitigated through the work of a leader with an empathetic and honest communication style.

12.3.1. Fear, Anxiety, Confusion, and Dread

In a crisis, you can expect people in your community are feeling fear, anxiety, confusion, and, possibly, dread. Your job as a leader is not to make these feelings go away. If that's the goal, failure is a certainty. Instead, these are the emotions that you should acknowledge in a statement of empathy. "We've never faced anything like this before in our community and it can be frightening." You may be an expert and not be feeling fear. That's OK. But the worst thing you can do is to tell a frightened person he or she has no reason to be frightened. Never utter the words "There's no reason to be afraid."

Instead, acknowledge the fear. Make no statement about wanting it to go away. Simply tell them what you know that makes you less afraid. "I understand that anything related to radiation can seem frightening. Let me tell you what I know...." Give people one good fact to "chew" on and then tell them where to get more information.

12.3.2. Hopelessness and Helplessness

Looking for a communication goal in a crisis? Here's the number one objective. If the community, its families, or individuals let their feelings of fear, anxiety, confusion, and dread grow unchecked during a crisis, psychologists can predict they will begin to feel hopeless or helpless. What leader needs a community of hopeless and helpless victims?

So, a reasonable amount of fear is OK. Instead of striving to "stop the panic" and eliminate the fears, help the community manage their fears and set them on a course of action. Action helps overcome feelings of hopelessness and helplessness.

Give people things to do. People want things to do. As much as possible, give them relevant things to do: Things that are constructive and relate to the crisis they're facing. Anxiety is reduced by action and a restored sense of control. The actions may be symbolic (e.g., put up the flag) or preparatory (e.g., donate blood or create a family checkin plan). Some actions need to be put into context. Be careful about telling people things they should do without telling them when to do it. Phrase these preparatory actions in an "if—then" format. For example, "Go buy duct tape and plastic sheeting to have on hand, and if (fill in the blank) occurs, then seal up one interior space in your house as a shelter place."

The public must feel empowered and in control of at least some parts of their lives if you want to reduce fear and victimisation. Plan ahead the things you can ask people to do, even if it's as simple as "checking on an elderly neighbor."

12.3.3. Managing Panic

Contrary to what one may see in the movies, people seldom act completely irrationally or panic during a crisis. We do know that people have run into burning buildings, have refused to get out of a car stuck on the tracks with a train speeding close, and have gone into shock and become paralysed to the point of helplessness. However, the overwhelming majority of people can and do act reasonably during an emergency. How people absorb or act on information they receive during an emergency may be different from nonemergency situations. Research provides some clues about the receiver of information during an emergency. It has shown that in a dire emergency, people or groups may exaggerate their responses as they revert to more rudimentary or instinctual "flight or fight" reasoning, caused in part by the increase of adrenaline and cortisol in the blood system.

In other words, that primitive part of our brains that we can credit for the survival of the human species kicks in. One can not predict whether someone will choose fight or flight. However, everyone will fall at some point on the continuum. "Fighters" may resist taking actions to keep them safe. "Fleers" may overreact and take additional steps to make them extra safe. Those extremes are what most of us see reflected back in the media. However, the overwhelming majority of people do not engage in extreme behavior. It just feels like they do when you're the one responsible for getting a recommended response from the community.

During the 2001 anthrax incident, media reported local shortages of the antibiotic known as "cipro" because people began to seek out prescriptions anticipating the threat of anthrax. Question: If I want a prescription of cipro in my back pocket even though I live on the other side of the country, is that a panic behavior? No, it's my survival instinct kicking into overdrive. If I hear my community leader saying "don't panic," I think that doesn't apply to me. While I'm chasing down a cipro prescription, I think I'm rationally taking steps to ensure my survival, and someone else must be panicking. If you describe individual survival behaviors as "panic," you've lost the very people you want to talk to. Acknowledge their desire to take steps and redirect them to an action they can take and explain why the unwanted behavior is not good for them or for the community. You can call on people's sense of community to help them resist individual grabs for protection.

When people are swamping your emergency hotline with calls, they are not panicking. They want the information they believe they need and you have. As long as people are seeking information, they may be fearful but they are not acting helpless, nor are they panicking.

Physical and mental preparation will relieve anxiety despite the expectation of potential injury or death. An "action message" can provide people with the feeling that they can take steps to improve a situation and not become passive victims of the threat. Action messages should not be an afterthought. Reduce the level of extreme reactions by reaching out early with a message of empathy and action.

12.3.4. Uncertainty

Have you ever had to wait over the weekend for the results of a life-or-death medical test? The not knowing quickly seems worse than dealing with a bad result. People hate uncertainty. We all spend a great deal of our time working to reduce uncertainty in our lives. The uncertainty that is inherent in most crises, especially early in the event, will challenge even the greatest communicator. Early in a crisis, typically there are more questions than answers. The full magnitude of the problem is unknown. Perhaps the cause of the disaster is unknown. Even what people can do to protect themselves may be unclear.

A danger early in a crisis, especially if you're responsible for fixing the problem, is to promise an outcome outside your control. Never utter a promise, no matter how heartfelt, unless it's in your absolute power to deliver. We can hope for certain outcomes, but most we can't promise. Instead of offering a "knee jerk" promise, "We're going to catch the SOBs who did this, promise." "We're going to throw everything we have at catching the bad guys, or stopping the spread of disease, or preventing further flood damage...."

People can manage the anxiety of the uncertainty if you share with them the process you are using to get the answers. "I can't tell you today what's causing people in our town to die so suddenly, but I can tell you what we're doing to find out. Here's the first step...."

Remember, in a crisis people believe any information is empowering. Tell them what you know and most important tell them what you don't know and the process you're using to try and get some answers. Mayor Giuliani cautioned, "Promise only when you're positive. This rule sounds so obvious that I wouldn't mention it unless I saw leaders break it on a regular basis".

12.4. Importance of First Messages

The public will be listening for factual information, and some will be expecting to hear a recommendation for action. Get the facts right, repeat them consistently, avoid sketchy details early on, and ensure that all credible sources share the same facts. Speak with one voice. Again, preparation counts. Consistent messages are vital. Inconsistent messages will increase anxiety and will quickly torpedo the credibility of experts. Your first official message in a crisis as a leader to the public, either through the media or directly, should contain the following six elements in the following order:

1. *An expression of empathy.*
2. *Confirmed facts* (who, what, where, when, why, how). It's not necessary to know all of them to go forward with a statement.
3. *What you don't know about the situation.*
4. *What's the process.* After acknowledging there are questions unanswered, explain first steps being taken to get the answers. What help can people expect next. (That first statement may be simply "We've activated the EOC.")
5. *Statement of commitment.* (You are there for the long haul. You'll be back to talk to them in an hour.) Be careful not to promise what is outside your control.

6. *Where people can get more information.* (Give a hotline number or a web site. Again, tell them when you will be back in touch with them.)

12.5. Make Your Message Work

Consider the following when creating your initial communication to your audiences:

— For the general public, *present a short, concise, and focused message (6th-grade level). It's difficult in a heightened* state of anxiety or fear to take in copious amounts of information. Get the bottom line out first. In time, the public will want more information.

— *Cut to the chase*—relevant information only at this time. Don't start with a lot of background information. Don't spend a lot of time establishing yourself or your organisation. One sentence should be enough.

— *Give action steps in positives*, not negatives (e.g., "In case of fire, use stairs," "Stay calm," are positive messages. Negative messages are "Do not use elevator" and "Don't panic.") Use positives, not negatives.

— *Repeat the message*—repetition reflects credibility and durability. Correct information is correct each time you repeat it. Reach and frequency, common advertising concepts, tell us that your message is more apt to be received and acted upon as the number of people exposed to the message (reach) and the number of times each person hears the message (frequency) go up.

— *Create action steps in threes or rhyme, or create an acronym.* These are ways to make basic information easier to remember, such as "stop/drop and roll" or "KISS—keep it simple, stupid." Three is not a magic number, but in an emergency you should expect someone to absorb three simple directions. Research indicates that somewhere between three and seven bits of information is the limit for people to memorise and recall. It makes sense in the stress of an emergency to ask your audience to remember fewer bits of information. (For example: Anthrax is a bacterium that is treated with antibiotics. Anthrax is not transmitted from person to person. Seek medical care if you believe you have symptoms of anthrax—fever, body aches, and breathing problems.)

— *Use personal pronouns for the organisation.* "We are committed to…" or "We understand the need for…"

Avoid:

— *Technical jargon* Cut the professional jargon and euphemisms; they imply insecurity and lack of honesty.

— *Condescending or judgmental phrases*—(e.g., "You would have to be an idiot and try to outrun a tornado." "Only hypochondriacs would need to walk around with a prescription for cipro.") Many of us are neither idiots nor hypochondriacs, and both ideas have crossed our minds. Don't insult your audience by word or tone. That doesn't mean condoning the behavior; instead, validate the impulse but offer a better alternative and the reasons why it's better.

— *Attacks*—Attack the problem, not the person or organisation.

— *Promises/guarantees*—only what you can deliver. Otherwise, promise to remain committed throughout the emergency response.

— *Discussion of money*—In the initial phase of a crisis, discussion of the magnitude of the problem should be in the context of the health and safety of the public or environment. Loss of property is secondary. Also, a discussion of the amount of money spent is not a surrogate for the level of concern and response from your organisation (What does that money provide?).

— *Humor*—Seldom is humor a good idea. People seldom "get the joke" when they are feeling desperate. Humor is a great stress-reliever behind closed doors. Anyone who has responded to emergencies knows that sometimes inappropriate humor creeps in as a coping mechanism. Be careful not to offend others responding to an emergency, even behind closed doors. Be especially sensitive when speaking to the public. One person's attempt at humor may be another's insult.

12.5.1. Expected Questions

No matter what the crisis, following are the questions that will always be asked and should be anticipated by you. Be prepared to address the following:

— What happened?
— Are my family and I safe?
— What have you found that may affect me?
— What can I do to protect myself and my family?
— Who caused this?
— Can you fix it?
— Who is in charge?
— Has this been contained?
— Are victims being helped?
— What can we expect, right now and later?
— What should we do?
— Why did this happen?
— Did you have forewarning?

12.6. Scientist as Spokesperson

Can what you say and how you say it be the difference between life and death during a crisis? Yes. The overwhelming research shows that a credible spokesperson can influence behaviors that could be life-saving. Oh, that it would be as simple as reading a prepared statement! It's not.

For a scientists to achieve such noble aims as saving lives, reducing anxiety and fear, and helping the community recover more quickly depends in great deal on not only the words delivered but also the way the words are delivered. A scientist who becomes a spokesperson during a crisis is endowed with special responsibilities. First, if you are representing a part of the official response, such as the incident commander or head of a response agency, you are the human embodiment of that command group or agency. You take the EOC or your agency from an "it" to a "we." You're the human face. That's a hefty responsibility. Use it strategically.

The public is looking for an expression of empathy from the "powers that be." You're it. If you express in words a sincere understanding of what the members of your community are feeling, you have just made a giant leap toward gaining their trust. Remember, you do not have to personally be afraid to be able to express "I can understand this situation may be frightening. I know you are looking for answers to important questions here. We want answers too and were taking steps to get them, including..." Or, "This is a confusing time for us. It's such a horrible tragedy we face today. My greatest wish is that we would never have to put into action the plans we made for just such an event. We are in pain but we are going to work through this pain and keep helping the people we can. We will not stop until we help every one of our neighbors. I'm going to ask you to help us too. We may be asking you to endure some hardships here. We may ask for your patience as we work to get answers. We may call on you to volunteer in some way. We're a strong community, built on a foundation of firm values and I know one of those is a willingness to help each other when we're in need. I'm counting on that help from each of you today and tomorrow."

It would be unwise to try to "can" statements of empathy in advance of a disaster. If you are a leader whose community is suffering, the words will come. Trust yourself that what you speak from your heart is what the public needs to hear. If you shut down emotionally and attempt to appear unfased by the event, you risk your credibility. Don't shed a tear if that's not you, but simply understand that some in your community are crying, are hurting, and want to know you understand. That sincere expression of empathy will help quiet anxious minds and allow people to hear your message. Express empathy and then give directions for action. These two steps, in this order, will help you and your community early in the disaster.

A leader has the ability in a crisis to rally his or her community. A leader who is sharing the risk, a part of the affected community, can call on his or her community to shoulder the burden and help others. A person frightened out of his or her wits will respond positively to a call for action and perseverance from an empathetic and committed leader. Ask your neighbors to be their strongest and they will be. Interestingly, following September 11, 2001, researchers discovered that able-bodied elderly people in lower Manhattan were an asset to the recovery of that community. They helped their younger neighbors cope with the worst tragedy of their young lives by telling stories about other trying times from the past. Young people wanted to hear that their elders faced tragedy and were able to recover. Stories about World War II and the Depression helped the young. In fact, Mayor Giuliani reached back to stories about the WW II bombings of London to help him keep hope for his city. An early reminder that we must "buck up" to help each other will give people something to concentrate on besides their own fears.

References

Bostrom, A., Fischhoff, B., & Morgan, M. G. (1992). Characterizing mental models of hazardous processes: A methodology and an application to radon. *Journal of Social Issues*, *48* (4), 85- 100.

Deetz S. A. (Ed.), *Communication Yearbook 15* (pp. 359- 373). Newbury Park CA: Sage Publications.

Fessenden- Raden, J., Fitchen, J. M., & Heath, J. S. (1987). Providing risk information in communities: Factors influencing what is heard and accepted. *Science. Technology, & Human Values*, 12 (3- 4), 94- 101.

Nelkin, D. (Ed.) (1985). *The language of risk.* Beverly Hills CA: Sage.

Sandman, P. M. (1986). *Explaining environmental risk.* Washington DC: U. S. Environmental Protection Agency.

13

Risk Communication and Food Safety

In 1997, the CAC adopted the following definition of risk communication: "an interactive exchange of information and opinions concerning risk among risk assessors, risk managers, consumers and other interested parties". Risk communication has also been described as all those integrated processes and procedures:

a) that involve and inform all interested parties within the risk analysis process;

b) that assist the development of transparent and credible decision-making processes; and

c) that can instil confidence in risk management decisions.

A wide variety of communication strategies can be used in the management of food-related risks, ranging from the development of international standards, to management of acute outbreaks of foodborne disease, to long-term programes aimed at changing food production, food handling and dietary practices.

The Consultation considered the Codex definition to be too narrow, since it does not take into account the need to communicate factors other than the probability of the adverse health effect and the severity and magnitude of that effect. Understanding and communicating risk has clearly been shown to be influenced by a host of additional factors, such as whether the risk is voluntary or involuntary; whether the distribution of risk and benefit is equitable; the transparency of the process; the extent to which risk managers are trusted; the degree of personal control; the individual dread of the adverse effect; and the extent to which the risk is unknown. To encompass this wider concept, the Consultation recommended that the Codex definition be modified by inserting the words "and risk related factors" so that the definition would read "Risk communication is the exchange of information and opinions concerning risk and risk-related factors among risk assessors, risk managers, consumers and other interested parties."

13.1. Goals of Risk Communication

The fundamental goal of risk communication is to provide meaningful, relevant and accurate information, in clear and understandable terms targeted to a specific audience. It may not resolve all differences between parties, but may lead to a better understanding of those differences. It may also lead to more widely understood and accepted risk management decisions. Effective risk communication should have goals that build and maintain trust and confidence. It should facilitate a higher degree of consensus and support by all interested parties for the risk management option(s) being proposed.

The Consultation considered that the goals of risk communication are to:

1. Promote awareness and understanding of the specific issues under consideration during the risk analysis process, by all participants;
2. Promote consistency and transparency in arriving at and implementing risk management decisions;
3. Provide a sound basis for understanding the risk management decisions proposed or implemented;
4. Improve the overall effectiveness and efficiency of the risk analysis process;
5. Contribute to the development and delivery of effective information and education programes, when they are selected as risk management options;
6. Foster public trust and confidence in the safety of the food supply;
7. Strengthen the working relationships and mutual respect among all participants;
8. Promote the appropriate involvement of all interested parties in the risk communication process; and,

9. Exchange information on the knowledge, attitudes, values, practices and perceptions of interested parties concerning risks associated with food and related topics.

For many years, those responsible for assessing and managing risks associated with hazards in the food supply have communicated information and opinion about those hazards in the interests of protecting and promoting public health. These communications were expressed mainly in qualitative terms regarding the hazards as there were often no clear quantitative data concerning the resultant risks. More recently, the formal development and application of risk-based approaches to food safety and the availability of quantitative information related to risks in human populations, has provided the opportunity for improved implementation of risk-based management strategies. Risk communication has played an important role in the application of such risk-based approaches, by providing a means to interactively consider all relevant information and data. Of course, risk communication is also applicable in the many situations where the qualitative consideration of hazards is undertaken. In such cases, the principles and strategies of risk communication as elaborated by this Consultation would still apply.

In the present Codex context, the CAC and its subsidiary bodies are responsible for establishing a risk assessment policy. This provides the guidance for those necessary value judgements and policy choices that may need to be applied at specific decision points in the risk assessment process. It is vital that risk managers and assessors maintain open communications with each other and with other interested parties in defining and applying policy in this area.

Before a formal risk assessment is initiated, appropriate information must be obtained from interested parties to prepare a "risk profile". This describes the food safety problem and its context, and identifies those elements of the hazard or risk which are relevant to various risk management decisions. This often involves a range of preliminary risk evaluation activities, which rely on effective risk communication (e.g., ranking for international standard setting or putting a food safety problem in an appropriate national or international context).

Risk characterisation is the primary means by which food safety risk assessment findings are communicated to risk managers and other interested parties. Numerical estimates in the characterisation, therefore, should be supported by qualitative information about the nature of the risk and about the weight of evidence that defines and supports it. There are inherent difficulties in communicating the quantitative aspects of a risk assessment. They include ensuring that the scientific uncertainties inherent in the risk characterisation are clearly explained and that scientific terminology and technical jargon do not render the presentation of risk less understandable to the target audience. Communications among risk assessors, risk managers and other interested parties should use language and concepts that are suitable for the intended audience.

Risk communication facilitates the identification and weighting of policy and decision alternatives by risk managers in the risk analysis process. Interactive communication among all interested parties tends to assure transparency, facilitate consistency and improve the risk management process. To the extent that it is practical and reasonable, interested parties should be involved in identifying management options, developing the criteria for selecting those options and providing input to the implementation and evaluation strategy. When a final risk management decision has been reached, it is important that the basis for the decision be clearly communicated to all interested parties.

During the selection of risk management options, the risk manager may often need to consider factors in addition to science in the evaluation of a risk. This is particularly important at the national government level. Interactive communications are essential to identify social, economic, religious, ethical, and other concerns, so that these can be openly considered and addressed. Preparation of risk messages for dissemination is an important part of the risk communication process. It is also a deliberate and specialised undertaking and should be treated as such.

13.2. Responsibilities for Risk Communication

13.2.1. The Codex system

The Codex Alimentarius Commission is an inter-governmental organisation with established procedures for input from member governments and other interested parties such as consumer and industry representatives as well as other international standards organisations. The organisational structure and processes of the CAC and its subsidiary bodies, provide many opportunities for effective risk communication, both within the Codex system (i.e., among the various Committees) and external to Codex.

13.2.2. Codex Committee on General Principles

The Codex Committee on General Principles (CCGP) deals with procedural and general matters, including establishment of principles that define the purpose and scope of Codex work. In the context of risk analysis, the CCGP is currently elaborating principles and guidelines for the application of risk-based approaches to food safety throughout the Codex system. These will allow all interested parties to understand the agreed framework for risk management decision making within Codex.

Normally, the general subject Committees are involved in risk management, such as the development of standards, guidelines and other recommendations. Their work is supported by risk assessment information often supplied by FAO/WHO expert advisory groups. These include the Joint FAO/WHO Expert Committee on Food Additives (JECFA) and the Joint FAO/WHO Meeting on Pesticide Residues (JMPR). Other international expert bodies such as the International Commission for Microbiological Specifications for Foods (ICMSF) also may provide scientific support. Established channels exist for co-ordination with other international scientific bodies. Co-ordination of Codex risk management activities is carried out by the FAO/WHO Codex Secretariat. The Secretariat is also responsible for some risk communication activities such as the publication of a variety of documents, including standards, reports and other texts from the Codex committees. Reports of Codex meetings provide a record of the deliberations and the outcome of food safety discussions leading to the elaboration of Codex standards.

13.2.3. FAO and WHO

The Food and Agriculture Organisation of the United Nations (FAO) and the World Health Organisation (WHO) provide advice to member governments and other interested parties from internationally recognised experts through consultations on specific issues. Technical and developmental assistance to member governments on matters related to public health and the quality and safety of the food supply are also provided. The agencies have a responsibility to develop and promote the principles and procedures of risk analysis and to communicate these to member governments to assist them in the development of effective strategies and information programes at the national level. Where FAO and WHO jointly undertake to conduct risk assessment activities (e.g., JECFA, JMPR, expert consultations), they communicate the results and recommendations to their member governments, as well as other interested parties, through published reports and the Internet World-Wide Web.

13.2.4. World Trade Organisation (WTO)

The WTO Agreement on the Application of Sanitary and Phytosanitary Measures (SPS Agreement) encourages harmonisation and places a strong emphasis on the risk communication principles of transparency and consistency in the development and application of food safety measures. Harmonisation includes the establishment, recognition, and application of common sanitary measures by different member countries, and this is clearly dependent on effective risk communication. The WTO SPS Committee manages the implementation of the SPS Agreement for WTO member countries and, through the notification procedure required by the SPS Agreement, it communicates risk management decisions among those member countries.

13.2.5. Governments

Governments have a fundamental responsibility for risk communication when managing public health risks, regardless of the management methods used. With the responsibility for managing risks comes the responsibility to communicate information about risks to all interested parties to an acceptable level of understanding. Decision-makers within governments have the obligation to ensure effective communication with interested parties when developing scientific and technical analyses and to appropriately involve the public and other interested parties in the risk analysis process. Risk managers also have the obligation to understand and respond to the underlying bases of public concerns about health risks.

Governments should work towards a consistent and transparent approach when communicating risk information. Communication strategies may differ for different issues and different target audiences. This is most apparent when dealing with issues where specific groups have differing views of a risk. These differences in perception, which may be due to economic, social or cultural differences, should be recognised and respected. It is the outcome, i.e. effectively managed risk, which is most important. Differing methods of reaching the outcome may be acceptable.

Governments that are members of the CAC have a responsibility to play an active role in the Codex process. They should ensure that all interested parties within their countries (industry, consumers, national organisations, etc.) have an opportunity to contribute to national positions on Codex matters, to the extent practicable and reasonable. They should also ensure that these positions are transmitted to Codex in a timely manner. Governments need to take an active role in the deliberations during Codex meetings and ensure that interested parties at the national level are aware of and understand the decisions reached at those meetings. The CAC is actively encouraging the formation of National Codex Co-ordinating Committees within member governments, to assist in meeting these responsibilities.

Governments are often responsible for public health education and delivery of appropriate messages to the health community. In these roles, risk communication enables the delivery of important information to specific target groups, such as pregnant women and the elderly.

13.2.6. Industry

Industry is responsible for the quality and safety of the food it produces. It also has a corporate responsibility to communicate information regarding risks to affected consumers. Industry participation in all aspects of risk analysis is essential for effective decision making and can serve as a major source of information for risk assessment and risk management. The routine information flow between industry and government usually involves communications necessary to set standards or gain approvals for new technologies, ingredients, or labels. In that connection, food labels have been and are routinely used to communicate information on the ingredients and instructions on the safe handling of food products, as a form of risk management using the label as the communicating device.

One goal of risk management is to identify the lowest reasonably achievable risk. This may require a knowledge of the specific process variables and capabilities within a food processing and handling system. The industry has the best understanding of those variables and capabilities and the information that they can provide would be vital for risk managers as they work with risk assessors to prepare the context and scenarios necessary for the risk assessment process.

13.2.7. Consumers and Consumer Organisations

Broad and open participation in risk analysis at the national level is viewed by the public as an essential element of what constitutes appropriate public health protection. Early participation in the risk analysis process by the public or consumer organisations can help to ensure that consumer concerns are addressed and will generally result in a better public understanding of the risk assessment process and how risk-based decisions are made. It can further provide support for the risk management decisions that result from the assessment. Consumers and consumer organisations have a responsibility to present their concerns and opinions on health risks to risk managers. International consumer organisations that are Codex observers have direct input into Codex discussions on these matters. International and national consumer organisations play an important role in disseminating information on health risks directly to consumers. Consumer organisations also often work with governments and industry to ensure that risk messages addressed to consumers are appropriately formulated and delivered.

13.2.8. Academia and Research Institutions

Members of the academic and research community may play an important role in risk analysis by contributing scientific expertise on health and food safety matters and assisting in the identification of hazards. They may be asked by the media or other interested parties to comment on government decisions. They often have a high level of credibility with the public and the media, and may serve as independent sources of information. Researchers involved in studies of consumer perception or communication methods and the assessment of communication effectiveness, may also be helpful to risk managers seeking expert advice on risk communication approaches and strategies.

13.2.9. Media

The media clearly play a critical role in risk communication. Much of the information that the public receives on food-related health risks comes to them through the media. The many varieties of mass media have roles which vary depending on the issue, the context and the type of media involved. The media may merely transmit a message, or they may create or interpret a message. They are not limited to official sources of information and their messages often reflect the concerns of the public and other sectors of society. This can and does facilitate risk communication since risk managers may become aware of concerns of which they were not previously cognisant.

13.3. Elements of Effective Risk Communication

Depending on what is to be communicated and to whom, risk communication messages may contain information on the following:

13.3.1. Nature of the Risk

— The characteristics and importance of the hazard of concern.
— The magnitude and severity of the risk.
— The urgency of the situation.
— Whether the risk is becoming greater or smaller (trends).
— The probability of exposure to the hazard.
— The distribution of exposure.
— The amount of exposure that constitutes a significant risk.
— The nature and size of the population at risk.
— Who is at the greatest risk.

13.3.2. Nature of the Benefits

— The actual or expected benefits associated with each risk.
— Who benefits and in what ways.
— Where the balance point is between risks and benefits.
— The magnitude and importance of the benefits.
— The total benefit to all affected populations combined.

13.3.3. Uncertainties in Risk Assessment

— The methods used to assess the risk.
— The importance of each of the uncertainties.
— The weaknesses of, or inaccuracies in, the available data.
— The assumptions on which estimates are based.
— The sensitivity of the estimates to changes in assumptions.
— The effect of changes in the estimates on risk management decisions.

13.3.4. Risk Management Options

— The action(s) taken to control or manage the risk.
— The action individuals may take to reduce personal risk.
— The justification for choosing a specific risk management option.
— The effectiveness of a specific option.
— The benefits of a specific option.
— The cost of managing the risk, and who pays for it.
— The risks that remain after a risk management option is implemented.

13.4. Principles of Risk Communication

13.4.1. Know the Audience

In formulating risk communication messages, the audience should be analysed to understand their motivations and opinions. Beyond knowing in general who the audience is, it is necessary to actually get to know them as groups and ideally as individuals to understand their concerns and feelings and to maintain an open channel of communication with them. Listening to all interested parties is an important part of risk communication.

13.4.2. Involve the Scientific Experts

Scientific experts, in their capacity as risk assessors, must be able to explain the concepts and processes of risk assessment. They need to be able to explain the results of their assessment and the scientific data, assumptions and subjective judgements upon which it is based, so that risk managers and other interested parties clearly understand the risk. They further must be able to clearly communicate what they know and what they do not know, and to explain the uncertainties related to the risk assessment process. In turn, the risk managers must be able to explain how the risk management decisions are arrived at as well.

13.4.3. Establish Expertise in Communication

Successful risk communication requires expertise in conveying understandable and usable information to all interested parties. Risk managers and technical experts may not have the time or the skill to perform complex risk communication tasks, such as responding to the needs of the various audiences (public, industry, media, etc.) and preparing effective messages. People with expertise in risk communication should therefore be involved as early as possible. This expertise will likely have to be developed by training and experience.

13.4.4. Be a Credible Source of Information

Information from credible sources is more likely to influence the public perception of a risk than is information from sources that lack this attribute. The credibility accorded a source by a target audience may vary according to the nature of the hazard, culture, social and economic status, and other factors. If consistent messages are received from multiple sources then the credibility of the message is reinforced. Factors determining source credibility include recognised competence or expertise, trustworthiness, fairness, and lack of bias. For example, the terms that consumers have associated with high credibility include factual, knowledgeable, expert, public welfare, responsible, truthful, and good "track record". Trust and credibility must be nurtured and can be eroded or lost through ineffective or inappropriate communication. In studies, consumers have indicated that distrust and low credibility resulted from exaggeration, distortion and perceived vested interest.

Effective communications acknowledge current issues and problems, are open in their content and approach, and are timely. Timeliness of the message is most important since many controversies become focused on the question, "why didn't you tell us sooner", rather than on the risk itself. Omissions, distortions and self-serving statements will damage credibility in the longer term.

13.4.5. Share Responsibility

Regulatory agencies of governments at the national, regional and local levels, have a fundamental responsibility for risk communication. The public expects the government to play a leading role in managing public health risks. This is true when the risk management decision involves regulatory or voluntary controls, and is even true when the government decision is to take no action. In the latter event, communication is still essential to provide reasons why taking no action is the best option. In order to understand the public concerns and to ensure that risk management decisions respond to those concerns in appropriate ways, the government needs to determine what the public knows about the risks and what the public thinks of the various options being considered to manage those risks.

The media play an essential role in the communication process and therefore shares in these responsibilities. Communication on immediate risks involving human health, particularly when there is a potential for serious health consequences, such as food-borne illnesses, cannot be treated the same as less immediate food safety concerns. Industry also has a responsibility for risk communication, especially when the risk is as a result of their products or processes. All parties involved in the risk communication process (e.g. government, industry, media) have joint responsibilities for the outcome of that communication even though their individual roles may differ. Since science must be the basis for decision making, all parties involved in the communication process should know the basic principles and data supporting the risk assessment and the policies underlying the resulting risk management decisions.

13.4.6. Differentiate between Science and Value Judgement

It is essential to separate "facts" from "values" in considering risk management options. At a practical level, it is useful to report the facts that are known at the time as well as what uncertainties are involved in the risk management decisions being proposed or implemented. The risk communicator bears the responsibility to explain what is known as fact and where the limits of this knowledge begins and ends. Value judgements are involved in the concept of acceptable levels of risk. Consequently, risk communicators should be able to justify the level of acceptable risk to the public. Many people take the term 'safe food' to mean food with sero risk, but sero risk is often unattainable. In practice, 'safe food' usually means food that is 'safe enough.' Making this clear is an important function of risk communication.

13.4.7. Assure Transparency

For the public to accept the risk analysis process and its outcomes, the process must be transparent. While respecting legitimate concerns to preserve confidentiality (e.g. proprietary information or data), transparency in risk analysis consists of having the process open and available for scrutiny by interested parties. Effective two-way communication between risk managers, the public and interested parties is both an essential part of risk management and a key to achieving transparency.

13.4.8. Put the Risk in Perspective

One way to put a risk in perspective is to examine it in the context of the benefits associated with the technology or process that poses the risk. Another approach that may be helpful is to compare the risk at issue with other similar, more familiar risks. However, this latter approach can create problems if it appears the risk comparisons have been intentionally chosen to make the risk at issue seem more acceptable to the public. In general, risk comparisons should not be used unless:

— Both (or all) risk estimates are equally sound;
— Both (or all) risk estimates are relevant to the specific audience;
— The degree of uncertainty in all risk estimates is similar;

— The concerns of the audience are acknowledged and addressed; and

— The substances, products or activities themselves are directly comparable, including the concept of voluntary and involuntary exposure.

13.5. Barriers to Effective Risk Communication

Effective communication about food-related health risks requires more than just an understanding of the risks in the context of the risk assessment and risk management processes. Barriers to risk communication exist and recognising those barriers and knowing how to overcome them are essential for effective risk communication.

Three categories of barriers to effective communication are addressed here. The first two include institutional and procedural barriers that can limit communication within the risk analysis process itself. Communication barriers in the third category apply to all contexts, and especially to efforts by the expert community to communicate with the general public and other interested parties about food-related health risks.

13.5.1. Barriers within the Risk Analysis Process

Communication plays a vital role throughout the risk analysis process to assure that risk management strategies effectively minimise foodborne risks to public health. Many communication steps in the process are internal, iterative exchanges between risk managers and risk assessors. Two key steps - hazard identification and selection of risk management options -require risk communication with all interested parties to help improve the transparency of decisions and increase the potential level of the acceptance of the outcomes.

13.5.2. Access to Information

Vital information needed to carry out the risk analysis process may not always be made available by those who possess it. Occasionally, industry or other private parties may have proprietary information about a risk, which they are reluctant to share with government agencies because of a need to protect their competitive position or for other business reasons. In other instances, government agencies may be unwilling to openly discuss facts they possess about food risks for a variety of reasons. Complete access to all relevant data about a food-related health risk, both for risk managers and for other interested parties, may not exist in all situations. Lack of access to critical data about a risk makes the communication steps involved in hazard identification and risk management even more difficult.

13.5.3. Participation in the Process

Lack of participation in the risk analysis process by those parties having a significant interest in the outcome, can be an important barrier to effective communication about the risk. Broad participation in the process improves risk communication by presenting opportunities to identify and address the concerns of interested parties when decisions are made. It increases the overall understanding of the process and the decisions, and makes it easier to communicate later with the public about those decisions. Those who were involved in the decision-making process are less likely to challenge the outcome, especially if their concerns have been addressed.

The Codex has made an effort to involve all interested parties in the risk analysis process. For example, at its 22nd Session in June 1997 (6), the CAC unanimously agreed on the importance of risk analysis in Codex work and adopted an Action Plan for Codex-wide Development and Application of Risk Analysis Principles and Guidelines. Despite these efforts, effective participation in the process by all interested parties has not been an easy goal to achieve. In general, governments and industry, at least from the industrialised nations, have been well represented, while many developing countries and consumer organisations have been under-represented in the risk analysis process. In theory, wider participation in the risk analysis process is more feasible at the national level than at the international level, but many national governments have not yet established mechanisms for involving all interested parties in the critical steps of risk analysis.

Some reasons for non-participation are external to the process itself. For example, most consumer organisations and some governments lack experienced, knowledgeable food safety specialists who can play effective roles in risk analysis. In some cases it is a lack of resources that prevents support for ongoing participation in international decision-making processes. There are also some barriers to participation within key steps of the risk analysis process itself. For example, certain critical sessions at which key decisions are made, such as meetings of JMPR and JECFA and the Executive Committee of the Codex Alimentarius, are closed to observers. While there are historical and administrative reasons why this is so, excluding interested parties from vital steps of the process is a communication barrier.

This barrier can be overcome through continuing and increasing efforts now being made by FAO, WHO and the Codex to involve consumer organisations and other interested parties more effectively in food safety risk analysis processes, especially at the international level. Consumer organisations should increase their efforts to identify and nominate experts for consideration as participants for international expert advisory committees. Training programes can be designed to provide the knowledge and skills needed for representatives from non-participating governments, consumer organisations and other interested sectors to participate effectively in risk analysis processes at the national and international levels.

13.5.4. Barriers within the Codex process

The workload of some Codex committees has increased while budgetary resources have remained fixed or shrunk, with a result that there is sometimes insufficient time during sessions to fully discuss the many agenda items. Many Codex documents are not available far enough in advance of meetings, and reports on Codex sessions tend to focus on what was decided, rather than how it was decided, which often leaves the basis for decisions unclear. At its 22nd Session (6), the CAC recognised these problems and expressed concern that reducing the duration of Codex sessions (proposed for budgetary reasons) would not allow sufficient time for consideration of the matters in question and that limiting the length of Codex meeting reports would make them less useful for understanding how positions were reached. This in turn could decrease the transparency and efficiency of Codex work.

Also at the 22nd Session, the CAC agreed to evaluate the application of "legitimate factors" other than science in adopting maximum residue limits for a specific veterinary drug. The lack of a general policy guideline on the application of factors other than science, in risk analysis, has been a barrier to communication as this results in a lack of clarity over which issues are or are not within the scope of Codex deliberations.

Elaboration of a policy on what legitimate factors other than science may be considered in risk analysis is a critical step towards removing this barrier and improving the context for risk communication in Codex. Efforts to improve the timeliness of documents might be increased, and the style of reports of meetings could be amended to explain more clearly the basis for decisions.

13.5.6. Barriers to Communication in All Contexts

Many barriers to risk communication are not specific to the food safety risk analysis process, but reflect difficulties intrinsic to most efforts to communicate about complex technical and value-laden issues. There is a large literature of academic research on the subject of risk communication and why it succeeds or fails in different circu

13.5.7. Differences in Perceptions

Individuals can perceive the risk from the same hazard very differently. Some of the public may disagree with risk assessors and managers regarding important hazard characteristics, the relative magnitude or severity of the risks associated with those hazards, the priority of risks, and other issues. Other segments of the public also may not pay attention to risk information if the message does not address their actual concerns, but instead addresses only technical risk assessments provided by the experts. For example, a low-risk hazard that some people perceive to be involuntarily imposed upon them, may appear more threatening than another, perhaps higher-risk hazard that those same individuals perceive to be under their personal choice and control.

The effectiveness of risk communication can be enhanced by efforts to establish dialogues with interested parties and the general public, through open meetings, focus groups, surveys and other methods. The goal of this effort should be to gain an understanding of how the public and other interested parties perceive the risk.

13.5.8. Differences in Receptivity

Many individuals believe they are personally less at risk from a given hazard than other people are, and perceive that risk messages concerning, for example, nutritional and food hygiene hazards are directed towards other people. Some people also tend to believe that they personally are more knowledgeable than the average member of society is, and will ignore risk messages they believe are directed toward less informed people. Also, some risk-taking behaviors may be perceived as normal or desirable within particular groups, and members of these groups may therefore discount risk messages as inappropriate.

To communicate effectively with such unreceptive groups, it is essential to understand their attitudes, beliefs and concerns, and to address those concerns in risk communication messages.

13.5.9. Lack of Understanding of the Scientific Process

Over-reliance on precise scientific terminology may obscure the meaning of facts for the general public. If messages are not kept relatively simple, they may be misunderstood. Unless scientific uncertainties are acknowledged and put into context, the public may not gain an accurate perception of what is and is not known about the risk. Also, unless value judgements that are necessary components of risk assessments and risk management decisions are explicitly stated, the public may not grasp the basis for decisions that are made. Public attitudes, once formed, are difficult to change as people tend to select information which supports already held beliefs.

To overcome these barriers, risk communicators should use non-technical terms to the greatest extent possible, and explain the technical terms that are used. Non-technical people should review proposed messages for clarity. Communicators should try to minimise the differences between themselves and the public and should address any uncertainties and value judgements involved in the risk analysis, both explicitly and clearly.

13.5.10. Source Credibility

The public does not equally trust all sources of information about food safety. In situations where different risk messages are received from different sources, the public will respond to the messages from the more credible source and discount the messages from the other sources.

Factors that enhance trust and credibility include public perceptions of the communicator's accuracy, knowledge and concern for public welfare. Addressing the public's concerns about risks will also facilitate trust. Distrust is associated with perceptions of bias or with failure by the communicator to provide accurate information in the past. Trust is more important under conditions of great uncertainty or when the public believes that accurate estimates of risk are unavailable. Trust also depends on the extent to which the risk assessment and risk management processes are believed to be transparent and open to public scrutiny. Once lost, trust is not easily regained. Communication is generally most effective when all sources, including those trusted most by the public, convey similar messages about the risk.

13.5.11. Media

The public generally gets their information on food safety issues from the media, as with other topics. Sometimes the mass media do not accurately convey risk information. Relatively few reporters have much experience with the complex scientific and policy aspects of food safety issues, and it can be difficult for them to prepare a story on highly technical matters, especially under deadline pressure. The media also have their own agenda and make their own independent judgements on what is newsworthy. It often may appear to risk managers and other technical experts that the news media focus unduly on conflict and controversy, and occasionally they sensationalise or exaggerate risks in order to draw attention to the story. While problems with media coverage of food-related risks are by no means universal, when they do occur they can make communication about risk more difficult.

Risk managers and others who serve as risk communicators often are not familiar enough with the media to understand how to work with reporters to enhance the quality and accuracy of media reports. During a food safety emergency, in particular, the urgency of the hazard and the high level of public anxiety tend to promote more co-operative relationships between media and risk managers, but communication problems may still occur.

Risk communicators need training in media skills and should work to establish long-term relationships with members of the media. In planning for, or responding to, emergency situations, it is essential tc include a person responsible for the media on any crisis response team. In those situations where certain necessary information is not considered newsworthy by the media and is therefore not disseminated by them, the authorities can still get the information to the public by considering the use of paid advertisements or public service announcements.

13.5.12. Societal Characteristics

Some barriers to risk communication are not associated with attributes of the senders or receivers of risk information or with the medium or the message itself, but with the nature of the society in which the communication occurs. Societal factors that can make risk communication more difficult include language differences, cultural factors, religious dietary laws, illiteracy, poverty, a lack of legal, technical and policy resources and a lack of infrastructures that support communication. These and other factors vary within countries and from one country to another.

Societal barriers to communication may be especially acute in those countries, where, in addition to the foregoing factors, there are extreme differences in socio-economic status among groups. Hunger and malnutrition may relegate food safety to secondary status among food-related concerns. Other barriers include physical or geographic ones - some geographic areas or groups of people can be physically inaccessible to risk communicators. Also, free exchange of information may be limited by political constraints.

To the extent possible, cultural and social attributes that hamper risk communication need to be identified and addressed, as part of the process of designing messages for target audiences. Targeted messages such as displays, posters and leaflets at market places, health centres, schools, bus terminals and the like can be used as suited to local social norms. In some countries, general improvements in the economic and social well-being of the citizens, including progress in alleviating poverty, increasing personal and political freedom, expanding access to education and information for all sectors, community involvement and ongoing training of key personnel, can all contribute to improved risk communication. Enhancing the status of rural women is likely to be a particularly effective social strategy for enhancing food safety communication.

13.6. Strategies for Effective Risk Communication

Risk communication occurs in many different contexts and both research and experience suggest that different risk communication strategies are appropriate for these different contexts. Although there are many similarities, the strategies needed during a food safety emergency differ in many respects from strategies needed to engage the public in dialogue about risks and benefits of new food technologies, and from those for communicating about chronic low-level food-related risks. Items to consider when developing strategies for risk communication during a food safety crisis are presented separately here, following a discussion of more general risk communication requirements.

13.6.1. General Considerations

Many considerations for effective risk communication, especially those involving the public, can be grouped in a sequence following the systematic approach of the risk communication process. This starts with gathering background and needed information, followed by the preparation and assembly of the message and its dissemination and distribution, with a follow-up review and evaluation of its impact.

13.6.2. Background/Information

- Understand the scientific basis of the risks and attendant uncertainties.
- Understand the public perception of the risk through such means as risk surveys, interviews nd focus groups.
- Find out what risk information people want.
- Be sensitive to related issues that may be more important to people than the risk itself. Expect different people to see the risk differently.

13.6.3. Preparation/assembly

- Avoid comparisons between familiar risks and new risks, as they may seem flippant and insincere unless presented properly.
- Recognise and respond to the emotional aspects of risk perceptions. Speak with sympathy and never use logic alone to convince an audience characterised by emotion.
- Express risk in several different ways, making sure not to evade the risk question.
- Explain the uncertainty factors which are used in risk assessment and standard setting.
- Maintain an openness, flexibility, and recognition of public responsibilities in all communication activities.
- Build an awareness of benefits associated with a risk.

13.6.4. Dissemination/distribution

- Accept and involve the public as a legitimate partner by describing risk/benefit information and control measures in an understandable way.
- Share the public's concern rather than deny it as not legitimate or as unimportant. Be prepared to give people's concerns as much emphasis as the risk statistics.
- Be honest, frank, and open in discussing all issues.
- If explaining statistics derived from risk assessment, explain the risk assessment process before presenting the numbers.
- Co-ordinate and collaborate with other credible sources.
- Meet the needs of the media.

13.6.6. Review/evaluation

- Evaluate the effectiveness of risk messages and communication channels.
- Emphasise action to monitor, manage, and reduce risk.
- Plan carefully and evaluate efforts.

13.6.7. Points to Consider regarding Public Concerns

Risks that involve some or all of the following aspects tend to concern the public more than those risks that lack these aspects:

— Unknown, unfamiliar or rare events as opposed to well-known or common hazards.

— Risks that are controlled by others, rather than those where the public or the individual is in control.

— Risks resulting from industry action or from new technology, rather than those perceived as natural.

— Risks where there is significant scientific uncertainty, or where there is open controversy among experts as to the probability and severity of the hazard.

— Risks that raise moral or ethical questions, such as the fairness of the distribution of risks and benefits, or the rights of one group in society to put others at risk.

— The decision-making process by which a risk is assessed is seen as being unresponsive or is unknown.

— Therefore, in order to mitigate public concern about risks, the following strategies may be used:

— Make risks voluntary by giving consumers choices, whenever possible;

— Acknowledge uncertainty;

— Show that expert disagreement on an issue is merely uncertainty, by estimating risks as a range that includes estimates from both sides of the debate;

— Determine where control is and look to share it with interested parties;

— Treat all interested parties with courtesy; and

— Always consider concerns and complaints seriously.

13.7. Strategies in Non-crisis Situations

Risk communication is obviously very important during a food safety crisis; however, it is equally important when there is no immediate crisis and routine risk analyses are being made to address identified hazards. The following should be considered in preparing risk communication strategies in such situations.

13.7.1. Background/information

— Anticipate emerging public health hazards before they become significant.

— Determine the public's perception of the hazard being considered and their knowledge and behavior regarding the risks involved.

— Analyse the target audience of a risk communication and understand their motivations. Try to determine the full range of the audience's concerns and their perceived importance.

— Analyse which information channels and messages are best to be used. Use the mass media and other appropriate channels to convey information.

13.7.2. Preparation/assembly

— Describe to concerned groups how risk is determined, how it can be monitored and how an individual can control or reduce risk.

— Identify shared values and help individuals identify an approach to meet their values.

— Make messages interesting and relevant by emphasising the human rather than the statistical aspects of a story.

— Use extra care to make a message interesting enough for the media to publish. Claims of risk are usually considered by the media to be more newsworthy than claims of safety.

13.7.3. Dissemination/distribution

— Use the mass media where possible to address those consumer concerns which have been identified. For example, public forums with local opinion leaders can be televised.

— Sustain communication, thus enabling the public to make decisions based upon personal values and goals and to gain a greater understanding of the potential risks and benefits involved.

— Make risk communication multi-directional, not just from technical experts to the public, but from the public back to the experts.

— Use participation to sustain efforts. People have to feel that they are at the centre of a health promotion action or decision for the process to be effective.

— Use health education and access to health information to foster effective participation of people and communities.

13.7.4. Review/evaluation

— Add an evaluation component into any risk communication strategy.

— Test the clarity and understanding of the message with a representative segment of the target audience.

— Integrate risk communication with risk assessment and risk management activities, toincrease the effectiveness of risk analysis and ensure proper utilisation of resources.

— Educate and train risk assessors and risk managers in the principles and uses of risk communication.

— Effective risk communication can break through traditional boundaries within government sectors, between governmental and non-governmental organisations, and between the public and private sectors. Co-operation is essential and this requires the creation of equal partnerships between the different sectors at all levels of governance in societies.

13.8. Facing a Food Safety Crisis

The typical food safety crisis envisioned here is one in which disease-causing organisms are discovered in a widely consumed food. The strategies suggested, however, also will apply to other kinds of crisis situations involving, for example, chemical contamination or physical adulteration of foods.

While the general strategies for non-crisis situations referred to previously still apply, a crisis situation calls for special considerations. Communication strategies should be an integral part of the crisis management plan. Effective crisis management requires a comprehensive plan that can be updated through periodic evaluations. Having good channels of communication to the public during a crisis is extremely important; first to prevent panic and second to provide positive information on the situation to help decide on what course of action should be undertaken. This should include information on:

— The nature and extent of the crisis and the measures taken to control it;
— The sources of contaminated foods and what to do with any suspected foods held in households;
— The identified hazard and its characterisation, and when and how to seek medical attention or other assistance as warranted;
— How to prevent further spread of the problem; and
— Safe food handling practices by the population during the crisis.
— To achieve these objectives the risk communicator may:
— Manage a series of media communications.
— Establish appropriate mechanisms to deliver information, e.g. local visits, radio announcements, a toll-free telephone help line, etc.
— Arrange for one-to-one advice on infection risk in a special clinic, if a foodborne disease is involved.
— Provide daily updates on the crisis and crisis management activities to all health care and other relevant professionals.
— Hold regular briefings for government officials, and other official representatives as well as representatives of the public. Involve the media.
— Evaluate the effectiveness of the crisis communications and make adjustments as appropriate
— Those responsible for managing a food safety crisis should establish a network for interactively sharing information. Central government research institutions, local governments, hospitals and private enterprises should make information accessible to each other in an accurate, concise and usable form.

13.8.1. Crisis Situations: International Responses

Early warning systems in countries or regions should be established to allow rapid communication of emerging crises. Once the cause of a foodborne disease outbreak has been established, action can be taken across international borders. For example, European Sal Net has helped prevent widespread illness due to specific outbreaks.

Member governments should follow the Codex Code for Ethics for International Trade in Food (8) and Guidelines for the Exchange of Information in Food Control Emergency Situations (9) which allows for rapid exchange of information during a crisis situation.

International organisations can serve as neutral fora for risk assessment and the development of appropriate risk management strategies and risk communication messages for national or international dissemination.

13.8.2. National Responses

National governments need to be prepared to rapidly disseminate accurate information to the mass media and the public when a food safety crisis arises. Essential steps in preparing for such a crisis include: identifying reliable sources of information and expert advice; arranging an administrative organisation to handle communications during a crisis; and developing staff skills in dealing with the media and the public.

A national government might consider opening a Food Safety Information Office which can serve as a crisis centre if needed, while serving as an information centre to receive routine inquiries from consumers about the safety of foods. Food control authorities may also consider developing a home page on the Internet World-Wide Web to provide information on food and food safety including questions and answers about issues of common concern.

13.8.3. Industry Responses

When a crisis is emerging or has emerged, the involved industry should assure that the public authorities are fully informed about the potential cause and extent of the problem, and the anticipated effectiveness of any recall of food products already on the market. In dealing with the public during a crisis, consumer safety comes first and company actions and communications should reflect this. The following policies and actions have proven to be effective:

— Assess the problem as if you were the consumer. Take responsibility for finding a solution to the problem and protecting and advising your customers by providing the facts to the public in a clear and reasonable way. This will demonstrate to the public that you are worthy of trust.

— Be certain that any company pronouncements are from a single unified source. Conflicting messages only confuse the issue, erode confidence and disrupt the process of crisis resolution.
— Choose a spokesperson who is trained and skilled in dealing with the media. Make the spokesperson accessible to the media at all times.
— The spokesperson should consider the public, not just the food company. Companies can appear to be impersonal and only concerned about profits and losses whereas an effective spokesperson would express concern for the people and their needs.
— Have an "open door" policy relative to communications with the media. Remember that communication messages must be consistent and should be updated as soon as new information is received
— Communicate quickly and often. Work with the media using the tools and timetables that work best for them. Communicate with those inside and outside the company who are working on the problem, especially government agencies.
— Inform company employees, especially those in sales and marketing positions, as to progress on the situation, what is being done to resolve it and the risk messages being communicated.
— Establish a mechanism for developing feedback from consumers. Free consumer call-in numbers and survey polls are ways of accomplishing this.
— Know your company's objectives and how they can be used to formulate risk communication messages.

13.8.4. Local Responses

The first lines of contact in a crisis are usually the local officials. It is critical that they communicate conditions to the appropriate authority quickly so a crisis can be contained and appropriately managed.

— Provide complete, up-to-date and accurate information. When the situation is resolved, tell the public that "it is over."

— Keep your message simple. Too many facts are overwhelming. If appropriate, use videotape or other communication means to emphasise your point.

— Chose a media-trained spokesperson. During a crisis, consumers should know who is responsible for information and updates. Make the trained spokesperson accessible to the media at all times.

13.9. Specific Guidelines for Communication

Risk communication about food safety within the risk analysis process is carried out on an ongoing basis from the local through the international levels. While many of the strategies presented above also apply in the risk analysis process, there are additional considerations that can help frame those risk communication strategies that are part of risk analysis.

13.9.1. International Considerations

Communication can be considered at two levels in the international context. The first level involves international organisations like FAO and WHO, and intergovernmental organisations like Codex. The second level involves national governments on bi-lateral and multi-lateral bases. At both levels, effective internal and external risk communication requires development and documentation of a comprehensive risk analysis policy. Matters of concern include:

— Continuing efforts to refine the concepts and understanding of food safety risk analysis in general and risk communication in particular;

— Improving the organisational infrastructure for internal and external risk communication to meet emerging situations;

— Addressing the critical role of effective risk communication in determining the equivalence of food control measures in different countries; and

— Establishing credible sources for risk assessments and technical advice.

In regard to the latter point, a joint FAO/WHO expert committee for food microbiological hazards (as is now the case for food additives, veterinary drug residues, pesticide residues and other food contaminants) would provide internationally recognised microbiological risk assessments for member governments and for Codex. The Consultation was aware that at its 22nd Session, the CAC recognised this problem and requested FAO and WHO to convene an international expert advisory body similar to JECFA and JMPR, to specifically address microbiological risk assessment in food.

Advice and assistance from international organisations may be sought when local authorities wish additional technical information and support. This may lead to specific international development projects. In such situations it would be necessary to maintain continuity in the composition of national counterpart staff. Co-ordination within such projects is essential.

13.9.2. National Considerations

National Codex Co-ordinating Committees should have responsibility and appropriate support to communicate issues involving risk to consumers, local food industry and those national authorities involved in risk analysis.

International organisations like WHO and FAO have, over the years, developed documentation related to risk assessment and management. National organisations should make use of this information. National organisations should integrate food safety into primary health care for the public. This should penetrate down to the local marketplace.

It was previously suggested that national governments consider opening a Food Safety Information Office to address routine food safety inquiries as well as serving as a crisis centre when needed. Governments may wish to consider establishing a Food Safety Council comprised of microbiologists, physicians and toxicologists and other scientists with appropriate public health and food control expertise, as well as representatives of consumer organisations and industry, to evaluate and advise government officials regarding food safety. The Council's deliberations and recommendations could be made available to the public through official bulletins or administrative notices as well as through the mass media. It could also provide input for national delegations to Codex meetings.

13.9.3. Industry Considerations

Industry should be more proactive and establish or strongly support non-profit information centres to provide science-based information on food safety and nutrition to the public, educators, health professionals, government officials and the media.

If consumer food handling, storage, or other practices can assist in controlling a food-borne illness or disease outbreak, then the industry should communicate clearly what actions the consumers should take. This communication should be based on a realistic estimate of the level of knowledge of the consumers. Safe handling, preparation and storage instructions should be presented in clear and unambiguous language, using graphics and pictograms when and where appropriate.

Judicious use of labelling holds promise as a risk management/ risk communication strategy but its effectiveness needs further study. Labelling has been extensively used to convey certain types of information to the consumer, e.g., product composition, nutrition, weights and measures, and warnings on certain health issues. Labelling should not be used as a substitute for consumer education. In assessing the use of food labels in risk communication, it is essential that the public's concerns be identified and addressed.

13.9.4. Local Considerations

Experience has shown that local government, being closer to the local population, is often more likely to be regarded as a trustworthy and credible source of risk information. Therefore local officials should be involved as key participants in ongoing risk communication activities. Local bodies should be encouraged to integrate food safety information into primary health care which should also include key risk communication messages using appropriate delivery systems .

13.10. Evaluation of Communication Activities

Risk communication efforts and programes need to be evaluated both regularly and systematically to determine their effectiveness and to provide for change where needed. Communication aims and objectives need to be clearly stated if an evaluation is to be effective. This could include the proportion of at-risk population to be reached, adoption of appropriate risk reduction practices, and the extent of resolution of the crisis. It is important to learn from both positive and negative risk communication experiences, in order to adjust and improve ongoing communication activities. Only through systematic evaluations, which are performed throughout the communication process, can that process be strengthened.

References

Hadden, S. G. (1989). *A citizen's right to know: Risk* communication *and Public policy*. Boulder CO: Westview.

Hance, B. J., Chess, C., & Sandman, P. M. (1988). *Improving dialogue with communities: A risk communication manual for government*. Report to the New Jersey Department of Environmental Protection, Division of Science and Research. Trenton: New Jersey Department of Environmental Protection.

Johnson, B. B., & Covello, V. T. (Eds.) (1987). *The social and cultural construction of risk:* Essays on risk *perception and selection*. Dordrecht, Holland: D. Reidel.

Krimsky, S., & Plough, A. (1988). *Environmental hazards: Communicating risks as a social process*. Dover MA: Auburn House.

Lave, L. (Ed.) (1987). *Risk assessment and management*. New York: Plenum Press.

Bibliography

Allen, F. W. (1987). Towards a holistic appreciation of risk: The challenge for communicators and policy makers. *Science, Technology & Human Values*, 12 (3-4), 138-143.

Andreasen, Alan R. (1995). *Marketing Social Change: Changing Behavior to Promote Health, Social Development, and the Environment*. San Francisco: Jossey-Bass Publishers.

Atman, C.J., Bostrom, A., Fischhoff, B. & Morgan, M.G.. (1994). Designing risk communications: Completing and correcting mental models of hazardous processes, Part 1. *Risk Analysis, 14*, 779-788.

Baird, B. R. N. (1986). Tolerance for environmental health risks: The influence of knowledge benefits, voluntariness, and environmental attitudes. *Risk analysis* 6, 425-435.

Bord, R. J., & O'Connor, R. E. (1990). Risk communication, knowledge, and attitudes: Explaining reactions to a technology perceived as risky. *Risk Analysis*, 10, 499506.

Borman, Ernest G. (1975). *Discussion and Group Methods. Second Edition.* New York: Harper and Row Publishers, Inc.

Bostrom, A., Fischhoff, B., & Morgan, M. G. (1992). Characterizing mental models of hazardous processes: A methodology and an application to radon. *Journal of Social Issues*, *48* (4), 85-100.

Chess, C., Saville, A., Tamuz, M., & Greenberg, M. (1992). The organizational links between risk communication and risk management: The case of Sybron Chemicals Inc. *Risk* analysis, 12, 431-438.

Cohn, Victor. (1990). *Reporting on Risk*. Washington D.C.: The Media Institute

Coleman, C. L. (1993). The influence of mass media and interpersonal communication on societal and personal risk judgments. *Communication* Research, 20, 611-628.

Cooper, Lane. (1932). *The Rhetoric of Aristotle*. Englewood Cliffs, NJ: Prentice Hall, Inc.

Covello, V. T. (1991). Risk comparisons and risk communication: Issues and problems in comparing health and environmental risks. In R. E. Kasperson & P. M. Stallen (Eds.), *Communicating risk to the public* (pp. 79124).

Covello, V. T., Sandman, P. M., & Slovic, P. (1988). *Risk* communication, risk statistics and risk comparisons: A manual for *plant managers*. Washington DC: Chemical Manufacturers Association.

Dear, M. (1992). Understanding and overcoming the NIMBY syndrome. *Journal of the American Planning Association*, 58, 288- 300.

Deetz S. A. (Ed.), *Communication Yearbook 15* (pp. 359- 373). Newbury Park CA: Sage Publications.

Dietz, T., Stern, P. C., & Rycroft, R. W. (1989). Definitions of conflict and the legitimating of resources: The case of environmental risk. *Sociological Forum*, 4, 47- 69.

DiGiovanni, C. (1999). "Domestic terrorism with chemical or biological agents: psychiatric aspects."*American Journal of Psychiatry*, 156, 1500–1505.

Douglas, M. (1990). Risk as a forensic resource. *Daedalus*, *119*, 1- 16.

Edwards, W., & von Winterfeldt, D. (1987). Public values in risk debates. *Risk Analysis*, 7, 141- 158.

Eggers, S.L., & Fischhoff, B. (2004). A defensible claim? Behaviorally realistic evaluation standards. *Journal of Public Policy and Marketing*, *23*, 14-27.

Everly, George S. Jr., Ph.D. (2001). "America Under Attack: The '10 Commandments' of Responding to

Fessenden- Raden, J., Fitchen, J. M., & Heath, J. S. (1987). Providing risk information in communities: Factors influencing what is heard and accepted. *Science. Technology, & Human Values*, *12* (3- 4), 94- 101.

Fessenden- Raden, J., Fitchen, J. M., & Heath, J. S. (1987). Providing risk information in communities: Factors influencing what is heard and accepted. *Science. Technology, & Human Values*, 12 (3- 4), 94- 101.

Fietkau, H. J. (1990). Accident prevention and risk communication in environmental protection: A sociopsychological perspective. *Industrial Crisis* Quarterly, 4, 277- 289.

Fiorino, D. J. (1989). Technical and democratic values in risk analysis. *Risk Analysis*, 9, 293- 299.

Fischer, Henry, W., III. (1998). *Response to Disaster*. Lanham, Md.: University Press of America.

Fischhoff, B. (2002). Assessing and communicating the risks of terrorism. In A.H. Teich, S.D. Nelson, & S.J. Lita (Eds.), *Science and technology in a vulnerable world* (pp. 51-64). Washington, DC: AAAS.

Graeff, Judith A., et. al. (1993). *Communication for Health and Behavior Change*. San Francisco: Jossey- Bass Publishers.

Hadden, S. G. (1989). *A citizen's right to know: Risk* communication *and Public policy*. Boulder CO: Westview.

Hance, B. J., Chess, C., & Sandman, P. M. (1988). *Improving dialogue with communities: A risk communication manual for government*. Report to the New Jersey Department of Environmental Protection, Division of Science and Research. Trenton: New Jersey Department of Environmental Protection.

Hornig, S. (1993). Reading risk: Public response to print media accounts of technological risk. *Public Understanding of Science,* 2, 95- 109.

Ice, R. (1991). Corporate publics and rhetorical strategies: The case of Union Carbide's Bhopal Crisis. *Management Communication Quarterly*, 4, 341- 362. (*)

Jasanoff, S. (1987). EPA's regulation of daminozide: Unscrambling the messages of risk. *Science Technology. & Human Values*, 12 (3- 4), 116- 124.

Johnson, B. B., & Covello, V. T. (Eds.) (1987). *The social and cultural construction of risk:* Essays on risk *perception and selection*. Dordrecht, Holland: D. Reidel.

Kasperson, R. E. (1986). Six propositions on public participation and their relevance for risk communication. *Risk Analysis*, 6, 275- 281.

Krimsky, S., & Plough, A. (1988). *Environmental hazards: Communicating risks as a social process*. Dover MA: Auburn House.

Lave, L. (Ed.) (1987). *Risk assessment and management*. New York: Plenum Press.

Leeds, Dorothy. (2000). *The 7 Powers of Questions*. New York: Berkley Publishing Group.

Lum, Max R., Ed.D.; Tinker, Tim L. Dr.P.H., M.P.H. (1994). *A Primer on Health Risk Communication Principles and Practices*. Atlanta: Division of Health Education, Agency for Toxic Substances and Disease Registry.

Mass Terrorist Attacks" *International Journal of Emergency Mental Health*, 3(3), pp 133–135.

Mazur, A. (1981). Media coverage and public opinion on scientific controversies. *Journal of Communication*, 31.

Morgan, M.G., Fischhoff, B., Bostrom, A., Lave, L., & Atman, C.J. (1992). Communicating risk to the public. *Environmental Science and Technology, 26,* 2048-2056.

Nelkin, D. (Ed.) (1985). *The language of risk.* Beverly Hills CA: Sage.

Novac, Andrei, M.D. (April 2001). "Traumatic Stress and Human Behavior," *Psychiatric Times*, website:http://www.mhsource.com.

Riley, D.M., Fischhoff, B., & Small, M., & Fischbeck, P. Behaviorally realistic regulation. (2001). In P.S. Fischbeck & S. Farrow (Eds.), *Improving regulation: Cases in environment, health, and safety* (pp. 145-164). Washington, DC: Resources for the Future.

Sandman, P. M. (1986). *Explaining environmental risk.* Washington DC: U. S. Environmental Protection Agency.

Schwarz, M., & Thompson, M. (1990). *Divided we stand: Redefininq politics technology and social choice.* Philadelphia: Univ. of Pennsylvania Press.

Slovic, P., Fischhoff, B., & Lichtenstein, S. (1981). *The assessment and perception of risk.* London: The Royal Society.

Smith, Larry. (2001). *The ICM Crisis Management Certification Course.* Louisville, Kentucky: Institute for Crisis Management.

Susskind, Lawrence, & Field, Patrick. (1996). *Dealing With an Angry Public.* NewYork: The Free Press.

Swets, Paul, W. (1992). *The Art of Talking So That People Will Listen.* New York: Simon & Schuster.

Timm, Paul, R. (1981). *Functional Business Presentations.* Englewood, NJ: Prentice Hall, Inc.

Turkington, Carol. (1999). *The Complete Idiot's Guide to Cultural Etiquette.* Indianapolis: Macmillan USA, Inc.

Ury, William. (1993). *Getting Past No: Negotiating your way from confrontation to cooperation.* New York: Bantam Books.

Yale, David, R. (1991). *The Publicity Handbook.* Chicago: NTC Business Books.

Index